D1231645

DATE DUE

WEST AFRICA 1860 – 1880

BRITISH CONTROLLED TERRITORY c. 1880

0°

R. NIGER

5° E

10°

15° N

R. VOLTA

(ASHANTI)

R. BENUE

•Ilorin

10° N

GOLD COAST

SLAVE

•Ibadan
•Abeokuta

COAST (YORUBA) Lokoja

(FANTI)

Lome
Grand Popo
Porto Novo
Lagos

Quittah
(Keta)

Accra

Mankessim
Cape Coast
Elmina
Secondee
(Sekondi)

(IBO)

OIL
RIVERS

FERNANDO
PO

5° N

0   100   200   300   400   500 MILES

0   100   200   300   400   500 KILOMETRES

0°

5° E

JCD/SJAN 196

Black Nationalism in Africa 1867

Extracts from the political, educational, scientific and medical writings of
Africanus Horton

chosen, edited and introduced by
Davidson Nicol

Africana Publishing Corporation

Published in the United States of America 1969
by Africana Publishing Corporation
101 Fifth Avenue
New York, N.Y. 10003

Library of Congress catalog card no. 77–94833
SBN 8419–0028–0

Printed in Great Britain

African Classics Series

The object of this series, planned in consultation with the Ghana Academy of Sciences and in co-operation with scholars throughout the continent, is to make available at a reasonable price the work of eminent writers, thinkers and professional men who witnessed the problems and growth of modern Africa in its early stages. All too often their publications are now to be found only in specialist libraries, or scattered in past volumes of periodicals where they may be sought by scholars already versed in the sources.

The series will present the writings, in whole or in selection, of these men, with introduction and notes by leading contemporary scholars in the field, in the belief that they will prove of interest and value to students in secondary schools and universities and, indeed, to general readers.

The following titles are in preparation

African Life and Customs and other essays by Edward Wilmot Blyden
edited by Edward W. Blyden III

Gold Coast Native Institutions by J. E. Casely Hayford
edited by W. E. Abraham

West African Celebrities by the Rev. S. R. B. Attoh Ahuma
edited by J. K. Fynn

Thoughts and Sentiments on the Evil of Slavery by Ottobah Cugoano
edited by Edmund Collins

Other titles will follow

Acknowledgements

I would like to acknowledge with grateful thanks the original suggestion and encouragement for writing this book from David M. Williams, editor of *West Africa*, in whose journal my first annotation on the late Dr Horton was published, and from whose unique library of eighteenth- and nineteenth-century Africana I started to study some of Horton's writings.

I wish also to thank Christopher Fyfe, Reader in History, Edinburgh University, John D. Hargreaves, Professor of History, Aberdeen University, and Brian Maegraith, Professor of Tropical Medicine, Liverpool University, all of whom made valuable suggestions after reading some of my introductory notes. I had helpful discussions on certain aspects of Horton's life and work with Mr James Pope-Hennessy, C.V.O., the writer and historian and Dr M. C. F. Easmon, O.B.E., Chairman of the Sierra Leone Monuments and Relics Commission. For the map of West Africa 1860–80 I am indebted to Professor J. C. Dewdney and Mr S. J. A. Nelson of the Department of Geography, Fourah Bay College, University of Sierra Leone.

Finally, I would like to thank my family and my secretarial staff, in particular Mrs Beryl Schweder, for their help in preparing this book for publication.

Davidson Nicol
Sierra Leone and Cambridge
1969

The publishers wish to make acknowledgement to Radio Times Hulton Picture Library for plate no. 4 and to the R.A.M.C. Historical Museum Trust for information. Plate no. 3 is from a photograph in the collection of the late Sir Mark Nathan.

To my wife
M.E.N.
another beloved physician
and nationalist

Contents

List of Illustrations

Editor's Preface

In February/May 1865, a motion was carried in the House of Commons in London that a Select Committee should be formed to determine whether the West African Colonies furthered or obstructed British policy. After sitting for some months the Committee passed several resolutions which were adopted by the House of Commons. These advised various local measures including the establishment of a central government in Sierra Leone for all four settlements—Gambia, Sierra Leone, Gold Coast (Ghana) and Lagos, the reduction of the settlement on Gambia by abandoning MacCarthy Island and the abolition of domestic slavery in Lagos.

The most important, however, was '. . . that the object of our policy should be to encourage in the natives the exercise of those qualities which may render it possible more and more to transfer to them the administration of all the Governments, with a view to our ultimate withdrawal . . .'

This particular resolution was greatly welcomed by the intelligentsia of West Africa; it was to make certain that both African and British in Africa should be fit in mind and body, and should also be prepared for the self-government of Africa by black Africans, that Dr J. A. B. Horton, a great African nationalist, wrote many articles and several books on politics, economics, science and medicine between that year and the end of his life in 1883.

The realisation of self-government which Horton and his compatriots thought was imminent did not materialise until almost a century later. These excerpts from his works are, however, of great interest and many of them are still relevant to the African situation.

Introduction: *African Self-Government 1865—The Dawn of Nationalism*

by Davidson Nicol

Dr James Horton, African physician, writer and army officer, was born on 1st June 1835 in a small village called Gloucester, near Freetown, Sierra Leone, in West Africa, of parents who originally came from Nigerian territory. He regarded himself as a Sierra Leonean. He spent most of his working life, however, in Quittah (Keta), in Ghana (then the Gold Coast) and in Gambia. He visited—for short periods—and occasionally worked in some of the other countries in West Africa; he may possibly have paid a short visit to the West Indies and the Americas in one of the troopships of the West India Regiments. He received his medical education in London and Edinburgh where he doubtless met students from all over the world, including some from Egypt, East and South Africa. In Britain he was considered a distinguished member of the African race. In almost every territory in West Africa in which he worked, he took a prominent part in the social and political life of educated local Africans, whilst carrying out his medical work amongst the military and civil population. His knowledge of the classics, history, anthropology, science and medicine was remarkable for a man of any race. It was to identify himself racially that he adopted the name Africanus Horton under which he wrote many of his books.

It is important to realise that, although their number was small, there were Africans living over a hundred years ago whose love of country and nation was matched by the extent of their scholarship and ability. Their thoughts and their dreams form part of the knowledge essential to any-one interested in the story of African advancement.

In the first half of the nineteenth century, the city of Freetown and the small area around it were known as Sierra Leone. The local community consisted of a handful of Europeans, their mulatto offspring, coloured Americans (called 'Nova Scotians' as they had been placed there temporarily after the American War of Independence) and coloured

Jamaicans of Maroon origin. The large majority of Sierra Leoneans, however, were settlers and their children from all over West and Central Africa including the country adjacent to Freetown, who were Africans who had been 'recaptured'—that is, set free by the British Navy whilst being taken to be sold into slavery in the West Indies and North America. It was from this group of recaptives that most of the distinguished West Africans of the latter half of the nineteenth century arose. Although they were called Sierra Leoneans their ancestors came from many African communities—over a hundred—including the Fanti, Mende, Bacongo, Yoruba, Ibo, Fulah, Jolloff and the Hausa-speaking group. The Yoruba and Ibo, however, predominated. From them were produced college lecturers, schoolmasters, physicians, lawyers, bishops, clergymen and farmers. Many of the schools and colleges in West Africa were concentrated in Sierra Leone at this time, and this produced the intellectual dominance then held by Sierra Leone but rightly shared by all Africa. A steady process of intermarriage and detribalisation, which was hastened by British education, produced in the second half of the century the group called Sierra Leone Creoles (the word 'creole' meaning, as it usually does, people born away from home), who were now speaking the Krio language as well as English. Some of them scattered back to the original land of their fathers (notably the Egbas to Lagos and Abeokuta), others went to other parts of Africa as far flung as Tanzania, Cape Town and Calabar. The majority remained in Sierra Leone to form the group called the Krio, one of the smaller communities in what is now the independent territory of Sierra Leone which is many times the size of the small original nineteenth-century Sierra Leone settlement.

Horton's life was etched out against this background. The village in which he was born was a small settlement named after the Duke of Gloucester. Its own particular inhabitants, then numbering under a thousand, comprised Africans who were Temne and Mende (from the territories adjacent to Freetown), Mandinka (from Senegal, Gambia and Guinea), Fanti (from Ghana), Ibo (from Nigeria) and Bacongo (from the Congo). The village still exists, four miles by road from Freetown, on a hillside near a valley through which a charming little stream flows by an old market-place. Few of the present inhabitants can recall their particular tribal ancestry and all now speak Krio.

The superintendents of the mountain villages were agents of the Church Missionary Society, a British organisation formed in 1799 for activities in India and Africa and stemming from the liberal evangelical wing of the Church of England. The Church Missionary Society (C.M.S.) was outstandingly successful in Sierra Leone where it started in 1804 and its agents were responsible for most of the major educational advances in West Africa in that period. It was to their village school that Horton went and he also attended the stone church which still stands on a hill in the middle of the village. Later, he attended their grammar school and at the age of eighteen, in 1853, their college, Fourah Bay College, which is now an independent institution and part of the present University of Sierra Leone.

Horton was one of seven students who entered the college in that year; his education was very sound and included studies in English, Mathematics, Classics and Theology. He seems to have received instruction in the Sciences too. The Principal was the Reverend Edward Jones, an American of African ancestry who had been educated at Amherst College in the United States before coming out to Sierra Leone. There were then two Professors at the College; one was a Professor of Languages and the other of Mathematics. The Principal taught Theology and the Greek Testament.

It was during the Principalship of Mr Jones that the large red laterite building known to many generations of West Africans as Fourah Bay College was put up in the district of that name near the present deep-water quay.

Henry Venn, the Secretary of the C.M.S. in London, recommended Horton to the War Office for a medical scholarship. Together with two others, he left for King's College, London, in 1855. Venn must have been partly responsible for getting him admitted to King's which because of its Christian background was then popular with African students. Horton's career there was brilliant, and he won prizes in Surgery, Physiology and Comparative Anatomy. His knowledge of Anatomy was amply demonstrated in his book *West African Countries and Peoples, British and Native . . . and a Vindication of the African Race* in which he challenged physical anthropologists who had asserted that the brain of an African was smaller than that of a European and that he was therefore less intelligent.

During Horton's period as an undergraduate at King's, the college was very much in a transitory state. The Principal was Dr Jelf, a theologian whose specialty was the Thirty-nine Articles which form the doctrinal basis of the Church of England. He stayed on as Principal long after it was clear to everybody that he should have left; eventually he was persuaded to leave and he retired to Oxford where he died of measles. There was a great move within the college to improve its teaching. The college, like Fourah Bay College of Sierra Leone, was founded to develop the ideal Christian gentleman of culture of that period. But around the time that Horton entered as a student, it was felt that it should be necessary to have some intellectual achievement, apart from compulsory attendance at chapel, to be awarded the college's diploma, the A.K.C.

3

(the Associateship of King's College). Science was taught, especially Geology and Mineralogy.

At the medical school itself, the medical and surgical Professors were compelled by college regulations to attend regularly instead of casually as had been the case before. The new timetable which was drawn up by the college authorities asked them to give demonstrations and lectures between one and two in the afternoon, and between two and three. They resented this because it interfered with dinner and their afternoon nap. The Professor of Midwifery successfully claimed exemption from these regulations as the necessity for his attendance at clinical cases was regulated by the laws of nature and not by those of man since children could be born at times other than those allowed for in college time-tables.

In spite of its theological background, King's College had a great reputation for Geology, through one of its Professors, Sir Charles Lyell. He and other scientists had done their best in the face of opposition from their colleagues in the Arts and Theology Faculties to show that Geology was not a science which undermined the Old Testament theory of the Creation or of the Flood and Noah's Ark. It is quite evident from his books that Horton's interest in Geology was developed and stimulated during his period at King's College. He gained his Associateship of King's College in 1858, after the regulations had been stiffened. He also took the membership examination of the Royal College of Surgeons of England (M.R.C.S.) which qualified him to be a doctor.

He next proceeded to Edinburgh for a year at the end of which he passed with commendation the examination for the Doctorate of Medicine (M.D.) degree which was then a first degree in Medicine and not a post-graduate one as it is now. During his period at Edinburgh he again showed himself an outstanding student and was president of several student professional societies at the University.

He joined the Army Medical Service as an Assistant Staff Surgeon in the West African Service and rose to the rank of Surgeon-Major in 1875, later ranking as Lieutenant-Colonel after twenty years' service and finally retiring on half pay in 1880. He was not the first African doctor, but he was one of the most versatile of his century.

During his Army career he served in all the military stations on the west coast as medical officer to Africans, West Indians and Europeans. He was in medical charge of a British military campaign in 1865 against the King of Boudou in Gambia who had invaded and destroyed towns and villages and he played a notable part in organising a militia in defence of MacCarthy Island when it was temporarily abandoned by the British in that year. He served throughout the Ashanti War in Ghana in 1873–4 and received a medal for this. His main achievement in Ghana,

4

however, was the help he gave to the Fanti Confederation in its organisation. His undergraduate and service career was paralleled by that of his countryman and colleague, Dr W. B. Davis who, however, did not see as much military action as Horton.

He was twice married in Freetown: first to Fanny Marietta Pratt, a member of a distinguished Creole family of Ibo origin, who died at the early age of twenty-two, and later to Selina Elliot, of coloured American (Nova Scotian) ancestry, who survived him. He left two daughters who later settled in Britain.

Horton's writings were on politics, education, medicine and science. They were to a considerable extent descriptive in nature, being composed of digests and excerpts from other authors. They all indicated wide and judicious reading and familiarity with the Latin, Greek, French and Hebrew he had learnt at Fourah Bay. He included in his books, however, personal observations and comments, ideas on the nature of self-government, simple medical and scientific experiments, and accounts of indigenous cures for some tropical ailments.

Horton's first book was printed in 1859 when he was twenty-four. Its title was *The Medical Topography of the West Coast of Africa*. It was this thesis which had won him the Doctorate of Medicine with commendation at Edinburgh University. It was largely a descriptive work on the natural vegetation, geology and animal life found along the African coast and islands from Tenerife to Fernando Po. It contained a description of the tropical seasons. There was not much that was medical or original in it, which was not surprising, as he had just qualified as a doctor and had not been home for some years. It was mostly a digest of existing published work.[1] It contained a short description of female circumcision as practised in the Gallinas district. He defined in it, also, two seasons which were particularly unhealthy in West Africa—the beginning of the rains and the harvest season; and his description of food plants was very thorough.

This book contained an advertisement for two forthcoming publications on medical matters: *A Manual of the Diseases of Tropical Climates with the Medical Topography of the West Coast of Africa* and *Diet and Regimen in Health and Disease*, but it does not seem that these were ever published. He wrote a short treatise on general medicine in the tropics two or three years later, however, which he sent to the C.M.S. in London where it still exists in the archives.

In 1865 he published a pamphlet entitled *The Political Economy of British Western Africa; with the Requirements of the several Colonies and Settlements (The African View of The Negro's Place in Nature)*. It was a

[1] He was indebted in this respect and in some of his later works to Dr Thomas Winterbottom's books. See Selected References.

5

lecture which he had given to the African Aid Society in London. This society, with Lord Alfred Churchill as President, had concerned itself with the spread of British influence and of Christianity in Africa and with assisting educated and trained Africans to develop their own countries. Its journal was *The African Times*, which was edited by the Secretary of the Society, Ferdinand Fitzgerald, a great champion of the African, who continued to edit the journal long after he had been asked to give up the secretaryship of the Society. *The African Times*, although published in Britain, provided the best information then available on current African affairs and served as a forum for the opinions of Europeans and educated Africans. Its circulation was small but its influence was great in London and West Africa. Much of what was in Horton's 1865 address to this Society was incorporated in his later work, *West African Countries and Peoples, British and Native . . . and a Vindication of the African Race*, which was published in 1868.

In the year before this, however, he had published the *Physical and Medical Climate and Meteorology of the West Coast of Africa*. This was well received in London. It was the only work extant in this field on Western Africa and was praised by some of the leading journalists of the day. It included *Valuable Hints to Europeans for the Preservation of Health in the Tropics*. It gave a thorough account not only of the subjects mentioned in its title, but also of the geological nature of coastal West Africa. It had many tables of observations of weather conditions— temperature, rainfall, humidity, wind velocities and atmospheric pressure over the preceding five years in Gambia, Sierra Leone, Ghana and the region bordering Western Nigeria. Many of these observations he must have made himself.

He provided some justification of his assiduity in taking readings by comparing some of his results with those taken forty years earlier by other observers. It would be equally interesting to compare the data he gave then with what obtains now.

He recorded interesting information of that period not easily found in other sources, such as the occurrence of snowfall, hail and earthquakes in West Africa. His descriptions of tropical tornadoes were particularly vivid.

His main concern, however, was about public health conditions, such as the bad drainage and poor sewage systems which then existed in these territories. He gave detailed and meticulous advice as to measures necessary for their improvement. He was particularly concerned with the high mortality of Europeans in the tropics and with the bad name which the West Coast then had in this respect. He obviously felt that the presence of skilled European personnel was necessary for the development of his country. His book also contained chapters on the effect of

6

tropical heat on its inhabitants; he tried to explain that the backwardness of Africans was possibly due to the effect of heat on the brain.

He propounded the thesis that the extreme blackness of the Jolloffs was due to the effect of the sun on their skin, and wrongly believed that this acquired characteristic was passed on to their children.

The details and number of cases of illness he treated, which he gave in this book, are of considerable interest to medical statisticians.

This book, more than any other, included most of his own personal observations, and extended the field he had opened with his first book. He was influenced by existing works of this nature which related to India, although his book was clearly the first of its kind on West Africa produced in mid-Victorian Britain.

He mentioned in one of its chapters that he had published a few years earlier a pamphlet on *The Geological Constitution of Ahanta, Gold Coast*. There is no copy of this pamphlet extant in major libraries, but most of it, as was his practice, was undoubtedly included in this book.

Some of the geological information about Ghana and other parts of West Africa mentioned in this book, and in the later *West African Countries and Peoples*, was surprisingly accurate. He mentioned the possibility of there being diamonds in Ghana, and searched for them unsuccessfully. He also mentioned the presence of iron ore in Sierra Leone. Sixty years later, the presence of these minerals in quantity was established in these territories and their exploitation has produced and is still producing vast financial returns.

West African Countries and Peoples, British and Native . . . and a Vindication of the African Race is the book by which he is most remembered. The first section was devoted to a reasoned but spirited reply to those scientists and anthropologists, among them Richard Burton, Dr Robert Knox and Dr James Hunt of the Anthropological Society, who had asserted that the Negro belonged to a lower order of the human species, and had physical and anatomical features which were more like those of an ape than those of European members of the human race. The arguments put forward in this section owed a great deal to William Armistead's *A Tribute for the Negro*, published twenty years earlier.

The second part of the book dealt with the capability of the African for self-government. He wrote a full account, based partly on personal observation, partly on hearsay and wide reading, of some of the peoples of West Africa, and he attempted to define what form of self-government —monarchical or republican—would be suitable for each group. He drew upon experiences gained during his residence in the different countries. Apart from short visits to Lagos, there is no record that he had travelled much in Nigeria. Most of his information about Nigeria he had probably gained from the many Nigerians and their Creole children

7

who resided in Gambia and Sierra Leone. His long chapter on the Ibo is of particular interest as his own parents were Ibos and he must have learnt a great deal about Ibo country from them and from those in the active Ibo community in Freetown who by then were calling themselves Sierra Leoneans. He must also have gathered contemporary information from alumni of Fourah Bay College, such as Bishop Crowther of Yoruba origin and the Reverend J. C. Taylor, himself of Ibo origin, who were then C.M.S. missionaries in Eastern Nigeria. The Principal of Fourah Bay College when Horton was a student there, the Reverend Edward Jones, had led an expedition to Iboland, Nigeria in 1853 whilst Horton was still at college, and on his return he must have given his students a vivid account of his journey.

Although the main theme of the book concerned the nature of self-government in the territories, the interspersed incidental accounts of the various peoples are of great interest, especially when they are from his own personal observation or when they reveal his personal prejudices. It is not surprising that the limitation of knowledge, then, of the interior caused him to omit many well-known hinterland communities except for a few scattered remarks about them. He ended by giving the requirements he considered necessary before self-government could be granted to each territory.

Some of his practical ideas, such as those regarding agriculture in Ghana, road building in Western Nigeria and building a bridge over the Oyster Creek in Gambia, all mentioned in his book, have been fulfilled. Some of his ideas, such as those on University education in Medicine and other subjects which he related to Sierra Leone, referred to that country more as being the capital of West Africa at that time than simply as a territory on its own. They are therefore justifiably meant to be applicable to all independent African territories. His ideas on female education also have universal African relevance to the present. The most important requirement for self-government in his view seemed to have been the organisation of a proper educational system at all levels, chiefly the University. The self-government he envisaged was one in which British influence would play an important part. It was not unlike what his contemporaries in Canada and Australia wanted, since in law —although they were black—the Creoles of the Sierra Leone peninsula were as British as the white colonial citizens of Canada and Australia. They too wanted self-government, but wished to continue under the influence of Britain. It will be observed that in all his writings, although he pressed for self-government for his people, Horton yet regarded himself as a British officer and a subject of the Queen.

The next background theme to this book on self-government was inspired by the resolutions of a Select Committee of the House of

8

Commons which had decided that self-government was necessary for the communities of West Africa. They had not reached this decision solely on the grounds of the ability of Africans to govern themselves. As Horton shrewdly points out, the high mortality of Europeans on the coast and the expense of maintaining armies and consular representatives on the west coast were burdens which the British government was unwilling to face. The annexation of further territories had been and continued for some years to be resisted, although it was strongly urged by traders and officials on the coast and even by educated Africans themselves who saw the trade routes to the interior threatened by neighbouring hinterland tribes. Paradoxically, Sierra Leone was made a possible exception for self-government, since although it was the most advanced educationally, it was, as the headquarters of the area, so much easier, more convenient and less expensive than the others to maintain. The port of Sierra Leone was also an imperial naval base and was important for the part it played in Britain's naval strategy.

It was not that the British government thought that the West Africans were fit to govern themselves. It was probably because it was felt that the price of governing it was too high in terms of finance and mortality. Horton, however, saw in this recommendation for future self-government a challenge to Africans to prove themselves capable of good and sound government in their respective countries.

Liberia was then self-governing, and its diplomatic and cultural ambassador, Dr Edward Blyden of Afro-West-Indian origin, was becoming well known in both African and European circles. Blyden's own view of the African was nearer that of our present concept as he felt that the African was unique, not in an inferior way as Knox and others had postulated, but in the fact that Negro civilisation had something positive to contribute to world culture and did not need to go through the processes of Christian and European acculturation before being able to make this contribution.

It may be that their differing backgrounds accounted for the different views of Blyden and Horton. Blyden, coming from the Danish West Indies at seventeen to receive his school and college education in an independent African country where his own Americo-Liberian immigrant group was supreme, having literally turned his back on America and Europe, could face Europe on his own terms afterwards and be accepted. Horton, born in the colonial Afro-European society of Freetown where his group, the liberated Africans, occupied the lowest social position among the literate classes (the Europeans ranked first, then their mulatto offspring and next above Horton's group the settlers from Nova Scotia and Jamaica), passed on to an even more competitive European society in the academic world of London and Edinburgh where he was not always at an advantage. From there he moved into the difficult and testing society of an Officers' Mess in Africa, containing British and white West Indians by whom the African was never regarded in the main as much more than a servant. In all these spheres, his ability was never questioned, but he was only partly accepted socially and he was always on trial. To him and his group, the one way by which they could gain complete acceptance was to acquire as completely as possible those ideals which they could see as if through a half-opened door. It was those British—like Henry Venn, of the C.M.S., Sir Arthur Kennedy, and John Pope Hennessy, Governor-General of West Africa and champion of Africanisation—who believed that they could achieve this goal, to whom they turned for encouragement and whom they most admired. It was to the first two particularly that Horton dedicated his books which dealt with questions of African self-government.

Horton's *Letters on the Political Condition of the Gold Coast since the Exchange of Territory between the English and Dutch Governments* was published in London in 1870. It was composed of a series of letters which had been sent by him to successive Secretaries of State for War and the Colonies in the preceding three years concerning conditions in the Gold Coast. It was this book that was dedicated to Sir Arthur Kennedy, about whom he made flattering remarks in one of his letters in the book. Horton, by gaining the sympathy of powerful patrons and friends in Britain and in the West African headquarters of Sierra Leone, protected himself from the criticism of local European officials which inevitably followed most of his controversial and polemical publications. The substance of the *Letters* was chiefly this: the majority of the forts along the coast of Ghana then belonged to the Dutch or the British; for administrative convenience these two powers had exchanged forts in 1869 so as to convert their haphazardly arranged forts and areas of influence into clearly demarcated and contiguous ones, which gave each imperial power a definite and uninterrupted area of influence.

By treaty, all the rights held by Europeans on the coast east of the Sweet River were allocated to the British and to the west of this river to the Dutch. Most of the people to the west were Fanti, who had long been in conflict with the powerful Ashanti in the interior. The Fanti were aware that the Dutch were particularly friendly with the Ashanti. The Elminas, under the Dutch, had also been hostile to the Fanti and friendly or sometimes even related by blood to the Ashanti. The Fanti had not been consulted about this transfer and felt that they were now at a disadvantage. They were very much opposed to being transferred. Horton's letters backed their contention and with some special pleading showed the disastrous consequences which had resulted from it. He had mentioned some of this in his *West African Countries and Peoples*.

The *Letters* also contained what was probably an eyewitness account of the expensive and inconclusive 1864 Ashanti War.

The last chapter contained an account of the Fanti Confederation which promised to be a self-governing unit and would in fact have formed a realization of Horton's scheme of monarchical self-government for that part of the coast as outlined in *West African Countries and Peoples*. Horton's *Letters* gained him great popularity with Ghanaians, but it caused consternation among the local officials who accused him of stirring up discontent amongst the Fanti by his attempts to unite them and his continued protests against the handing over of the British forts to the Dutch. The Governor asked for his transfer from Ghana. The officials in the War Office and the Colonial Office in London and the Governor-General in Sierra Leone had, however, already read the *Letters* before publication and did not see any reason for alarm; they took no disciplinary action.

The Dutch territories were finally bought by the British in 1872, thus solving that particular problem. The Fanti Confederation was never encouraged or accepted by the British but it formed, like the more short-lived Accra Native Confederation, one of the first attempts at self-government by local Africans under European sovereignty.

After 1870, Horton published no more political books and pamphlets. In 1872 he had unsuccessfully applied for the vacant post of Governor of the Gold Coast, after the holder of that office had been invalided home. He was supported by the temporary Administrator or Governor-General of West Africa, the liberal Irishman, John Pope Hennessy, who described him as being 'a perfectly black man of considerable integrity and zeal'. Horton's application was not as unreasonable or premature as it may now seem. European members of the Army Medical Service—Dr Samuel Rowe and Dr Gouldsbury—were later appointed Administrators or Governors of territories in West Africa. His application showed, however, a certain imperviousness to the hostile feelings which he knew he must have aroused in the local European officials. He was again severely criticised soon after, whilst stationed in Sekondi as Civil Commandant (see Chapter 16). All this may have led to an understandable reluctance to publish any more books or articles on local political situations. The Ashanti War of 1873 broke out soon after, and he was in active service throughout, under Sir Garnet Wolseley who is said to have made use of Horton's geographical knowledge of the area in planning his campaign.

During this period of respite from political writing, he turned with more resolution to the compilation of his work on tropical diseases. This resulted in the appearance of his *Diseases of Tropical Climates and their Treatment* in 1874. It was very well received in medical circles. His promotion to the substantive rank of Surgeon-Major from that of Surgeon had been anticipated by his publishers, who described him as such in the book. All went well, however, and he achieved the senior rank soon afterwards. His book incorporated as one of its chapters another smaller work on *The Guinea Worm, or Dracunculus* which had been published about ten years earlier as a pamphlet, and it also included with minor modifications the *Hints to Europeans* which had been published in the earlier *Physical and Medical Climate and Meteorology of West Africa.*

This substantial textbook on tropical medicine chose examples from the wide experience which fifteen years of practising medicine in West Africa had given him. Another edition was published five years later. He retired soon afterwards, in 1880, on half pay, at the age of forty-five.

He returned to Freetown on his retirement, a relatively wealthy man, and embarked forthwith on commercial ventures. He opened a bank to provide cash advances for local *entrepreneurs*. His interest in Ghana still remained and he became actively engaged in suggesting plans for the construction of a railway there, and in obtaining concessions for gold-mining. He joined in awarding scholarships to promising Africans to go abroad and study.

He died of severe erysipelas three years later at the early age of forty-eight. His friends subscribed to the erection of a memorial tablet, which is situated, still legible, in the south-eastern corner of the Cathedral of St George in Freetown; this tablet summarises his career, giving his age at the time of death as fifty-one instead of forty-eight. The F.R.G.S. (Fellow of the Royal Geographical Society) inscribed after his name, and now a little worn, was misquoted as F.R.C.S. (Fellow of the Royal College of Surgeons) in an earlier essay on Horton. In fact, the distinction of being the first African F.R.C.S. and thus a surgical specialist, belonged to his neighbour at Gloucester Street, Freetown, Dr Robert Smith, who was of mixed ancestry.

True to his belief in the importance of education, Horton left a substantial part of his estate for the furtherance of scientific education at both school and college level in a way which would benefit West Africa. He had lived long enough to see his vision of a University of West Africa begun by the affiliation in 1876 of his *alma mater*, Fourah Bay College, to Durham University in Britain for the award of University degrees and diplomas.

The settlement of his estate took some time and in the end most of the money was lost by depreciation of shares and legal expenses. The remainder was used towards the foundation of a Diocesan Technical

Institute in Freetown, as this was felt to have been within the intention of one who was so passionately interested in the industrial advancement and technological development of Africa.

After his death, there followed a period of seventy years of colonial domination during which African advancement was held back. The Westminster policy of self-government was forgotten or reversed. Many of the British officials on the coast had never really believed in it and some never did to the end. Domestic rivalries in Europe, the problem of Egypt, the energetic policy of annexation in Africa by the French, the ambitions of Bismarck the Prussian Chancellor, of King Leopold of Belgium, of Goldie the British merchant-adventurer on the Niger River; all this against the background of the understandable aggressiveness of the hinterland tribes in barring the opening up of new trade routes into the rich interior, led to the partitioning of Africa among imperialistic European powers, which culminated in the Berlin Conference of 1885.

Advances in tropical medicine and public health, some of which had been advocated by Horton himself, made it easier for Europeans to live with relative safety in tropical Africa. They did not in the main, however, come in the rôle of visiting advisers and sympathetic purveyors of Christian civilisation and western culture, ready to hand over rapidly to self-governing Africans, as Henry Venn and Ferdinand Fitzgerald in Britain had desired, and as Africans like Bishop Adjai Crowther and Africanus Horton had hoped. They came instead ready to stay for a long time to govern men who they felt needed centuries of guidance before they would be able to govern themselves. The reactionaries had won, but their victory proved only partial and temporary.

Horton's educational and cultural background (as we have seen) made him believe that the technology and culture of Christian Europe were the highest and best ideals worth striving for. This concept has now been long abandoned in Africa, and even then was challenged by his friend Dr Edward Blyden. The protests of most educated Africans who felt as Horton did, were directed against those who felt that the Negro was incapable of achieving these European virtues. It must be remembered, to understand their viewpoint, that within two generations they had risen from a background of warring tribes, to an ordered and peaceful community where they could study Plato's *Republic* in the original Greek, carry out experiments in chemistry, make accurate meteorological measurements, and where the Victorian concepts of industry and self-help leading to settled prosperity were desirable goals which they had in some cases successfully achieved.

The group of educated Africans who had made this achievement possible was proportionately small but very impressive. It included not only Africanus Horton, the most prolific in writing, but also Samuel Lewis, a distinguished barrister, later to become the first African to receive the honour of knighthood; George Blankson of Ghana, merchant prince of Anomabu, and a member of the Legislative Council; Adjai Crowther of Nigeria with an honorary doctorate of Divinity from Oxford University and the first non-European to be consecrated a Protestant Bishop since the Reformation.

It is important for our present era that these men succeeded in the European Victorian context. They had first to prove to the world that it was possible to do so before the particular and unique contribution of the African could be made and readily accepted. They were essential as a bridge to make it possible for their descendants to cross over to the distant side of the river where African political and cultural independence lay. Edward Blyden was before his time in insisting that the total African contribution could then be made at once. But he was necessary to the others as a warning that the situation had a dynamism which carried beyond mere European acculturation.

Those who were against African advancement held their victory for many long decades before a combination of educational progress, freedom fighters in Africa and liberal forces in Europe, which had never been completely extinguished, broke through into a new day in the second half of the twentieth century.

Nevertheless, in that false dawn, a century ago, we can still discern from Horton's works glimmerings of future institutions of self-government and beginnings of the concept of African unity. We can see them in the bodies formed in that period like the Egba Administration, the Fanti Confederation (many of the principles of which were Horton's ideas), the Liberian Republic and the Committee of Gentlemen at MacCarthy Island in the River Gambia which he himself had led.

Now that the true dawn has appeared and great nations in Africa have been liberated into the complex, arduous yet rewarding responsibilities of independence, the call for integrity and courage which Horton addressed to the predecessors and ancestors of the modern African in 1866 must be remembered:

The rising generation especially should bear in mind that they have a special mission to fulfil on earth; that they are not exclusively their own property, but that by industry and perseverance they might so better their circumstances and position as to give material aid to those less favoured than themselves. . . .[1]

[The youth of Africa] should make it their ruling principle to con-

[1] *West African Countries*, p. 274, l. 20 ff.

14

centrate their mental powers, their powers of observation, reasoning, and memory, on the primary objects of their engagement. . . .[1]

Let them consider that their own interest is intimately bound up in the interest of their country's rise; and that by developing the principle of public interest they will bring the Government to take an interest in themselves, and thus their interest and that of their Government will not clash, but become identical. . . .

Let the rising generation, therefore, study to exert themselves to obtain the combined attractive influence of knowledge and wisdom, wealth and honesty, great place and charity, fame and happiness, book-learning and virtue, so that they may be made to bring their happy influence to bear on the regeneration of their country . . . tutu, cito, et jucunde. [2, 3]

[1] *Ibid.*, p. 275, l. 13 ff.
[2] 'Safely, quickly and with joy' (Ed.).
[3] *West African Countries*, p. 273, l. 20 ff.

Note: in the chapters which follow, the editor's introductions to the different sections are printed in italics.

I

The Capability of Africans for Self-Government

Dr Horton eloquently states his thesis that on historical, cultural and economic grounds Africans are capable of political self-government and national independence. The African nations he had in mind were large communities like the Fanti, the Ga, the Yoruba, the Ibo and the Sierra Leone Creoles.

Modern African nations as we know them now had not yet been formed. Horton, however, would have welcomed them as he felt federated units were more useful than fragmented ones.

Mankind by the knowledge of metallurgy and other useful arts emerged from a primitive state of barbarism, and have gradually brought to themselves the benefits of a civilised life. Of this primitive state little is furnished us in history, and very little is actually known; but we are led to believe the speculative traditions of the ancient Romans, that 'mankind', as the state of political community now exists, advanced from a rude and helpless state to the formation of political society; and entirely disapprove of the Greek mythological legend, that 'mankind emerged from a state of innocence and bliss'.

Bearing in mind the foregoing, it will be my province to prove the capability of the African for possessing a real political Government and national independence.[1]

Such being the tendency of all national greatness, the nations of Africa must live in the hope, that in process of time their turn will come, when they will occupy a prominent position in the world's history, and when they will command a voice in the council of nations.[2]

Africa, in ages past, was the nursery of science and literature; from

[1] *West African Countries*, p. 1, l. 4 ff.
[2] *Ibid.*, p. 68, l. 16 ff.

thence they were taught in Greece and Rome, so that it was said that the ancient Greeks represented their favourite goddess of Wisdom— Minerva—as an African princess. Pilgrimages were made to Africa in search of knowledge by such eminent men as Solon, Plato, Pythagoras; and several came to listen to the instructions of the African Euclid, who was at the head of the most celebrated mathematical school in the world, and who flourished 300 years before the birth of Christ. The conqueror of the great African Hannibal made his associate and confidant the African poet, Terence.

'Being emancipated by his master, he took him to Rome and gave him a good education; the young African soon acquired reputation for the talent he displayed in his comedies. His dramatic works were much admired by the Romans for their prudential maxims and moral sentences, and compared with his contemporaries, he was much in advance of them in point of style.'

Origen, Tertullian, Augustin, Clemens Alexandrinus, and Cyril, who were fathers and writers of the Primitive Church, were tawny Africans of Apostolic renown. Many eminent writers and historians agree that these ancient Ethiopians were Negroes, but many deny that this was the case. The accounts given by Herodotus, who travelled in Egypt, and other writers, settle the question that such they were. Herodotus describes them as 'woolly-haired blacks, with projecting lips'. In describing the people of Colchis, he says that they were Egyptian colonists who were 'black in complexion and woolly-haired'. This description undoubtedly refers to a race of Negroes, as neither the Copts, their descendants, nor the mummies which have been preserved, would lead us to believe that their complexion was black. Even the large sphinx, which was excavated by M. Caviglia in Egypt, and which is regarded by all scientific men as a stupendous piece of sculpture, has its face 'of the Negro cast', and is said to be of a mild and even of a sublime expression. 'If it be not admitted that these nations were black, they were undoubtedly of very dark complexion, having much of the Negro physiognomy, as depicted in Egyptian sculpture and painting, and from them the Negro population, indeed the whole race of Africa, have sprung. Say not, then, I repeat it, that Africa is without her heraldry of science and fame. Its inhabitants are the offshoots—wild and untrained, it is true, but still the offshoots of a stem which was once proudly luxuriant in the fruits of learning and taste; whilst that from which the Goths, their calumniators, have sprung, remained hard, and knotted and barren' (Armistead: *A Tribute for the Negro*, p. 123). And why should not the same race who governed Egypt, attacked the most famous and flourishing city—Rome, who had her churches, her Universities, and her repositories of learning and science, once more stand on their legs and endeavour to raise their characters in the scale of the civilised world?

In the examination of the world's history, we are led forcibly to entertain the opinion that human affairs possess a gradual and progressive tendency to deterioration. Nations rise and fall; the once flourishing and civilized degenerates into a semi-barbarous state; and those who have lived in utter barbarism, after a lapse of time become the standing nation.[1]

Examining Western Africa in its entirety, we find it to be composed of a number of political communities, each ruled by a national Government, formed in many cases of distinct nationalities occupying determined territory; but some national communities are broken up into innumerable fractional sections, governed by rebel chiefs, or satraps; others depend upon a political body whose sovereign chief rules over life and property; and others, again, are under well-regulated civilised government. But in order to develop among these different nationalities a true political science, it is necessary that the inhabitants should be made acquainted with the useful arts, and the physical conditions which influence other more civilised and refined political Governments.

What, it may be asked, are the different forms of government now in existence on the West Coast of Africa? The two principal forms are the monarchical and the republican.

In the purely native community we observe the recognition of power, in many cases, vested in a single individual, variously called by the different tribes, but to which we apply the names of basileus, or king; surrounded by a number of headmen, who pledge themselves to do his will. Some of these basileus, such as those of Ashantee and Dahomey, have implicit power over life and property, and therefore are held in dread by their subjects.

Among other political native communities we find that in some the form of government resembles very closely a limited monarchy—in others a democracy, in which all the caboceers or head men stand almost on equal terms.

In matters of great interest, in many cases a whole nation assemble together for deliberation; but the counsels of the aged, from their experience, especially when backed by previous sage advice and reputation of wisdom, a sober and thoughtful deportment, and a vigorous and energetic character, generally decide the will of the multitude.

Some towns there are which are governed entirely by chiefs, who exercise an uncertain rule over the inhabitants and who are regarded more as a father of the community than a political head; some of them

[1] *Ibid.*, p. 66, l. 15 ff.

19

are nomadic in their nature, but others constitute themselves into a political society of the most primitive order.[1]

Among those tribes who have made some onward step in the career of civilisation we observe that agriculture is supported by regular labours at the proper season, the produce of which they bring to European markets, to exchange for useful implements, cotton goods, and rude luxuries; they weave a kind of cotton or fibre cloth, which they employ as wearing apparel and for exportation, and some of it is much prized, even by Europeans, for the dexterity of the workmanship; and a particular rough kind (Bandy cloth) forms an important medium of commerce in Western Africa. The inhabitants collect themselves in large and populous towns, with the idea of strengthening their powers of defence, as in Abeokuta. Some, as the Fantees (Cromantees), in whose region gold forms the medium of commerce, are fully aware of its value, and possess a knowledge of the means of working it into various trinkets and articles of domestic importance. . . .

Some, such as the Fans, show considerable ingenuity in the manufacture of iron. In their country, interior of the Gaboon, iron ore is found in considerable quantity, cropping out at the surface. To obtain the iron, they 'build a huge pile of wood, heap on this a considerable quantity of the ore broken up, then come with more wood', and apply fire to the whole; wood is continually being thrown into it until the ore becomes fluid, when it is allowed to cool down, and cast iron is obtained. To temper and make it malleable, 'they put it through a most tedious series of heating and hammerings, till at last they turn out a very superior article of iron and steel', which is much better than the trade quality brought out from Europe. Of this they make their knives, arrow-heads, and swords. . . .

Fishing and hunting form also a part of their pursuits, and in many cases they excel in these to an appreciable degree. In North-Western and Central West Africa, the regions of the Gambia and Sierra Leone (as also in Dahomey) the inhabitants are accustomed every summer to set fire to the bush, and thus consume the grass and underwood, giving the country an open appearance. But in other parts there are large, dense forests, impenetrable to man, and with difficulty penetrable to the larger quadrupeds.

Some of the languages of the tribes are harsh and guttural, such as the Jollofs and Calabars; others are soft and mellowy, as the Mandingos, Temineh (Temne), and Fantee; and others again are palatal, as the Accra, Awoonah, and Dahomey. The trading propensity is most extensively developed among every tribe; in their native state, money, as

[1] *Ibid.*, p. 2, l. 21 ff.

a coin, is unknown to them; in many places cowrie shell is the prevailing medium—as from Accra to the Niger; in Bonny and Calabar, iron bar; in the Gambia and Senegal and the Casamangs, native-made cloth called bandy cloth; in Fantee, Bassa, Ahanta, Apollonia, Ashantee, and Sooso, gold; In some places, however, domestic slaves form the principal article of barter.[1]

Some of the tribes make canoes from the trunk of the silk cotton-tree, the bombax, which they hollow out and afterwards burn; those on the river Gambia make their canoes out of the mahogany tree, which is very strong and durable, resisting the action of the powerful rays of the sun, and with the effects of the water, easily destroys other boats. They mould their rude cooking utensils—water pots, plates, and dishes—from the clay of the land, and cut out their spoons and combs from different kinds of wood. . . .

Personal cleanliness is a chief trait in the character of most tribes; gambling forms part of the amusement of some; they practise several athletic games, such as wrestling, boxing, and running for sport and exercise. In some tribes they build large stockades of wood or mud, which on examination exhibit evidence of design and labour.

After the death of a near relative in some tribes there is great moaning, weeping, and lamentation; but among others, as is the practice on the Gold Coast, as soon as the funeral party returns from the graveyard they are regaled with champagne and other wines and with spirits; a dancing party is invariably given, either in the same evening or a few days afterwards, in the house of the deceased, the chief mourner being the chief dancer.

In a few isolated spots the chastity of the young female is carefully watched by the priests of the country, and the girls are known by peculiar names; in the Sherbro and Quiah (Koya) countries they are called 'Boondoo girls', and in the Adogma and Crobboe 'Fetish girls'. They are kept under strict surveillance, no intrusion is permitted; a discovery of any irregularity is attended with a heavy fine, slavery, or even death on the part of the male. After remaining for some years, varying from two to six, certain rites are performed by the priests, and they are then allowed to return to their homes.[2]

The African, in common with the most enlightened people, may be impelled by events into philosophical speculations; and this is proved by the existence of a written language amongst them, designed entirely by themselves. The origin of this language, if their legend is reliable, was in the wonder excited by some messengers of the Quiah (Koya Temne,

[1] *Ibid.*, pp. 6, 7, 8.   [2] *Ibid.*, p. 10, l. 12 ff.

Sierra Leone) tribe carrying a letter from an educated person of a more civilised nation to an individual at a distance, the reading of which conveyed to him the information of what had taken place in their own town. Possessing clearly a philosophical turn of mind, they became curious to discover the contrivance which so struck their observation; and from that time began to put in writing on leaves and barks of trees the language of their country. . . .

Where they have nothing to stir up the latent powers of improvement in them but the book of nature, whose pages, truly, are filled with objects of wonder and admiration, Africans do, in many cases, show signs of possessing wonderful powers of observation; and when once they acquire the necessary information respecting natural objects by habits of patient attention, which must be the inevitable result, when those powers are brought into play, they are indelibly riveted in their memory. Too true, the majestic trees of the forest, covered with their evergreen foliage of a thousand variegated colours; the numerous gay tropical birds with beautiful plumage; the solitary and melancholy grandeur of many of the scenes with which they are surrounded; the magnificent rivers which run through their country; the ocean, in all its forms of sublimity and terror; the tremendous rocks which resound with the ceaseless roar of the billows, and the numerous shells which stud the shores of their country, form in a scientific point of view but a small portion of their consideration, from their seeming insignificance, and from a want of scientific knowledge in the beholders; yet still, the brilliant stars, the splendid midday sun, the resplendent full moon, and the terrific tornado, with its thunder and lightning, all call into exercise the peculiar disposition and talents of their mind.

They calculate figures in their memory to an extent which would surprise the most practised mathematician, without using any mechanical means for their aid.[1]

In 1818, the immortal Clarkson, in the Congress of Aix-la-Chapelle, exhibited certain articles of native African manufacture to the Emperor of Russia, whilst endeavouring to secure support in the suppression of the slave-trade; viewing the articles, the Emperor said, 'You astonish me; you have given me a new idea of the state of these poor people; I was not aware that they were so advanced in society. The works you have shown me are not the works of brutes, but of men endowed with natural and intellectual powers, and capable of being brought to as high a degree of proficiency as any other man. Africa ought to be allowed to have a fair chance of raising her character in the scale of the civilised world.'[2]

[1] *Ibid.*, p. 22, l. 3 ff.　　[2] *Ibid.*, p. 26, l. 6 ff.

I (thus) claim the existence of the attribute of a common humanity in the African or Negro race; that there exist no radical distinctions between him and his more civilised confrere; that the amount of moral and intellectual endowments exhibited by him, as originally conferred by nature, is the same, or nearly so, as that found amongst the European nations; and it is an incontrovertible logical inference that the difference arises entirely from the influence of external circumstances. Truly—

Natura una et communis omnium est.[1,2]

[1] 'Nature is one and shared by all' (Ed.).
[2] *West African Countries*, p. 29, l. 14 ff.

Refutation of the Alleged Inferiority of the Negro Race

The Anthropological Society of London in its early days had amongst its members many who were convinced that the Negro was inferior to other races and that in the development of mankind he was midway between the European and the ape. They based their theories on the development and the size of the brain.

*Amongst them was Dr Robert Knox, an anatomist who had been involved in a scandal and had given up his professional career to become instead a popular lecturer and racial theorist. His pupil Dr Hunt had the same racialist convictions. Dr Hunt's disparaging book **The Negro's place in Nature** had evoked a reply in a subtitle from Dr Horton in his pamphlet **The Political Economy of British Western Africa with the Requirements of the several Colonies and Settlements (The African View of the Negro's place in Nature)**, published in London in 1865 and also in a letter in **The African Times** of April 1866; the latter comprises the second extract in this chapter.*

Carl Vogt, the German anthropologist, was also one of the scientific anthropologists who in Germany and Switzerland had propagated similar theories.

Horton had won a Certificate of Honour at King's College, London, in Comparative Anatomy, and this was a field in which he took a special interest. He produced evidence from his own medical and educational experience to refute the allegations of Negro inferiority and showed by the experience of his own people, the Sierra Leone Creoles, that there could be a swift rise from apparent barbarity to a civilised community in one generation. He wanted to prove by this that Negro backwardness was not intrinsic but the result of adverse circumstances and lack of opportunity.

*Philip Curtin in his book **The Image of Africa** (Madison, 1964) gives a full account of the racialist theories of this particular period.*

It is in the development of the most important organ of the body—the brain, and its investing parieties—that much stress has been laid to prove the simian or apelike character of the Negro race. . . . The skull is, as regards the sutures, intimately connected with the brain; in man, we find that the posterior sutures first close, and the frontal and coronal last, but in the anthropoid ape the contrary is the case. Among the Negro race, at least among the thousands that have come under my notice, the posterior sutures first close, then the frontal and coronal, and the contrary has never been observed by me in even a single instance, not even among Negro idiots; and yet M. Gratiolet and Carl Vogt, without an opportunity of investigating the subject to any extent, have unhesitatingly propagated the most absurd and erroneous doctrine—that the closing of the sutures in the Negro follows the siminious or animal arrangement, differing from that already given as the governing condition in man.[1]

Dr. Knox regards everything to be subservient to race; and his arguments are brought forward to show that the Negro race, in spite of all the exertions of Exeter Hall, or as his commentators most sneeringly call them, the 'broad-brimmed philanthropy and dismal science school', will still continue as they were. To him, as he says, 'Race is everything—literature, science, art—in a word civilisation depends on it. . . . With me race or hereditary descent is everything; it stamps the man'.

Of late years a society has been formed in England in imitation of the Anthropological Society of Paris, which might be made of great use to science had it not been for the profound prejudice exhibited against the Negro race in their discussions and in their writings. They again revive the old vexed question of race, which the able researches of Blumenbach, Prichard, Pallas, Hunter, Lacépéde, Quatrefages, Geoffroy St. Hilaire, and many others had, years ago (as it is thought) settled. They placed the structure of the anthropoid apes before them, and then commenced the discussion of a series of ideal structures of the Negro which only exist in their imagination, and thus endeavour to link the Negro with the brute creation. Some of their statements are so barefacedly false, so utterly the subversion of scientific truth, that they serve to exhibit the writers as perfectly ignorant of the subjects of which they treat. The works of Carl Vogt, 'Lectures on Man' of Dr. Hunt, 'Negro's Place in Nature'; and of Prunner Bey, 'Mémoire sur les Nègres', 1861, contain, in many respects, tissues of the most deceptive statements, calculated to mislead those who are unacquainted with the African race.

M. Prunner Bey rests his description on observations of the most narrow nature confined to Egypt; his 'Memoirs on the Negro Race', which has been made so much of, and which forms the keystone of writers on Negro formation in these days, was made on slaves, who for the last two thousand years have been subjected to the most damnifying

[1] *West African Countries*, p. 44, l. 1 ff.

degradation by their most austere Mohammedan masters; yet still this description is held up as the standard. We can, therefore, account for his opening fallacy: 'The stature of the Negro approaches the middle size. . . . I know of no instance of dwarfism among Negroes; though the monuments of Egypt show that there were dwarfs among Negroes at a very remote epoch'. . . . Now, from the above statement it would appear that there are no dwarfs among the Negroes, and in fact those who quote or comment on his statement affirm that to be the case, which is a great mistake; there are very likely none amongst the serfs of Eygpt whilst before me now, in Jamestown, Accra, on the Gold Coast, there are three dwarfs, and in every part of the West Coast I have met with them, except in the Gambia.[1]

From the starting point of Dr. Hunt we perceived the partiality which all writers of the same prejudiced mind as himself are subject to—viz., to select the worse possible specimens, and make them typical of the whole African race. *Contra*, when they attempt to describe the European race, no man comes to their standard but the most perfect and model form, or the most angelic woman.

Dr. Hunt states that the average height of the Negro is less than that of the European, the skeleton heavier, the bones larger and thicker. I can assure him that I have seen men in Africa, and not a few, taller men than any Yorkshire man I have ever come across, some of whom have been regarded as unproportionately tall. What will he say of the tall Sonninkers and Marabouts of Bathurst? What will he say of the gigantic Awoonahs in the Slave Coast? As regards the weight of the skeleton, I deny its being heavier in many instances, whilst it might be in others, just as the skeleton of a navvy in England is far heavier than the skeleton of a philosopher like Dr. Hunt. The Negro chest, he says, is laterally compressed; but for the dysentery, I should like him to visit the interior of the Gold Coast, and examine some of those Caboceers there, and then let him say whether he has seen better-developed chests in any part of the world. . . .

That Dr. Hunt was very much prejudiced before he commenced his writings may be proved from the fact that he condemns as false and unsatisfactory the favourable records of writers on the African race. Thus, he condemns the opinions of Tiedeman as unwarranted—viz., that the brain of a Negro is, upon the whole, quite as large as that of a European and other human races; the weight of the brain, its diameter, and the capacity of the *cavum cranii* prove this fact; whilst he agrees with the damnifying accounts of the American writers, Morton and Meigs, with M. Broca and Theodor Wartz, and the villainous accounts

[1] *Ibid.*, p. 35, l. 28 ff.

of Count Gorz and Van Amringe, as well as the one-sided and notoriously partial researches of M. Prunner Bey.

Some writers have said that great improvement has taken place in the intellect of the Negro by education. Dr. Hunt said such is not the fact. M. Quatrefages, with M. Elisée Reclus, made the statement that the Negro in America advances in intellect and in social scale in every generation. Dr. Hunt says he believes it not to be the fact. Dr. Hunt decries every writer who states that a pure Negro has ever exhibited mental distinction. If he should inquire in schools and colleges in England, where pure Negroes have been educated, he will easily be undeceived in that point, and he will find that in many competitive examinations these 'analogies of the *anthropoid apes*' have taken the first place, above several European students; but Dr. Hunt will perhaps say that was accidental.

The statement of Consular Agent Captain Burton, quoted by Dr. Hunt—viz., 'ever remember, that by far the greater number of the liberated were the vilest criminals in their own lands, and that in their case exportation becomes, in fact, the African form of transportation'— is as false as it is unargumentative. Slaves are sold by the hundreds and the thousands, and where are these thousands of criminals of Burton's to be obtained? Why, this question is answered by the yearly expedition of the King of Dahomey, who falls by night upon a defenceless city, panyarres the whole inhabitants, and sells them as slaves. Ninety-nine-hundredths of the slaves sold are obtained by war expeditions, and it is worse than nonsense to say that after they have been liberated, that they were 'the vilest criminals in their own lands'. The great drawback for the African is that there is no field in Africa for him in which to prosecute and put to a more practical use the knowledge he has obtained; he has no learned society to go to, and he has not sufficient money to continue independent researches, so that when he comes out to the Coast, he turns all his attention to the making of a livelihood; and he meets with discouragement everywhere he turns. In Europe the case is different; we meet with men of means and learning who could afford time for great researches.

To show more fully the partiality of Dr. Hunt, and his determination to bring the Negro out in his worst possible light, he made the quotation from Hutchison's writings, as the type of the Negro—that a Kruman after twelve years' attendance at the mission school at Cape Palmas, was asked what he knew of God; that he replied; 'God be very good. He made two things—one sleep, and the other Sunday, when no person had to work'. This Dr. Hunt singles out as the result of twelve years missionary operation. Dr. Hunt should be transported for half-an-hour to the examination of the Grammar School at Sierra Leone, conducted by a pure Negro, and in his next scientific paper we should hear another tale from him, should he be just. . . .[1]

It may be asked, what advances in civilisation have the negro race exhibited since their free contact with civilised nations untrammelled by the slave trade and slavery, that may tend to prove them not to be behind the most favoured nations in their moral and intellectual qualifications?

Leaving unnoticed many genuine evidences of civilisation to be found nowadays amongst the coloured inhabitants of Barbadoes and other West Indian Islands, and bearing in mind that mankind (in all ages) in different communities, when subject to proper cultivating influences, do not show an equal rate of advance within a given period, I shall endeavour to point out what improvements have taken place amongst the Negroes in one of the colonies on the West Coast of Africa only within the last fifty years.

As Sierra Leone is the headquarters of the possessions there, I shall select it as the subject of the example, and will commence from the liberated Africans, who were there freed from the fetters of slavery. Prior to their being kidnapped they were governed by kings, or chiefs, who had a complete sway over life and property; they possessed no written laws, and no proper religion, but worshipped wood, stones, and other material substances; they were extremely cruel to each other; polygamy was carried on to a fearful extent; the lower class were kept in a state of slavery; warfare was carried on in a most cruel style and all conquered populations were enslaved; they lived in huts, made either with mud or cane; they made only one kind of cloth; they lived either wholly naked or partially so, they tilled the ground; and the Cramantees, from having gold as the medium of commerce, knew weights and measures.

On their arrival at Sierra Leone, landed naked and in a state of abject rudeness and poverty, without the least knowledge of civilisation, they are placed under Government supervision for a few months. A portion of land is given them, to cut down the woods and build towns; then commences cultivation; missionary schools are established; gradually they begin to read and write; commerce, by degrees, forms a part of their occupation; they begin slowly to throw off their air of serfdom, which they had imbibed from previous treatment; and become interested in the nature of their Government, so as to require improvement in its administrative and judicial departments. The worship of the living and true God is strictly observed by them, and they manifest great sympathy for the condition of their countrymen. In time they begin to inquire how

[1] *The African Times*, 23rd April, 1866.

their children are to be educated, and what are the best means at their disposal for doing so. These, as they grow up (which is the generation at present occupying Sierra Leone) seek after and obtain justice; preach loudly the Christian ethics—viz., mutual charity, forgiveness of one another, fraṯernity, and equality. Science and literature are taught in some of the schools; the generation feel themselves to possess great liberty, physically and mentally; philanthropic views are extensively circulated amongst them; they build large and expensive dwelling houses; buy up the former abodes of their European masters [employers, not slave masters—Ed.], carry on extensive mercantile speculations; seek after the indulgences of civilized life, and travel in foreign countries to seek after wealth. English newspapers are very much circulated amongst them, and are read with eagerness; and they require a voice in their legislative administration. They look out for a better form of governmental administration, and desire to attain it; and they use the best means for arriving at their wish;—the essentials for political progress.[1]

But it is not only the pure Negro that has received so pernicious a handling from the anthropologists of this day; they have been unsparing also to their mixed production—the Mulattoes—who are said to be the most immoral people on the face of the globe. Of them, Captain Burton says, 'The worst class of all is the Mulatto, under which I include the Quadroon and Octaroon. He is everywhere like wealth—irritamenta malorum. The "bar sinister", and the uneasy idea that he is despised, naturally fill him with ineffable bile and bitterness. Inferior in point of morale to Europeans, and as far as regards physique, to Africans, he seeks strength in making the families of his progenitors fall out.' The description of Bosman, in his work on Guinea, published at the end of the seventeenth century, is singled out as the most true and perfect picture of Mulattoes as a class. '. . . I cannot help giving you an account of a wonderful and extraordinary sort of people—I mean the Tapaeyers or Mulattoes—a race begotten by the Europeans upon the Negro or Mulatto-woman. . . . I can only tell you whatever is in its own nature worse, in Europeans and Negroes is united in them, so that they are the sink of both. The men, most of whom are soldiers in our service, are clothed as we are, but the women prink up themselves. . . . In process of time, their bodies become speckled with white, brown, and yellow spots, like the tigers, which they also resemble in their barbarous natures. But I shall here leave them, for fear it may be thought that I am prejudiced by hatred against 'em; but so far from that, there is not a single person who hath anything to do with them, but he must own they are not worth speaking to.'

[1] *West African Countries*, p. 59, l. 1 ff.

Such is the description which is now regarded as typical of the mulattoes on the Coast.

[My own view is that] . . . these people, when properly educated, adorn and enliven society, and are chaste and faithful when properly married. But in the generality of cases we find that whilst the European and the coloured women get married, the Mulattoes, especially if not properly educated, are very seldom so, and are therefore placed in a position where they are obliged to live a disreputable life. I have met with several Mulatto ladies, who are ladies in every sense of the word, agreeable, amiable, sociable, chaste, and possessing a happy tact of making themselves agreeable with every class; and as regards their broods being frightfully ugly, I emphatically deny this as the general rule.[1]

[1] *Ibid.*, p. 53, l. 16 ff.

3

African Nationality and Recommendations for Self-Government in the African Settlements of Nigeria, Ghana, Sierra Leone and Gambia

It should be remembered that the region of West Africa to which Horton referred in all his books was more limited than that which we now know. Little was known of the hinterland tribes, and some of them, because of their attacks on the coastal settlements, were regarded as hostile. The excerpts in this anthology from this section of his book on African nationality defined the boundaries of what he regarded as West Africa.

(a) **Nigeria** *was divided into two coastal kingdoms, the Aku and the Ibo. The kingdom of the Akus (Yorubas) would have Lagos as its chief seaport, and Abeokuta as its headquarters. There was not much known of the Yoruba country beyond Abeokuta and Ibadan, and he put the capital of the region at Ilorin instead of old Oyo. He felt that the hostility of neighbouring Dahomey and the hinterland tribes might make it dangerous to grant self-government to this region without protection.*

(b) *He similarly divided* **Ghana** *into two regions—the country of the Fanti, which he felt needed a monarch, and the country around Accra, for which he decided a republican form of government was more suitable.*

(c) **Sierra Leone***, which he felt needed a monarchical form of government, consisted of the area around Freetown and Sherbro, the islands of Bulama (now in Portuguese Guinea) and the Iles de Los (now in the Republic of Guinea).*

(d) **Gambia***, which he decided needed a similar form of government, consisted of a small area around Bathurst and MacCarthy Island.*

African Nationality

Africa, through Britannic influence, is free from foreign slavery, and through that same influence has made, and hopes still to make, important progressive improvements in her history.

The desire to give an impetus to this grand development seemed to have pervaded the minds of the members of the late African Committee of the House of Commons. Their third resolution lays it down plainly that the policy of the British Government henceforth in Africa, 'should be to encourage in the native the exercise of those qualities which may render it possible for us more and more to transfer to the natives the administrations of all the Governments, with a view to our ultimate withdrawal from all, except probably Sierra Leone'. This indeed is a grand conception, which if developed into fact, will immortalise the name of Britain as the most generous and enlightened nation that has adorned the face of the globe. It is indeed a glorious idea to contemplate that the sun never sets in the vast dominions where the British flag flies, and that the name of England is always associated with liberty, justice, and humanity; but it will be still grander to contemplate that same powerful nation, setting on foot the nationality of a race down-trodden for ages, and giving to those whom she has nurtured and fostered in the principles of government 'a chance of raising their character in the scale of the civilised world'.

The Committee felt bound to come to some such a decision, because in private as well as public, in the daily press and in written works, when the subject of West African Colonies is under consideration, we find the following questions in one form or other repeatedly asked—Why are we there? Why not give it up? It is no country for Europeans? It is the worst climate in the world? It is impossible for Europeans to civilize it? A white man can't live there? Give it up! It is a mistaken philanthropy! &c., &c., &c.

In the tropical countries of Western Africa the idea of a permanent occupation by European settlers, if ever entertained, is impossible of realisation; it is a mistake and a delusion. Again, we find that wherever the African race has been carried to, except, perhaps, the East Indies, they increase, no matter under what depressing and burdensome yoke they may suffer; from which it may be safely inferred that the African people is a permanent and enduring people; and the fancies of those who had determined their destruction will go in the same limbo as the now almost defunct American slavery. The English Government is conscious of this; and the House of Commons Committee has now set on foot by resolution (and we hope it will soon be by actual practice) that great principle of establishing independent African nationalities as independent as the present Liberian Government. But simple written resolutions without being carried into practice are worse than waste paper, because they encourage hopes which may never be realised; and the absence of the necessary means to effect such realisation destroys all confidence of belief in several separate nationalities. There is, however, every hope that the contemplated reform will be happily carried into effect. It will, therefore, be well to make a review of the different Colonies, and examine how far they are capable of upholding an independent separate nationality.[1]

Self-Government of Lagos and its Interior Countries—
Kingdom of the Akus

The Committee of the House of Commons, in their report, state that 'the annexation of Lagos was a strong measure, of which not only the wisdom may be questioned, but the alleged justification also—viz., the incapacity and faithlessness of a king, who was first set up by the English against a very doubtful usurper, and whose powerlessness over his subjects was much caused by their interference. The wisdom of the act may be tested by the consideration that, had we refrained from assuming the government, we need not have been complicated in the Egba Wars, nor in the perplexity of having to recognise at the same time that we prohibit slavery within our own territory'.

From the foregoing evidence it will be supposed by the casual reader that the existence of British rule was a curse to this part of the Coast; that the country was infinitely superior, commerce much more advanced, and life and property safer in the hands of the superseded native government than under the sovereignty of Britain. But viewing the growing civilisation of Lagos and its suburbs, the immense and progressive improvement going on, the march of intellectual development among the mass of the population, the increase of commerce both in imports and exports, the sanitary improvements everywhere observed, and the imitation of the civilised mode of government among surrounding potentates, we must unhesitatingly state that it was the greatest blessing that could have happened to Lagos and the whole of the Yoruba or Aku tribe, that such a responsible, civilised, and powerful government should have at that opportune moment commenced her regeneration.

I do not at all by this intend to justify the means adopted, but, looking to the results achieved, we must forget the past and hail what has been so instrumental for the country's good.

Lagos is a star from which must radiate the refulgent rays of civilisation into the interior of the Yoruba or Aku Country, and every effort must be made, especially by the native inhabitants, to support the hands of the Government in their work of regeneration. It should have been expected that the assumption of the territory would have, at first, led to internal rows and distrust on the part of the interior population, who knew nothing of arms and power, and after this storm which might have

[1] *West African Countries*, p. 73, l. 27 ff.

led to destruction of trade, and even to open hostility, with all its concomitant woes, there would be a happy lull, and things would take an entirely opposite turn. . . .

But Lagos is only an isolated and important seaport town in the kingdom of the Akus. From want of a more specific name and from the whole of the tribes being once subjected to the king of Yoruba, the Church Missionary Society has designated it the 'Yoruba Country', but as most of the tribes, such as the Egbas and Egbadoes, have objected to their being called Yorubas, and as there is no national name by which all the tribes speaking the same language but differently governed is known, I have employed the name which is given to the whole nation at Sierra Leone, and which is generally adopted in every part of the Coast—viz., the Akus. The kingdom is bounded on the north by the right or Quora branch of the River Niger, and on the south by the Atlantic, on the east by Benin, Kakanda, and part of Igara, and on the west by the kingdom of Dahomey.

The kingdom is divided into various tribes who are governed by their own chiefs and by their own laws, but who are extremely jealous of one another. The principal tribes are the Egbadoes, which includes 'Otta and Lagos, near the seacoast, forming a belt of country on the banks of the Lagoon in the forest, to Ketu, on the border of Dahomey. The next tribe occupy Ketu and Shabe, on the border of Dahomey on the west, then comes Ijebu on the east, on the border of Benin, then the Egbas of the forest, now known by the name of Egbas of Abeokuta; then comes Yoruba Proper northward of the plain. Ife, Ijesha, Iyamo Efou, Oudo, Ideko, Igbomma, and Ado, near the banks of the Niger, from which the creek or stream a little below Iddah is called Do or Ido'. Years ago all these tribes were politically united under one head as tributaries to the King of Yoruba, amongst whom were included Benin on the east and Dahomey on the west. A large proportion of Yoruba Proper is governed by a Mussulman king, who is subject to the Sultan of Sokoto, on the other side of the Niger; the principal town and seat of government is Ilorin. . . .

The country is governed by separate kings, whose right is hereditary, but only in the male issue of the king's daughter; his power is, in many instances, absolute; his person and those of the royal family, sacred. He is assisted in making laws and settling palavers by the elders in the kingdom, who are designated in Yoruba, Iweffa.

The capabilities of the kingdom of the Akus are very great and extensive; populated, as it is, by a hard-working, persevering people, with a rich, well-watered country. This territory, when fully developed and explored, bids fair to become one of the richest in Western Africa. The conversion of Lagos into a Colony, with a display of all the improvements, power, and civilisation of a European nation, is a work of vast importance to those regions.[1]

Self-Government in Ibo Country

Egbo, Igbo, Ebo, and Ibo are the various spellings met with in books describing the race inhabiting this part of the Coast. Among the soft Isuama and Elugu, the soft Ebo and Ibo is used; but among the inhabitants on the coast, such as Bonny and Okrika, the harsher name Egbo is prevalent. In the interior north of the Territory, the nations are called Igbo, which approaches more to the original name of the inhabitants.[2]

In those early days Africa was known and famous amongst the then civilised portion of the world, and the Assyrians and Babylonians were among its earliest conquerors, so that about sixty-seven years after the destruction of the Temple, we are told, in Esther i, 1, that Ahasuerus, the king of Assyria, reigned from India unto Ethiopia, over one hundred and seven and twenty provinces. And since the king of Egypt was considered lord of the people of Ethiopia or Soudan, we read in Isaiah that the 'king of Assyria led away the Ethiopians captive, young and old, naked and barefooted, to the shame of Egypt.' Northern Egypt then was the most known portion of the globe, and into it vast immigration took place from time to time, even to the most remote period. The ten tribes of Israel, after they were left to follow the dictates of their own mind, and during the commotion and destructive warfare which ensued, to escape utter extermination, migrated, according to the usage of the time, in vast numbers into various countries, but principally into Northern Africa, as it then presented the safest and easiest route. Once settled, every commotion and intestine war had the most powerful effect of inducing these migratory bands to shift their abode still further, and so lose all connection with the other branch of the tribe. As hundreds of years pass on, and generation after generation roll away, they lose a great many of their habits and customs, becoming more amalgamated with the population with which they associate. But when Mohammedanism overspread Northern Africa, destroying by fire and sword all those of other religions, the Israelitish descendants, or the inhabitants occupying the central portion of Africa, passed forward, seeking shelter to the south and west; a part, namely those from the east central, crossing the Benue or Joliba branch of the Niger, descended gradually southward, and became intermingled with the original inhabitants. Protected from incursion on the north by the Benue River, and quietly settled between the Great Niger

[1] *Ibid.*, p. 152, l. 1 ff.   [2] *Ibid.*, p. 171.

35

and Old Calabar Rivers, they remained in peace, and grew from one generation to another in idolatry, but still leaving tangible proofs in the form of their religion of the Judaistic origin of the inhabitants.[1]

Thus situated between the Rivers Niger and Old Calabar, and bounded on the north by the left or Benue branch of the first river, on the south by the Atlantic, on the east by Old Calabar and the Dwalla Countries, and on the west by the River Niger, Benin, and Igara, lies this extensive and well-watered tract of territory which is included in the Empire of the Egboes. According to Dr. Baikie, Egboe extends east and west from the Old Calabar River to the banks of the Niger, or Kwora (Quora), and possesses also some territory at Abo, in the westward of the stream; on the north it borders on Igara and Akpoto, and is separated from the sea only by petty tribes, all of which trace their origin from the great race.

It is divided into several districts or countries, each speaking different dialects, although derived from one root. The principal counties are Isuama, Elugu, Isielu, Isiago, Abaga, Mitshie, and Djuku, all of which are situated on the north; in the middle are Abo, Abazim, Aro, and Amazunie; and in the south are Brass, Nimbe, Okrika, Ebane or Bonny and Adony. Very little is known of these districts; their histories are shrouded in impenetrable darkness; expeditions have been made through the great water course into the interior; but no cross expedition, starting from the eastern banks of the Niger to the Old Calabar River, has as yet been attempted.

In the south the districts are intersected by numerous streams and rivulets, which enter to form the delta of the Niger; mangrove swamps are abundant in various places and except between Bonny and Old Calabar, the soil is rich and fertile. Further up, the country is more open and elevated, and numerously populated. In Isuama most of the towns are built on rising ground, dry, and well selected; so that Isuama, Elugu, and Isiago, are far healthier and dryer than the seacoast towns. But there are yet several large and important countries in the interior of Egboe of which nothing is known, as the country has not received that attention among civilized settlers that other parts of the Coast have. After the great failure of the expedition of 1841, no adequate attempt was made to open the River Niger until 1854, when a new impetus was given by the complete success of that year, but which, unfortunately, has been followed by tardy operations. The country is governed by independent kings and chiefs, whose extent of dominion varies greatly; some exercise authority over large and extensive districts; others rule over a town or village. The title of king, unlike in the countries west of the Niger to as far as Senegambia, is hereditary in the male line. After the death of the

[1] *Ibid.*, p. 188, l. 9 ff.

father, the son is proclaimed king; in default, the brother. This may be seen in the coronation of the kings of Bonny. So far back as could be remembered, Papa reigned for a certain period, and was succeeded at his death by his son Zhedie, who was also succeeded by his son Peppel I, who was succeeded by his son Peppel II, then by his son Opubu, who was succeeded by his son Peppel III. Bribo, his cousin, then succeeded him, or Peppel IV, and on his death, Dappa, the son of Peppel III, ascended the throne, and was succeeded by George, his son, the now reigning king.

In some of the districts the people endeavour to assume the elective power; thus, after the death of King Obi, of Abo, two parties sprung up, one supporting the claims of the king's sons, whilst the other advanced an influential person named Orisa as a candidate for the vacant crown; these two sections were known respectively as king's people, and the Oshiodapara party. Whilst the rights of the parties were still in dispute, law and justice were administered by a neutral party, having no connexion whatever with either side. The kings exercise very extensive powers over their subjects, but they are not absolute monarchs, as any excessive use of power may lead to dethronement; they are assisted in making laws and transacting public business by councillors, who in Isuama are generally four principal persons: here the king is called Obi, and is addressed by his subjects kneeling, by the title of Igue, or supreme head; in Abo the king is called Ese. His revenue consists of a portion of the fines inflicted for misdemeanour and a portion of the game obtained in hunting. His throne 'is a raised bank of mud in the verandah, about four feet long, two wide, and two feet high from the level of the floor'; on this is spread a mat and a white piece of calico over it, which cloth is also spread on the walls against the king's back, extending from the top of the wall to that spread on the floor of the throne. 'This is a sign of royalty and the prerogative of the king, which no one in the country is to imitate.' No stranger is allowed in the king's palace a seat of any kind before his majesty, whether mat or stool, excepting the loose red earth, as the king took an oath to that effect.

Among the Egboes, women hold a very superior rank in the social scale; they are not regarded, as among other tribes as an inferior creation and doomed to perpetual degradation, but occupy their 'rightful status in society'. Nothing would, however, induce them to place a woman on the throne as their ruler; this they consider as subverting nature itself. In colloquy with the King of Nsube, Mr. Taylor was asked what was the name of his king. On being told that he had no king, but a queen, the king drew back in astonishment and said, 'What! Can woman rule over man?' This, he afterwards said, accounts for the greatness of England, as there is no partiality among her people.

37

The language of the whole of the district is Egboe, but there are strong dialectic differences as we recede from the interior to the Coast towns. In Isuama, or by contraction Isu, the purest and softest Egboe is spoken, and from it more or less differences occur as we enter different districts; even the language spoken in Old Calabar and Dwalla is derived from the great family of Egboe, only far removed. Oru, Brass, Bonny, Okrika, and Andoney bear dialect affinity to Isuama Egboe, and are derived from the same root, as may be noticed in the following collections made by the late Dr. Baikie:—

English	Isuama Egboe	Bonny	Nimbe	Oru
Water	minyi	mingi	mindi or migi	megi
Fire	oko	fene	fendi	fini
Firewood	unyi		fingia	fendia
God	Orisa	Tamono	Orisa	Orisa
Idol	dju-dju	dju-dju	owu	owu
House	ulo	wari	wale	wale
Mat	ute	bile	ute	ute

The language of the Egboes differs entirely from that of the Yoruba or Ewe westward of the Niger; after crossing that great river we are brought at once among an entirely new and distinct tribe, who are allied in tongue to the Lichuana, the Gala on the north, the Tumali, and the Kaffir, which ethnologically forms the South African Alteral family; this relation of the Egboe to the Kaffir tongue has been also pronounced by the great ethnologist, Dr. Latham.

The population of Egboe is unknown. Unlike the countries between the River Volta and the Niger, Egboe, since 1835, has been freed from internal convulsions. There is no large, independent, warlike power in its neighbourhood, as in Ashantee and Dahomey; but the population, since the limitation of the external slave-trade has been known to be wonderfully increased; and, judging from the extent and population of the known towns along the banks of the river and on the sea-coast, it will not be far short of the mark if we state the whole at from 10,000,000 to 12,000,000, all of whom speak one language with slight dialectic differences.

In stature the Egboes differ very considerably according to the region whence they are taken. In Isuama and the north central districts the inhabitants are tall and majestic looking, some well formed and shaped; they carry themselves very erect and consequentially. In other parts they are of a middling size, averaging five feet two. In the deltas of the rivers the inhabitants are short, stout, bull-necked, and very strong; specimens of them are even now to be found in Sierra Leone or the Gambia; they

38

are scarcely above four and a half feet, having very broad shoulders, and are stoutly built.

The Egboes are considered the most imitative and emulative people in the whole of Western Africa; place them where you will, or introduce to them any manners and customs, you will find that they very easily adapt themselves to them. Stout-hearted, or, to use the more common phraseology, big-hearted, they always possess a desire of superiority, and make attempts to attain it, or excel in what is praiseworthy, without a desire of depressing others. To them we may well apply the language of Dryden:—

'A noble emulation beats their breasts . . . '[1]

The introduction of the new yam is, as among other Coast tribes, an occasion for the performance of several rites and ceremonies. Here the doctor figures conspicuously. The Fetish custom is called Waje, or the eating of the new yam. It is not, as in other parts, participated in by the general public, but is performed by a certain class of people who carry a long trumpet tusk about them. Mr. Taylor gives the following as the manner in which the custom is performed: 'Each head-man brings out six yams, besides some kola nuts and fish, and cuts down young branches of palm leaves, and places them before his gate; three of the yams are roasted, after which the dibia, or doctor, takes and scrapes them into a meal, and then divides it in two. He then takes one piece and places it on the lip of the person who is going to eat the new yam. The eater blows out the steam from the hot yam, and afterwards pokes the whole into his mouth and says: "I thank God for being permitted to eat the new yam". He then begins to chew it heartily, with fish. The doctor receives as a fee for performing the ceremony the three remaining yams.'

In their salutation, individuals of an inferior position, on meeting their superiors, place one knee on the ground and then bow with great reverence. Among equals they shake hands, which is performed first in the regular manner, but before separating the hands, they partly take loose hold of the fingers of each other, and then sharply slipping them so as to make at the same instant a snapping sound; this process is assisted by the thumb.

In Yoruba, Nufi, and many other parts of the Coast, the mothers carry their children about on their backs, but not so in Egboe; there they are carried chiefly in their arms. The children are very seldom punished, consequently are found to be self-willed and have their own way: 'yet they are docile and imitative, and with very little trouble will soon be made intelligent scholars'. Life for life is a law throughout the country; whether taken accidentally or not, one life must go for the other; this is

[1] *Ibid.*, p. 171, l. 1 ff.

39

imperative. If the murderer himself manages to escape, some one of his family must be killed in his stead. If the murderer or homicide be inferior in rank to the murdered man, some one of equal rank in the family must be delivered in his stead. Neither the king nor any individual member of a family has any right to alienate land; and before any sale or gift of land belonging to any family is made, the consent of the leading members of the family must first be obtained, as amongst Egboes land is possessed by inheritance.[1]

In the foregoing we have seen that the Egbo nationality is divided into numerous independent tribes, governed by their own laws, but having one national sentiment: that they are still unlettered and unchristian. The question arises, how is it possible to form an independent, united, Christian, and civilised nation, having the same laws and governed by one imperial head? This at once presents a question of vast importance and great difficulty. In the first place, the seat of the *ab initio* Government should not only be near to, or on, the sea-coast, but also be a place of commercial importance. Bonny, having all the advantages above described, is most adapted for the commencement of such an important undertaking; but there are serious prejudices among the neighbouring tribes, which would present great obstacles to their union under the leadership of its king. The chiefs composing the different sections in that country are very jealous of one another, and particularly of the reigning dynasty, and to effect an agreement on this point an individual from without should be elected by the universal vote of not only the kings and chiefs of Bonny, but also the kings and chiefs of all the neighbouring towns.[2] The elected individual must of necessity be well acquainted with the different departments of a political government, and capable of introducing such institutions, with such modifications as would suit the conditions of the governed. A treaty of unity, or of alliance, offensive and defensive, should, in the first place, be entered into by all the various kings and chiefs in the neighbouring provinces.

The next, and most important, consideration would be the raising of a sufficient revenue to carry out the various improvements which it will be found absolutely necessary to make, and this he must do by giving the greatest encouragement to trade. . . .

To ensure the establishment of a firm central Government in such a primitive state of existence, it will be found necessary that the responsible power should in a great measure be vested in the king elect for at least a time, although a representation of all the chiefs in the bond should take

[1] *Ibid.*, p. 180, l. 26 ff.
[2] A step similar to, but differing, however, in details from, the Egba United Board of Management now established in Abeokuta.

place at certain fixed periods to discourse on State matters. This Government should be the starting point for the regeneration of the interior of the Egboe tribe. The more firm, strong, and conciliatory are its measures, the greater influence would it exercise over surrounding tribes, and the more easily would they rally around it. Let the civilisation of those tribes near the seaboard be well secured, and those small divided states in the interior would of themselves seek protection from the stronger Government. If we see this accomplished in Ashantee and Dahomey, both of whom rose from a trifling state, how much more shall we see in a kingdom based on religious principle and on the civilization of the nineteenth century?

When once established, the king's authority should not be easily gainsaid by any turbulent and refractory chief. He must make himself powerful enough to be feared, whilst at the same time respected. . . .[1]

Self-Government of the Gold Coast—Kingdom of Fantee

The Gold Coast under British influence extends over a coast-line of not more than three hundred miles, comprising Appolonia, Ahanta, Fantee, Winnebah, Accra and Adangme. The inhabitants are the possessors of the lands they now occupy from time immemorial. The natives are almost all alike in habits and customs, in their mode of living, and almost in that of thinking. . . .

As, according to the decision of the Home Government, the Protectorate of the Territory is to be retained, whilst the 'chiefs may be, as speedily as possible, made to do without it', and that they are on no account to lean on British help, or trust to British administration of their affairs, let us consider what would be the most judicious and most fitting self-administration of such an extensive Coast. The British Gold Coast must be divided into two parts, each governed separately, called respectively Fantee and Accra. The form of government best suited to Fantee is monarchical; and that to Accra, a republic. I shall, therefore, consider these two separately, under the heads of the Kingdom of Fantee, and the Republic of Accra . . . the Kingdom of Fantee, extending from the Sweet River to the borders of Winnebah; and the Republic of Accra, extending from Winnebah to the River Volta; the former to comprise the kingdom of Denkera, Abrah, or Abacrampah, Assin, Western Akim, and Goomoor; the latter Eastern Akim, Winnebah, Accra, Aquapim, Adangme, and Crobboe.

The next point to be considered is the political union of the various kings in the kingdom of Fantee under one political head. A man should

[1] *Ibid.*, pp. 192, 193, 195.

41

be chosen either by universal suffrage, or appointed by the Governor, and sanctioned and received by all the kings and chiefs, and crowned as King of Fantee. He should be a man of great sagacity, good common sense, not easily influenced by party spirit, of a kind and generous disposition, a man of good education, and who had done good service to the Coast Government. He should be crowned before all the kings and caboceers within the kingdom of Fantee; the kings should regard him as their chief; his authority should be recognised and supported by the Governor of the Coast, who should refer to him matters of domestic importance relative to the other native kings, advise him as to the course he should pursue, and see that his decisions be immediately carried out.

He should be assisted by a number of councillors, who, for the time, should swear allegiance to the British Government, until such time as the country is considered fit for delivery over to self-government. They should consist not only of men of education and good, sound common sense, residing in the Coast towns, but also of responsible chiefs, as representatives of the various kings within the kingdom.

One most important consideration is the yearly vote of a round sum out of the revenue as stipend to the king elect whilst under this probationary course, such as would allow him to keep up a certain amount of State dignity, and would enable him to carry out his authority over the kings and chiefs. Each State should be made to contribute towards the support of the temporary Government; a native volunteer corps should be attached to the Government, officered by natives of intelligence, who should be thoroughly drilled by paid officers and sergeants, supplied from West Indian regiments stationed on the Coast. The English language should be made the diplomatic language with foreign nations; but Fantee should be made the medium of internal communication, and therefore ought at once to be reduced to writing.

The territory of the kingdom of Ashantee is larger than that of the Protected Territory of the Gold Coast, but we find the reigning king possesses absolute power over the different tribes composing it. True enough, the edifice was constructed on the blood of several nationalities, which gives it greater strength; but the kingdom of Fantee must be directed on a peaceable footing, supported, for a time at least, by a civilised Government, with a prince at the head who is versed in native diplomacy, and well known and respected by the various kings; such a man is the Hon. George Blankson, whose experience and deserved fame would make his appointment meet with universal support; a prince who would be able, like the potentate of Ashantee, to concentrate a large force at a very short notice, at any given point, when menaced by their powerful neighbours.

The appointment is absolutely necessary, since King John Aggery, of

Cape Coast, has been dethroned by the local government, and this has been sanctioned by Her Majesty's Government. . . .

It is evident that from the unsatisfactory political state of the Western District of the Gold Coast, it cannot, at present, be left to govern itself; that radical reforms are imperatively necessary before this can be done with safety to the population. . . .

Before the country should be given up to self-government, a responsible king, of education and experience, must be crowned, assisted, acknowledged and supported by the British authority, both on the Coast and in Downing-street; and a British Consular Agency should be formed, and the Consul appointed be a man who would aid and advise the native Government, and guarantee it against European invasion.[1]

Self-Government of the Gold Coast—Republic of Accra

The territory to be included within this Republic should extend from Winnebah to the River Volta. Awoonah, at present, should be no part of it, as it would only be a point of weakness to the young Republic. The constitution of the several states in it, the feelings of the inhabitants, the physical geography of the country, as well as the peculiar habits and customs of the people, lead me to believe that no form of government would be suited to their wants and requirements as the republican form.

If this place must ultimately be left to govern itself, a republican form of government should be chosen. An educated native gentleman, of high character and good common sense, who has the welfare of his country at heart . . . should be selected by the Government as a candidate for the presidency, and offered for the votes of the populace in the various districts; and, when once elected, he must be regarded as supreme in everything, and the natural referee in all their quarrels and differences. He should be assisted by counsellors chosen by the people as their representatives. The term of office of the president should not be less than eight years, and he should be eligible for re-election.

The absurd custom of having kings in every petty town should be, as speedily as possible, abolished. They should be called by other names than that of kings, and in case of their death the 'stool' should be done away with. The president for the time being should be recognised constitutional king. A good strong government would thus be formed, which would receive the assistance of the European residents. If a proper custom-house be established a large revenue will be collected.

Before the place should be given up to self-government (say two or three years before) the different kings and headmen should be assembled at Accra and a treaty drawn up binding them, offensive and defensive,

[1] *Ibid.*, pp. 105, 123, 125, 126, 135.

with one another. The Government should introduce to them one of the natives, whom it may consider to be of good practical common sense, educated, and possessed of influence in the country, as their nominee for the post of head centre, or President of the Republic of Accra—such a man, for instance, as Libercht Hesse, Esq., of Christiansborg. They should give in their votes, and, when elected, he should be inaugurated in their presence, and considered as their chief. As soon as this is done, he should be made to regulate the internal government of the country, under the supervision of the Governor. A yearly grant out of the revenue should be voted him; schools and educational seminaries should be established in every town. A militia force should be enrolled, and drilled by paid officers and sergeants of West Indian regiments. In all such efforts I am certain that he would receive the assistance, not only of the educated natives of the place, but also of the Europeans of long residence in the country, who would lend him the weight of their influence, as well as assist in developing the resources of the country.

It is, therefore, evident from the foregoing that there are more advantages in the Eastern District than the Western for forming a good, useful, native self-government, which should ultimately be profitable to the British Government and the native population; but that there are vast rooms for improvement in the various branches. That if the kings be left as they are to govern themselves, the base being rotten, the whole fabric will, within a very short time, tumble to the ground. Confusion, massacre, and bloodshed would be the inevitable result. That before the people be given up to govern themselves a new order of things must be established, and an entirely new government formed, under the auspices of the British Government, supported by all kings of the districts; and the British Consul of the Gold Coast should always be ready to advise them in political matters, and preserve the country from foreign invasion.[1]

Self-Government of Sierra Leone—Kingdom of Sierra Leone

There are several peculiarities characteristic of the physical geography of Sierra Leone, which will enable her to sustain a good and powerful self-government, not threatened by any native tribe of consequence in its neighbourhood, and not easily by any European or foreign nations. Sierra Leone possesses a safe haven where distressed vessels can put in and refit, and the entrance of its harbour is through a narrow channel completely covered by several important elevations and hills. In her claim for independence she ranks with Liberia, her immediate neighbour, having a strong, vigorous, and persevering population, who speak one

[1] *Ibid.*, p. 136, l. 1 ff., p. 150, l. 31 ff.

44

language. Education of the masses has been going on to a very encouraging extent, and missionary efforts have had most salutary and beneficial results on the population who are holding their ground in various self-supporting systems.

Sierra Leone is, to a certain degree, the place on the Coast that the British Government (to carry out their laudable intentions for Africa) could give up to self-government with hope of success, and a due appreciation of the advantages granted thereby. It has a better and more increasing revenue than any other part of the Coast; in it are congregated all the blood and sinews of the various tribes in every part of the Coast; and, according to Koelle's polyglot calculation, there are more than a hundred different tribes among its inhabitants, the principal, both in numbers and influence, being the Akus and Egboes.

The inhabitants of the Colony have been gradually blending into one race, and a national spirit is being developed. The language of self-government when formed must of necessity be English, and all official and private business be done in it. It comes readily to all those born in the Colony. There will be no spirit of a native language counteracting, modifying, and balancing it, because it is now the universal language of the Colony.

When Liberia was given up to self-government, the progress previously made as regards the working of state government, was not at all to be compared with what now exists at Sierra Leone; yet still we find that the Liberians have maintained their own ground, have extended their dominions, and are making every year great and rapid progress. Might we not hope that if the latter country were to be placed under somewhat similar circumstances a material progressive advance would take place, which would ultimately lead to a greater consolidation of power, aided and assisted by the fostering mother government?

Of the government of Sierra Leone, the most important town is the city of Freetown, situated at the foot of the hills which run in an easterly direction, of which Leicester Mountain is the highest. It contains a population of more than twenty thousand inhabitants, which is yearly increasing. The wealth of the Colony is in Freetown; in it are the best educational establishments, the centre of the various missionary establishments, and the seat of government. It possesses many large substantial buildings and a thriving commerical prospect. It extends from Granville Brook to Congo Town Bridge, a distance of nearly two and half miles. There is no fertile land about its neighbourhood, so that people depend on the other parts of the Colony for articles of food, although a small quantity of the garden and surrounding arid land is cultivated. The harbour can receive vessels of any tonnage, being very deep; and from the circumstances of its entrance being completely commanded by hills

45

and elevated lands, it can be easily protected from hostile inroads by good artillery properly arranged and manned. Freetown, therefore, as a safe haven and as a capital, is well chosen, and would form a nucleus of a very extensive power over the countries north and south of it. The increase of population, the wealth and strength of the city, will ever form a great barrier to its being threatened by the surrounding native tribes, who, I am certain, would never harbour the remotest idea of attacking it.

As it is proposed to teach the people self-government, to the ultimate withdrawal of British influence or power, and to leave the natives to govern themselves, there must be chosen either a monarchical or republican form of government. . . .

As in the Gambia a republic is unsuited to the taste of the people, so it is at Sierra Leone. It will never have among the native inhabitants, who have always looked up to their king, the same influence and effect. A national government should be selected, which should be made so powerful and influential as to create an interest in its support, extensive and strong enough to counterbalance all other influences. A monarchical government, then, will be the only form, and the king should be elected by universal suffrage, supported for some time by the British Government; he should for a short period be initiated into the art of governing, by serving the subordinate position of a governor over the Colony and its Dependencies, whilst the English Governor should act as Governor-General of all the Coast.

His first policy should be to show himself to be on the popular side, identifying himself with the growth of the people's liberties, by which means he will secure an under basis of popular affection, which will be an important auxiliary in his infant kingdom, where, at the commencement, conflicting views and opinions are possible. He should make merit the great high road to public trusts, honours, and rewards, thus proving to every one that he measures the intellectual worth and dignity of a man, not by the truths which he possesses, or fancies he possesses, but by the sincere and honest pains which he takes to discover them. He should be a native-born Sierra Leonean or a citizen by constitutional adoption. On his accession he will find that his treasury is not impoverished, that his people are intelligent, industrious, and willing to give him every assistance in establishing and completing the national edifices. He will have a population comparatively well advanced and progressing in civilization, who, by the zealous efforts of the missionary societies, have nearly one-fifth of the whole of the inhabitants at school, which is an unusually large proportion in any country.

One of his principal objects should be to annexe the neighbouring territory as an integral part of his kingdom, and to endeavour to give protection and support to the merchants trading in it; this will in every way improve his growing revenue, which it should be his utmost endeavour to increase, as a good and healthy revenue is indispensable for the support of his authority.

A constitutional form of government must form the basis of his administration, consisting of a House of Assembly which should be composed of men elected by the people, as it will be difficult for his Government to stand without popular confidence, and the only means by which that can be secured is by giving the people the power of election of one branch of the Legislature; they will be required to direct their attention to the internal government of the State, to sanction the amount of duty to be levied on foreign importation, and regulate the trade with foreign nations, and the imposition of stamp, postal, and other duties. Each member should possess landed property, be over the age of twenty-two, and be properly educated. Besides the House of Assembly, there should be the senate, consisting of men above the age of thirty-five years, and having extensive means, and who may be recognised by all as possessing good practical common sense. The senator should be chosen by the king-elect, and should retain office so long as his character is unimpeachable, either for life or a period not less than ten years, and then be eligible for re-election.

From the foregoing it is evident that there is growing at Sierra Leone an enlightened population, and that under the fostering care of the mother Government the people can, within a short time, be left to govern themselves; that with an enlightened monarch, elected by universal suffrage, and an efficient legislation, the African element, so essential to African civilization, will receive a powerful impetus to intelligent progress, and then will Sierra Leone be able to compete with Liberia in virtuous emulation towards progressive civilization, and in endeavours to raise their much-abused race and country in the scale of civilized nations.[1]

The Creoles of Sierra Leone have been stigmatized as the most impertinent rogues in all the coast, even by men who know nothing of them. They will not wait for the truth, the whole truth, and nothing but the truth; no—but they rant upon the platform, seeing who can crow the loudest, or 'forge red-hot sentences at their pens' points'; and when investigation is made as to whether the assertion be true, it is found to be some mere phantom of ignorance and credulity which has been exaggerated in the repetition by those who have had occasion to complain. There is undoubtedly among the low, reckless class, a certain amount of roguery, such as is found among a parallel portion of the whole world; but the stigma is here applied to the whole population; for those who propagate the would-be extraordinary intelligence, magnify the tale to such a

[1] *Ibid.*, pp. 87, 89, 97–9, 102.

degree, that the story in its progress through the fancies and mouths of those who represent it, assumes great magnitude and importance. But we find, nevertheless, that these Creoles of Sierra Leone occupy lucrative subordinate positions of trust in both the military and civil service of the Government in the four colonies and settlements on the coast—viz., Sierra Leone, the Gambia, the Gold Coast, and Lagos; which speaks volumes for the indomitable and arduous exertions and perseverance of the missionaries who formed the educational body of the colony. Besides this, they are to be found in every part of the coast sighing after gold in the capacity of merchants, traders, and clerks—in the French colony of Senegal; in the Rivers Gambia, Casamanza, Nunez, Pongas, Sherbros and Gallinas; in the Liberian Republic; on the Gold Coast; in the Kingdom of Dahomey; in Lagos and Abeokuta; in the Niger; at Bonny; old and new Calabar, the Cameroons, Fernando Po, the Gaboons, and the Islands of St. Helena and Ascension. If they were not an industrious, exploring race, determined to advance their position in life by speculation and other legitimate means, would they not have confined themselves within the limits of the Peninsula of Sierra Leone; and do not their exertions above alluded to, point to a similar trait in the character of Englishmen, who are to be found in every part of the known world where money can be made?[1]

Self-Government of British Gambia

British Gambia consists of the island of St. Mary, situated on the left bank and at the mouth of the river, on which is Bathurst, the capital of the settlement; beyond this is a large tract of land ceded by the King of Combo, known as British Combo, in which is Cape St. Mary, which latter had, prior to the cession, been obtained by purchase. On the right bank of the river a strip of land, one mile in width, extending from Boonyadoo Creek to Swarra Cundah Creek, beyond Albredah, became, in 1846, British territory by cession, and about 150 miles from the mouth of the river is M'Carthy's Island. These constitute the British possessions in Gambia. The principal native inhabitants of the British possessions are the Jollofs and the liberated Africans and their descendants; there are besides a few Serias, Jolahs, Mandingos, and Footah Foolahs. The Jollofs are a fine race of people, who originally came from Senegal and Goree and the countries between that and Gambia, as well as from Goonjour, and are, therefore, intimately connected with families in these two places. The mulatto Jollof at one time had extensive influence in the colony, but it is now gradually decaying; they, or two

[1] *Ibid.*, p. 61, l. 24.

families (viz., the Lloyds and Hughes) are owners of most of the large and substantial dwelling-houses in Bathurst. . . .[1]

The population of British Gambia is barely fifteen thousand souls; the Marabouts around number several hundred thousands. If the inhabitants of the former were to be left to govern themselves, there must be either a monarchical or a republican form of government instituted. The latter is unsuited to the taste and feelings of the people. A monarchical government must be chosen, and the king elected by universal suffrage. If once left to himself, without military support for a time, he would find his movements hampered by contending views; his territory, especially British Combo and British Barra, exposed to the inroads of his most powerful enemy. The Marabout chieftains would get sufficient information of all his internal arrangements, and would take the earliest opportunity of trying his strength. In a financial point of view, his revenue would be increased or diminished according to his capacity of affording protection to the merchants and traders. He would find nine-tenths of his population very ignorant and uneducated; that his kingdom lacked good educational seminaries; and that his greatest attention would require to be immediately devoted to political economy and social details. His registrar-general would report to him that the death-rate exceeds the birth by nearly a half; that depopulation to a vast extent is going on every year. On examining into the sanitary condition of his state, he would find it to be truly deplorable; that there is a large and extensive marsh which stands out as a great barrier to the healthiness of his capital, and which will require a large amount of money to drain, altogether beyond the power of his exchequer to afford. The language of his kingdom is in Babelic confusion, being Jollof, Mandingo, Serere, Foolah, Jolah, and English; and although four-fifths of the population do not understand English, he would have gradually to develop it among the mass, and make it the spoken and diplomatic language. Having no military at his command, he would find his untrained volunteers unable to stand before the impetuous charge of the Marabouts.

The Marabouts, finding that the king was not powerful, and not supported by any European powers, would make an unprovoked attack on Combo and Sebbajee, and, before a sufficient force could be collected to oppose them, destroy the whole of the towns, and massacre and enslave the inhabitants. And even were the volunteers to meet them in a pitched battle, unless well supported by regular artillery, they would not be able to stand the impetuous attack and cavalry charge of the daring Marabouts; and a victory gained by them would be fatal to the commercial interests of the country. Bathurst will always be protected against any number of the Marabout force, who will find Oyster Creek a good barrier

[1] *Ibid.*, p. 74, l. 13 ff.

against their onward progress; as fifty volunteers, with good rifles and well officered, could resist the landing of two thousand Marabout warriors from the mainland.[1]

From the foregoing it is evident that in the present condition of the Settlement of Gambia it cannot be left to govern itself. An esteemed Governor remarked, after reading the third resolution of the Parliamentary Committee, that it will take a hundred years before Gambia will be capable of self-government; but I say that if the present system of governing the people be persisted in, it will take more than two hundred years; while if radical reform be made, and if the people be properly trained, it will take less than a quarter of a century to bring the country into such a state of improvement as might enable it to be left with safety in the hands of an enlightened native king, chosen by universal suffrage.[2]

[1] *Ibid.*, p. 81, l. 6 ff.   [2] *Ibid.*, p. 86, l. 14 ff.

4

Existing Institutions of Self-Government

Horton describes attempts at self-government on the pattern of European models. Abeokuta was then the centre of an independent state of the Egba group of the Yoruba community in Western Nigeria. The Egba United Board of Management had as its leading protagonists not only the local aristocracy but also educated Christians of Yoruba ancestry who had received their education in Sierra Leone. It was not strictly correct that the Board was always active in spreading Christianity or protecting the property of European merchants, as Horton wrote. George Johnson, the secretary, was nicknamed 'Reversible Johnson' probably because of his frequent changes of policies. He may have been known personally to Horton as he was born in Sierra Leone.

Abeokuta was on one of the main trade routes from the interior to Lagos for the export overseas of natural products.

The Fante Confederation was one of the most important manifestations of self-government in nineteenth-century Africa. The Fante along the coast of Ghana had combined for purposes of defence and for negotiation with the colonial powers of Britain and Holland. They attempted several times at Mankessim, a Fante city of considerable importance, to organise a confederation. These moves were, however, repeatedly resisted by local officials of the British government.

Horton's ideas and his encouragement to the Fante to build up their confederation were of great influence in that period and with his suggestions, as set out in the previous chapter for a kingdom of Fante, were perhaps his most notable contribution to the political history of Ghana.

His chapter in West African Countries and Peoples on a republic of Accra aroused a great deal of interest locally. There is a letter[1] to him by James Bannerman on the Accra Native Confederation which is clear evidence of this and of the esteem and high regard in which Horton was held by the élite and intelligentsia of Ghana. James Bannerman (jnr) was a Ghanaian who had been a magistrate and during a short period of municipal

[1] Quoted by Horton in *Letters on the Gold Coast* as a footnote pp. 34–41 (Ed.).

government had held the position of Mayor of James Town, Accra. His father was of part Scottish ancestry and had held the high appointment of Lieutenant-Governor of the Gold Coast. The Accra Native Confederation was unfortunately a short-lived affair.

The section on 'The Presidential Elections in Liberia' illustrates the state of affairs then existing in the only independent republic on the Western Model in West Africa and the important part Dr Blyden played in the affairs of his country for most of that century.

The 'Gambian Defence Militia' showed Horton as an active and constructive administrator and soldier. It followed the implementation of the 1865 Select Committee resolution when MacCarthy Island up the river Gambia was temporarily abandoned by the British Army. Horton who was then the resident army surgeon called together the leading citizens of the island and organised a militia as a defence measure against the hostile tribes in the surrounding mainland.

MacCarthy Island had been ceded to Britain in 1823 in an effort to stop the slave trade in that region. It was named after Sir Charles MacCarthy, the Governor-in-Chief, then stationed in Sierra Leone. The Wesleyan Methodists founded a mission and school there, and settlers from other West African countries were sent there. A small garrison of troops was stationed on the island most of the nineteenth century.

After Horton had organised his defence militia, the authorities eventually decided to assume again the defence of the island, and once more sent a Manager and some Police constables to be stationed there.

The Egba United Board of Management

The spirit of self-government seems to be taking a healthy hold on the inhabitants of the metropolis of Aku—viz., Abeokuta; the savage old native government is now undergoing a very decided change for the better, and it is modelled according to civilized constitutions, which shows the happy influence which British civilization has upon minds otherwise disposed to improvement. It is true that in Abeokuta, liberated slaves (and their descendants) of the country, who had been instructed and educated at school at Sierra Leone, had returned and made it their permanent abode and rendered the existing native government great service; but it was not until there was established in Lagos a European Christian power that we saw the march of improvement rapidly advancing.

At present, there is established at Abeokuta a board of management for the express purpose of directing the native government, of forwarding civilisation, and promoting the spread of Christianity, as well as of protecting the property of European merchants and British subjects. The

Secretary and Director of this Board, which is styled the Egba United Board of Management, is an educated native of Sierra Leone.[1] The first ordinance enacted related to the imposing of custom duties, which is necessary for the development of the Government. Such duties are imposed on exports, which must have an injurious effect on trade. The conditions of the ordinance are:—

1. That it shall be lawful for any person or persons (without exception) to have free access in Abeokuta for the purposes of trade, and to export therefrom any goods or produce, passing from Abeokuta to Lagos by the River Ogun, or elsewhere, subject to the regulations hereinafter mentioned.

2. That on all goods exported from Abeokuta to Lagos, by the River Ogun, or elsewhere, there shall be paid the following duty in cowries or produce, at the time of such exportation—viz., ivory and shea butter, three strings of cowries on every pound; palm and nut-oil, one string on every gallon; cotton, twenty cowries on every pound.

3. That all other goods not named shall be charged or chargeable with a duty of three per cent on the marketable value of such goods and produce at Abeokuta at the time of such exportation.

4. That such duty shall be payable and paid at the Customs-house of Abeokuta, on all such goods and produce as shall be intended to be exported by the River Ogun, and that on such payment a permit for the export thereof shall be granted by the collector, deputy collector, or such other person or persons as shall be sent with and accompany such goods or produce on their exportation and shall be produced if required by any person or persons in charge of such goods or produce, and that the payment of the duty on goods and produce exported will and shall be payable at such place as shall be from time to time appointed.

5. That any goods or produce being exported from Abeokuta by the River Ogun or elsewhere, for which a permit shall not on demand be produced to any person appointed for the examination of such permits, shall and may be seized, and on proof before the Board of Management, or any four justices of the peace appointed for that purpose, and the non-production of such permit, the goods or produce shall be declared forfeited; and on sale, the produce of such sale shall, after deducting the necessary expenses, be paid as follows: viz., one-third thereof to the seizer and collector, and the balance to the Treasurer of the Board of Management for the use of the Egba Government.

6. That this ordinance shall take effect immediately on publication thereof.

[1] George W. Johnson. See introductory comments to this chapter. He later adopted the name Oshokale Tejumade Johnson (Ed.).

Passed in the Board of Management, this 11th day of October, in the year of our Lord One Thousand Eight Hundred and Sixty-five, and confirmed on the 23rd day of March, 1867.

By command,

Shomoya, Bashorun, President-General

George W. Johnson, Secretary and Director.

The most powerful and troublesome neighbour to Aku or Yoruba Land is the kingdom of Dahomey, which has for a long time been looking eagerly for the destruction of Abeokuta; twice has the Dahomean potentate attempted to destroy that town, and twice has he received a signal thrashing, with the loss of several thousands of his warriors; the last was so terrific, that it is certain that Abeokuta will never again be made a point of attack. It will still continue to harass the small towns on the frontier, until such time as a combined action of all petty kingdoms is made against the common enemy, and Dahomey receives a final check in the slave-hunting exploits eastward of its dominion.

The natural capital of the Aku or Yoruba Territory is Abeokuta, and its best seaport town—or Liverpool—is Lagos. As yet the country and people are unprepared to be thrown on their own resources, it still requires more nursing. There are no roads in the interior, the water communications are not yet properly opened, and no regular native police or soldiery is paid by the native government. Things are only just germinating, and it would be an unwise step in the British Government were it to withdraw at once from the place. Abeokuta is by no means strong enough to withstand the several native growing powers. Ibadan, for example, will not receive any dictation from it, and it is not in a position to make it do so; should, therefore, the country be given up, anarchy and disorder will run riot throughout all the territory, and the slave-trade in its worst possible form will devastate the healthy growth of the kingdom of the Akus.[1]

The Fantee Confederation, Ghana (a letter)

The political constitution of the interior tribes on the Gold Coast is of a very primitive order, and their social organization resembles most closely the feudal system of Europe in the middle ages. A king is acknowledged, who in former years exercised the most unbounded authority as feudal lord, retaining paramount right or *dominicum directum* over the life and property of all the wealthiest nobles or caboceers of his kingdom. Under the kings are powerful chiefs (barons) and princes of the blood, who exercise considerable authority over their vassals, levy taxes, command a division (cohort) of the army, undertake distant expeditions,

[1] *West African Countries*, p. 167, l. 16 ff.

receiving under their protection inferior chiefs or free families who are wealthy, but who do not possess sufficient number of vassals to protect themselves from the influences of neighbouring powerful caboceers or chiefs. These families consent to hold their property and estate as their feudatories, and may be regarded as the *inferior nobility* of the ancient feudal states. Then come the free inhabitants, who, although not wealthy, have considerable influence in the country; these people are dependent on or claim vassalage to powerful feudal caboceers for protection. Then come the real vassals or serfs (*villicus*), who cultivate the land, and who are generally slaves received into the inheritance of a feudal caboceer (baron) or their vassals.

Before the English became influential on the Gold Coast this feudal system was carried on to a very high degree. The feudal kingdoms were conglomerations of many heterogeneous states, who acknowledged a king as their feudal lord, and he, on his part, was to a considerable extent a vassal of the powerful King of Ashantee. But since the English Government has had a complete hold on the sea-coast towns, and made the feudal lords or kings independent of the Ashantee potentate, as well as since it has exercised considerable influence over the institutions of each feudal kingdom, a universal spirit of disaffection and sedition reigns in the interior; the influence of each regal government has declined in a very considerable degree; each feudal-baron or chief, according to his strength, power, and audacity, finding that he is not dependent on the king or feudal lord, but the kings on him, according to the number of vassals under his command, pays but very little attention to his orders, in many cases, in fact, defying him openly. In many places the king is deprived of all regal power, and his retinue or *comitatus* of the poorest order, and even the external honour of royalty is but meagrely accorded him. Internal convulsions without much violence are not infrequent; and now a state of agitation exists in the interior; the feudal system is tottering to its foundation; a more enlightened Government is earnestly demanded by even the nominal feudal lords or kings and the wealthy caboceers (barons) and people. But the people are most woefully deficient in the two essential elements of real liberty and the means of having a settled order of things—viz., *education and industry*.

If the Government of the interior tribes is to be continued in the very unsatisfactory and undefined manner in which it has been carried on for the last century by the Government on the Coast, it will take more than three hundred years to bring it to that state of political civilisation which will fit them for independence after fully shaking off the yoke of their feudal lords. And I hazard the opinion, my Lord, that if the regeneration and civilisation of the fine race of interior tribes is to be left to the present system of Coast Government, it will certainly take another hundred years to infuse only the germ of civilisation amongst them and to enlighten them in the true principles of a civilised Government. Examining the country in the light which I have had the honour to bring before your Lordship, it will be conceived that nothing but narrow-minded prejudice or low servility to principles and policies of government already exploded since the conclusion of the ill-fated Ashantee war can induce any one to hamper any legitimate, loyal, and democratic measures tending to improve the tribes in the interior.

I do not believe, my Lord, that any European Government can effect this improved state of things in the interior without an enormous outlay, and we natives of the Coast believe your Lordship personally, and the Government of Her Majesty the Queen, whose Secretary of the Colonies you are, hail with delight any loyal, legitimate, and approved means employed by the natives of the Coast to further any political improvement amongst their countrymen, so as not only to relieve the Imperial exchequer from its heavy outlay, but also to lessen the awful responsibility of the Home Government on matters relating to so distant and unhealthy a colony. That means, in the interior of the Gold Coast, is the formation of a Confederation of all their kings, recognising one person of influence as their superior, and organising a constitutional Government, loyal to the British sea-coast Government.

The Fantee Confederation, as I have stated in my letter No. II, sprung into existence soon after the exchange of territory between the English and Dutch Governments, and its main object is to advance the interests of the whole of the Fantee nation, and to combine for offence and defence in time of war; the tentative manner in which it has been carried on for nearly two years, and the influence and power which it had over the kings in the interior, especially when not hampered by petty annoyances from the sea-coast Government, is a sufficient guarantee that it is the most needful and necessary constitution to advance the civilisation of the interior tribes, which, if left dependent on the narrow and limited Government of the sea-coast, will remain in utter barbarism. It is, therefore, the anxious wish of every civilized native of the Gold Coast, who has the interest of his country at heart, that in this agitated political state of the interior, a great desideratum to their country would be to get a *Codex Constitutionum* from the British Government on the sea-coast, defining their powers, giving them extensive latitude to improve the interior, without their President, or whatever the head of the Government might be called, being subjected to constant humiliation by being ordered up to Cape Coast; in fact, so as to give 'stability, distinctness, and extent to principles before unsettled, indefinite, and limited in their operations', such law as would form the basis of further political development.

The Fantee Confederation is necessary to be established as a compact Government of the Fantee race:—

FIRST. Because in a despatch from the Right Hon. Edward Cardwell, when Secretary of State for the Colonies, to the Government of Cape Coast in 1864, after the disastrous and ill-fated Ashantee expedition, the kings were ordered to be told that they were *not to receive protection* in future from the British Government. Lieutenant-Governor Conran, in a despatch to the Secretary of State for the Colonies, dated 7th October, 1865, informed him that he had put up a notice defining the limits of British territory to a distance of cannon shot or five miles from each castle or fort, so as to bring the natives within our laws, and check lawlessness amongst them, but not interfering with domestic slavery. Mr. Cardwell, in a reply dated November, 1865, distinctly informed him that he was 'unable to approve the step which he' (Colonel Conran) 'had taken in declaring the territory within five miles of eight separate British forts to be British territory', and requested him to 'recall the notice in which he had done it;' and in a subsequent despatch, dated December 22nd, 1865, he expressly told him to 'avoid any expression,' in any notice issued by him, 'which bore the appearance of extended jurisdiction over territory at the Gold Coast'.

SECOND. Because the Confederation will in no way interfere with the British authority on the sea-coast, but will aid greatly in putting down cruel punishments and exactions which are practised by native interior chiefs.

THIRD. Because it will form a compact governing body, composed of men of intelligence, protecting the boundary line on the frontier of Ashantee, their implacable enemy, and capable of exhibiting such force as would resist any attempt at invasion.

FOURTH. Because the Coast Government had done nothing, nor is it likely to do anything in years to come, towards the improvement of the interior towns.

FIFTH. Because in all previous invasions of the Fantee territory, the Ashantee forces, since the battle of Dodoowah in 1822, have cunningly avoided the sea-coast towns where British troops are stationed, but have ravaged the interior towns; and there being no compact government body, and no superior leader, the Ashantee forces have succeeded in destroying each province in detail.

SIXTH. Because the Dutch Government is an ally of the constant enemy of the Fantees—the Ashantees; and the exchange of territory, if accepted by the Wassaws and Denkeras in the interior of the Dutch sea-coast towns, will open a high road immediately for the Ashantees, which would give them considerable power over the Fantee nation, and would lead to constant trouble on the sea-coast. That the Wassaws and

Denkeras, who had thrown off the yoke of Ashantee for the flag of England, having refused to accept the Dutch flag, and having made overtures to the Fantee nation, who are composed of innumerable kings governing various provinces, to form an alliance with it, it was absolutely necessary that there should proceed the wishes of the nation from recognised and approved authority.

SEVENTH. Because the Coast Government declines giving sufficient and adequate protection to those who might attempt to develop the mineral resources of the country, by placing officers of the peace in the districts or provinces where the diggings are worked, so as to prevent the chiefs from molesting them, as the chiefs in the interior exhibit very little respect towards the interference of the Government on the Coast in their social arrangements, unless the Governor is able to march troops into their provinces and compel the execution of his orders.

EIGHTH. Because wars have broken out in the interior towns in the neighbourhood of the towns on the sea-coast; the country had been invaded by hostile tribes; treaties signed and sealed by these hostile tribes with the British authority have been broken; and no physical force was sent by the Governor (nor by orders can he do so) to quell the disturbance, but guns and ammunition were given to the natives, who were left to do the best they could to repel the invaders.

NINTH. Because education and industrial pursuits have never been encouraged by the authorities on the Coast amongst the interior tribes, and there is no reason to believe that they will ever be encouraged. Consequently it requires the interior tribes to organise a body of men who will give the subject that attention and consideration which it deserves, without, however, interfering with the Coast authorities.

TENTH. Because the Gold Coast is considered by the Home authorities as an expensive Protectorate, and authority of the British Government is limited to a very great extent to the sea-coast towns, and the people still maintain their time-honoured customs and practices, which, although in direct opposition and repugnant to the British Colonial Constitution, are tolerated and allowed free latitude. That in the interior the Coast Government cannot put down the more abominable practices; and a native Government, whose authority is recognised and accepted by all the kings, will have a great deal more power to put them down.

These are, my Lord, the reasons which I am able to discover, and which, if carefully considered by an unprejudiced mind, will be regarded as sufficient inducement to give the Fantee Confederation all the support requisite for its compact formation.

Since the formation of the present Confederation the whole of the Fantee nation has been combined under one Government, whose status, although ill-defined, carries great weight and influence amongst the interior tribes. It forms a representative body, to whom the various tribes who are anxious to become allies of the Fantee race have been able to communicate their wishes. It is the pivot of national unity, headed by intelligent men, to whom a great deal of the powers of the kings and chiefs are delegated, and whose advice would have considerable weight and power. Through it the whole of the Fantee race, numbering some 400,000 souls, can now, for the first time, boast of a national assembly, in which have congregated not only various kings and chiefs in scattered provinces, far and wide, but also the intelligence of Fantee-land. It makes the King of Ashantee for the first time throw off his supercilious disregard of the formerly disunited Fantee race, and tremble for the safety of his kingdom. When the Confederate tribes menaced it with the weight and power of their combined army, even the King of Ashantee felt the influence of the Confederation, and sent conciliatory messages to its Court at Mankessim. It enables the whole of the Fantee race to possess a national purse, by which it is enabled in time of war to supply each province with means for the purchase of war materials, and also to send material aid to its allies in men and money. The utility of the Confederation to the interior tribes is undoubted, and its power and influence are increased in arithmetical progression according to the support and countenance it receives from the Governor or Administrator on the sea-coast. When it is befriended by the Governor, when he lends it his advice and counsel, when he supports its legitimate measures, and does not regard it with a jealous eye, the Confederation grows strong for good, its officers receive great respect, the kings and chiefs have great confidence in it, and its commands are greatly respected. But when the Governor or Administrator circumvents the officers of the Confederation with petty annoyances and humiliations, its President humiliated in every possible way before the eyes of the nation, then the interest of the Confederation, and the good results which its formation prognosticated, become checked; and the Coast Government, which at present does not attempt to develop the interior provinces, retards rather than supports its organization.

It is on this ground that there is now a loud cry for a *codex constitutionum* for the Confederation from the Government of the Coast. It is essential so that every branch of the Government should have its power and limits well defined, protecting it against aggression, and 'ascertaining the purposes for which the Government exists,' and the rights which are guaranteed to it; securing its rights in the various provinces, and restraining it from exercising functions which would endanger liberty and justice. The present drooping state of the Confederation can say with great truth, *novus rerum nascitur ordo*—a new order of things is generated.

There are, no doubt, many intelligent natives on the sea-coast who are

59

well disposed towards the Confederation. Some of these men have told me that, on account of the undefined and unstable state of the Confederation, they have been afraid to act their part towards it according to their feelings and influence, which they would immediately do were the British Government on the Coast to countenance and support it in such a manner as to lead them to believe that it would not, on slight occasions, use its power to embarrass and ultimately suppress it.

In a pamphlet on the political economy of British Western Africa, with the requirements of the several colonies and settlements, published by me in 1865, I remarked in paragraph 1, page 6, that 'it will be necessary for the Government to be very circumspect in the selection of its officials for the Coast, and that the Governor-General, in particular, should be a man who possesses a happy tact and natural sagacity combined with experience, so as to hit the right course, since to him will be given the ground-plan of the future political government. He should make it his first object to discover those salutary measures which are necessary and endeavour to counteract those noxious influences which may sap the healthy action of the community. He must make himself perfectly acquainted with the internal affairs of each colony, its revenues and expenses, its commerce and agriculture, with the national character of the inhabitants, and each section of their Government. He should form a correct judgement of the character of every prominent official in his Government, and he should possess a talent for comprehensive and rapid observations in the selection of fit instruments for different appointments'. I am happy to say, my Lord, that the present Governor-in-Chief of the Western African Settlements, Sir Arthur Kennedy, is one who has fulfilled the hopes of the general public—one who answers to the general description of the high official necessary for the whole Coast. He is the right man in the right place, and to him must the people on the Gold Coast look as the steersman at the helm of the Fantee national vessel to guide it safely into a quiet and peaceful haven.

The following memorial portrays in an especial manner the feeling of the public in Western Africa:—

To His Excellency Sir A. E. Kennedy, C.B.
Governor-in-Chief of the West African Settlements

Freetown, Nov., 1869

May it please your Excellency,

The Memorial of the Sierra Leone native pastors in connexion with the Church of England, under the auspices of the venerable Church Missionary Society, humbly and respectfully sheweth:—

That your memorialists hail with unmingled pleasure the recent appointment of the Rev. George Nicol, late pastor of St. Charles, Regent, to the vacant chaplaincy of the Gambia, as an era in the history of the West African settlements; and that, whilst your memorialists thus give expression to their feelings for the honour conferred on one of their body, they cannot let pass this opportunity without expressing with thankfulness to your Excellency their firm conviction that to the influence of your high position is due the credit of this appointment.

Your memorialists will ever regard with unfeigned gratitude to Almighty God the consecration of the Rev. Dr. Crowther to the bishopric of the Niger territory, as a crowning act of British Christian philanthropy; the admission of Drs. Horton and Davies as staff assistant-surgeons in the service of Her Most Gracious Majesty as a proof of British goodwill for the sons of Africa; but they regard the present appointment with a lively interest as peculiar in its character, in that whilst Dr. Crowther is a missionary bishop, exercising the functions of his office in a territory not under British rule, and Drs. Davies and Horton are employed in an entirely military capacity, this is a civil ecclesiastical appointment to a post not hitherto known in the history of these settlements to have been filled by any in a full capacity except by Europeans.

Your memorialists regard the appointment as an earnest of a happier day for the West African settlements, when the prejudice of race, so prevalent in countries where civilisation, literature, and refinement in manners are in the growth, will be at an end. They need hardly say that to you, dear Sir Arthur, they look with eager expectations for the speedy fulfilment of this blessed time, for in this appointment, as in others of inferior though not of small importance otherwise, you have shown a just appreciation of merit and character, and not a regard to mere accident.

Your memorialists cannot conclude without assuring your Excellency of their affectionate goodwill towards you personally, and recording their gratitude to Earl Granville (to whom may it please your Excellency to convey these expressions of our feelings) and the British Government, and to the venerable Church Missionary Society, to whose untiring and praiseworthy efforts three-fourths of the educated portion in this colony are indebted.

God save the Queen!

(signed)

The Native Pastors

The Constitution between the English Government on the sea-coast and the Fantee Confederation should be somewhat distinct from that of the Act of Confederation between the kings themselves; but this latter Act should be supervised and modelled according to the position of the different kings and their provinces, as well as the condition of the people, by the administrative power on the Coast, by which means it will carry a far greater degree of power, weight, and influence amongst the kings themselves. The position and jurisdiction of the British authority and the Fantee Confederation must be strictly defined and definitely laid down, the position of the Administration of the Gold Coast to the Confederation properly regulated, and the sources of revenue, whether by a grant from the custom dues or by a small export duty on produce, considered. Ample provision should be made for the education of the young in every province, either by the employment of teachers by the officers of the Confederation, or by subsidizing the Wesleyans for that express purpose. A distinct plan should be laid down for the purpose of improving the industry of the interior tribes, and for developing the mineral resources.

The object of the Confederation being not only for social improvement, but also to secure external as well as internal peace, the Administrator of the Gold Coast should be *ex officio*, by the Act of Confederation, the *Protector of the Fantee Confederation*. There should then be elected a president, two ministers—viz., one who superintends internal and external affairs, and the other industry and education—and a chief justice. For the purpose of deliberating on the mutual affairs of the Confederate states, a Confederate Diet should be established at Mankessim, having two divisions—the Royal, in which all the kings, with the principal chiefs or grandees, should have seats; the other, the Representative Assembly, to which each province should send a certain number of representatives, obtained by the votes of all citizens. The fundamental law of the country should guarantee to every citizen equal rights and protection, and direct or indirect participation in the Government. These Assemblies should have the power of legislating for the Confederate provinces, the right of declaring peace or war (when the interest of the Government of the Coast is not concerned), of forming alliances, of regulating the taxation, the police, industrial pursuits, education, &c. Disputes of the Confederate provinces to be decided at the Royal Diet, and the decision open to appeal to the Governor. The President of the Confederation should be made, *ex officio*, a member of the Legislative Council, where his presence should be only required when subjects affecting or relating to the interest of the Confederation are about to be discussed; and should he hold that appointment as a Government nominee prior to his election, he should be called upon to resign it as such, but assume the position of membership as President of the Confederation.

Ce n'est que le premier pas qui coute.

I have the honour to be, my Lord,
Your Lordship's most obedient servant,
J. A. B. Horton, M.D.[1]

[1] *Letters on the Gold Coast*, p. 149, l. 9 ff.

For the last twenty years the people of Liberia have enjoyed an independent political existence. Experiments have been assiduously made in the various branches of the political affairs of the nation, and at present the constitution, as it now stands, is found to be lamentably deficient in many points of vital importance to the State; and however sacred and venerable the document may be, the national existence and prosperity demand that it should receive a thorough revision. The first point requiring amendation, as recorded by Mr. Blyden, is the increase of the Presidential term of office. At present it is limited to two years only. This term is so short that the President, instead of devoting his attention and ability to measures that will develop and advance materially the prosperity of the State, is tempted to direct his administrative power to electioneering expedients. The President, instead of becoming an able statesman, becomes an electioneer; the body politic of the nation suffers most severely, the whole nation consequently do not sufficiently pride themselves on their President; they do not sufficiently venerate him as the sovereign power of the whole nation, and thus in the election of a new President, party feelings run high, the President is traduced in the most violent manner by the opposite parties, his most laudable undertakings are scoffed at and greatly misrepresented, and the whole nation is convulsed for a time by violent political conflicts. That the President ought to be elected for a longer period is self-evident; a period of six years should be the minimum term of office, and he should not immediately be re-eligible.

Again, by the constitution, after the election of a President, a period of eight months is allowed to elapse, namely, from May to January, before the new President can be inaugurated. The consequences are pernicious to the nation, as the defeated President has ample opportunity of carrying out such party views and adverse plans as suit his purpose.

A third amendment necessary in the Liberian constitution is to remove what is found to be a prolific source of mischief in a large republic, and still more so in a small but rising State, such as Liberia—viz., the power conferred upon the President of dismissing Government employees indiscriminately at his pleasure. Mr. Blyden shows the deteriorating effect of this power when it was first introduced into America, and how manifold and all mischievous the consequences have been; indeed, so great has been the evil resulting from its introduction, that in 1859, he says, the fact that a man holds a removable Government office is a presumptive evidence that he is either an adventurer, an incompetent person, or a scoundrel. The evils are threefold—first, 'Few men can obtain any skill or experience in their offices, and the official capacity of the civil service must be deplorably impaired. Secondly, every man,

63

knowing that he has only a four years', or, at most, and by every exertion, an eight years' tenure of office, will be inclined to feather his nest as fast and as daringly as he can. Thirdly, it renders it impossible for men of intelligence, ability, and virtue, who wish for a reasonable permanence and a decent independence, to become servants of the State'. If in America where there are thousands of men of ability, education, and experience in political matters, the experiment is found to work so badly, how much worse must it be for the small state of Liberia, where the Government ought to concentrate around it the best abilities of the land. We hope that the national Representatives in the House of Assembly will not consider themselves helplessly bound to each item of a constitution which their political existence and scientific experiments have proved to be practically unsuited to the national prosperity and advancement, but make such amendments as shall place their executive administration on a better and far healthier foundation.

The inhabitants now elect their own President and Representatives in a National Congress, according to a constitution framed on the principles of the American Republic. They 'display a degree of intelligence in managing their affairs highly creditable to their ability, and calculated to rebut the insinuations which have sometimes been put forth by the enemies of freedom, as to the supposed mental inferiority of persons of African descent'.

The Liberian Government had its trials and difficulties to encounter, but experience has proved that they are perfectly competent to carry on their own Government; and having mastered a great many of the vicissitudes and drawbacks which a Government brought to existence in the form in which they have been brought must expect to meet with, they bid fair to occupy an important place in regenerated Africa.[1]

Whilst we rejoice with the Liberians on their yearly accession of emigrants from America, it behoves us to remind them that unless certain improvements are made among the aboriginal inhabitants whom they meet in the country, in order that they may be brought to the scale of equality with themselves, there will be a poor chance for the prosperous futurity of the Government. These original inhabitants are a firm able-bodied race, who unlike the American Indians, would withstand 'wave after wave of destructive and malignant tempest,' were it ever to be brought against them. They are a perpetual race, and the climate is more likely to devastate the emigrants than them—*i.e.*, if the former continue to remain pure and unmixed with the aboriginal inhabitants. The improvement in the position of the coloured population of America would lead *a priori* to the belief that ere long there would be but very few

[1] *West African Countries*, p. 17, l. 28 ff.

emigrations from that country and consequently a general diminution of the civilized population.[1]

A Gambian Defence Militia

M'Carthy's Island, being the entrepot of the trade in the upper portion of the River Gambia, where the best quality of ground-nuts is obtained, could not be relinquished. It is surrounded by a natural stockade, impassable by the Marabouts—namely, the river; and a handful of troops and a few good field-pieces, with proper management, would be able to prevent any crossing of a hostile force. The inhabitants are ready and willing to defend themselves against their enemy; and although the unhealthiness of the place has led to an unparalleled yearly depopulation, yet still those who remain are willing to aid in maintaining it against any attack of the Marabouts; and this is evident from the resolution passed by the people, who were represented by the merchants and principal inhabitants in a council (holden a day after the island was totally abandoned by the British troops) called together by the Commandant. The following were the members present, and the resolutions passed (vide *African Times*, July 23, 1866):—

'President: J. Africanus B. Horton, M.D., Provisional Civil and Military Commandant; Members: James Gray Savage, J.P., Edward Dusseault, John Melbury, John D. Attride, James Dodgin, Joseph I. Owens, George Randell, James Bell and George Robert.

The President explained that his intention in calling them together was to deliberate on the best means they should adopt in protecting themselves against any outbreak among their warlike neighbours, as all the soldiers had now been removed, and the island left in a very defenceless state; that any measure now adopted would be only provisional until the Manager who has been appointed takes over the command of the place. . . .

Among others, a resolution—moved by Dr. Horton, seconded by Mr. John D. Attride, and agreed to, "That special constables be enrolled out of the respectable portion of the inhabitants, and that the subjoined oaths be taken by each".

Oath administered to each Special Constable:
No. 1.
"I swear that I will be faithful and bear true allegiance to Her Majesty Queen Victoria so help me God." '
No. 2.
"I swear that I will well and faithfully serve our Sovereign Lady the Queen provisionally in the capacity of a special constable in the

[1] *Ibid.*, p. 271, l. 15 ff.

65

Settlement of M'Carthy's Island, and that I will not conceal any apparent danger, damage, or harm which may likely or possibly arise, without giving, or causing to be given, speedy notice thereof; and that I will truly, faithfully, and disinterestedly endeavour to use calm and peaceable means to quell any and every disturbance that may arise in any part of the said Island, or give immediate notice to the Sergeant of Police, or to any of Her Majesty's Justices of the Peace. So help me God".'

This is an excellent manifestation of a spirit of self-government, *esprit de corps*, and of mutual support against a common enemy—a spirit which, if always encouraged, would lead to most happy result. The whole of the inhabitants went cheerfully and heartily to work in carrying out these resolutions; there was not the least trouble experienced in enlisting the volunteers, and every one threw in his mite towards their support.'[1]

[1] *Ibid.*, p. 83, l. 26 ff.

5

Events in Ghana 1860–9: *The Qualities needed for a Ruler of Ghana; Comments on the Colonial Policy of the French and Dutch; The Ashanti War of 1863 with Britain—an African Victory*

The qualities needed for a ruler of Ghana, as enumerated by Horton, are of considerable interest. Ussher, the British administrator at the time, probably felt that attention was being drawn to qualities which it was felt he did not possess. Horton himself, however, aspired to the post, and this possibility had been favourably urged by John Pope Hennessy who had been administrator-in-chief of West Africa and was a great champion of Africanisation. Horton might therefore have been thinking more of his own qualities than those of Ussher when he wrote his letter on this subject.

The colonial policies of France and Holland are viewed by Horton from the standpoint of himself as British. After all, he was a commissioned officer of the Queen, and the word 'we' meant 'the British', whose colonial policy seemed to Horton unquestionably good, since it would lead ultimately to self-government.

The 1863 Ashanti war was one which caused great concern to the British Parliament. Both the British and their local allies suffered losses, and it was really an Ashanti victory. It was felt in Parliament that British commitments in the area should be reduced. The concern over the losses suffered in this war was one of the factors which led to a parliamentary enquiry into the state of the West African Settlements; this eventually resulted in the 1865 Select Committee being formed which later advocated the Resolution on Self-Government for West African territories. It was this which inspired Horton's major work, **West African Countries and Peoples.**

The Administratorship of the Gold Coast

Unlike all the other Governments on the Western Coast of Africa, that of the Gold Coast is influenced by many surrounding circumstances which make it the most difficult of them all, and require great tact and magnanimity in the executive. Its close proximity to the settlement of a very small European Power,[1] whose policy of government is totally different from that of the British; its position on the sea-coast, in front of a powerful potentate, who has a compact Government; its commerce being almost wholly dependent on that interior tribe—the Ashantees—who have the power of putting a check to the wants and requirements of the commercial population on the British territory; its inhabitants, claiming British protection, but disclaiming themselves as British subjects, each regarding himself as an independent individual in alliance with the British Government;—these circumstances make the Gold Coast by no means an easy Government. Besides, the extent of country is so large, the views and wishes of the people in each province so different, the difficulty of access to the country so great, the orders for non-intervention which the Administrators are constantly receiving from the Home Authorities are so general, and matters of importance within the Protectorate are so frequently arising requiring prompt, decisive, and immediate action, that it is no wonder that the Gold Coast Government is considered by men of experience as a trying ordeal for one who is appointed to fill the important post of head of the executive there.

The Governor or Administrator of the Gold Coast should be a man of tact, resolution, and great independence. Whilst firm in his decision, which should only be arrived at after matured consideration, he should be most magnanimous and conciliatory to the inhabitants over whom he exercises supreme authority. He should be a man who, by long experience in the manners, customs, and habits of the peculiar people of this coast, could form an adequate judgment as to the measures necessary to avert internal disturbance, and to give them a generalised conception of the interest the Home Government has always manifested, and will still continue to manifest, towards their advancement. . . .

I verily believe, my Lord, that in the government of a developing race, where the aim is to bring up the governed rapidly to advancement in industrial pursuits, education, and general social condition, *a little despotism is absolutely necessary*. But it must be understood that this despotism must not be used for the exertion of uncalled-for arbitrary power, which an intelligent race might think, simply from its superior intelligence, it ought to exact over the other as being less informed. But it should be more on principles of equity, having this object in view—the *material advancement* of the people. It will, however, be a most deplorable thing for any Government if this little despotism is exercised for revenge, or for the purpose of satisfying private pique.[2]

[1] At that time, the Dutch (Ed.).
[2] *Letters on the Gold Coast*, p. 136, l. 7 ff.

An African's View of the Colonial Policies of Holland, Britain and France in the Nineteenth Century

Events have now taken such a fearful turn in the Government of the Gold Coast, that nothing but a complete transformation of the mode of governing the Dutch territory can lead to a happy conclusion of the difficulties hanging over the political atmosphere of the settlement. Every day the difficulties of the question become more and more apparent. The insubordination of even the Elminas to the direct commands of the Dutch Government, or their tardy obedience to its rule; the atrocities of the few Ashantees who have found their way into the Dutch capital, unparalleled in the civilized history of the Gold Coast; and the enormous expenditure which the Dutch Government at the Hague are, through the unsettled state of the country, bound to keep up—are sufficient *a priori* arguments to prove that the present state of the Gold Coast politics is untenable.

There are two courses opened to the Dutch Government—viz.:—

First—To declare against Ashantee, and induce their subjects to enter into an alliance with the Fantee, offensive and defensive.

Second—To get rid of their possessions in the best possible way.

It is not likely that the Dutch Government nor their subjects would break up their alliance with Ashantee, which from time immemorial has been cemented through various phases of struggles which the Ashantees have had with the Coast tribes. The Dutch Fantees or Ashantees would rather maintain the *status quo* as long as they are under the Dutch flag; the first course is consequently not easily admissible.

The second course is the only one by which the Dutch will be able to close their affairs on this coast honourably. They may come to terms for the sale of their possessions either to the English, French, or North German Confederation. If sold to the English, we shall have under command the whole of the Gold Coast, with the exception of a small portion to the westward, now occupied by the French; and, with the judicious supply of custom officers, the revenue will be vastly increased, so that from being now between £20,000 to £30,000 a year, we can safely reckon, when trade in the interior is opened, on from £70,000 to £100,000. We shall then be able to bring the Ashantees to terms more easily and readily than before. But the material advancement of the Coast would be exceedingly slow; the field would be too large for the means of improvement at the Administrator's command, a scattered machinery would most likely be put to work, and the result would be unsatisfactory.

If sold to the French, they would have a continuous possession from Assinee to the Sweet River, a country of unknown mineral wealth. They would disdain to uphold the pretensions of Ashantee; and such is my knowledge of them in the Senegambia, that I most assuredly believe they would quickly form an alliance with our Government against any native Government, and would put down within a very short time the waywardness of the Elminas. The Wassaws and Denkeras would submit to their dictation, they would open roads into the interior to the boundary of Ashantee, and the capital of Ashantee—Coomassie—would soon fall into their hands. They would improve the country and people, make good Catholics of the latter, put down their barbarous customs, and teach them the mechanical arts. Indeed their occupation, as measured by the improvements accomplished by them at Dakar, near Goree, only lately annexed by the French Government, would be of immense advantage to the Gold Coast.[1]

The 1863 Ashanti War

Up to the end of 1862, when Richard Pine, Esq., landed here as Governor of Her Majesty's Forts and Settlements on the Gold Coast, the country was in a most prosperous state; the blessings of peace had been felt and enjoyed for many years; all the kings and chiefs in the interior were in perfect amity and concord with one another; the Ashantees were in the most friendly relations with Fantees and the British authorities; trade was in the most flourishing condition; bands of Ashantee merchants poured daily from the interior into the coast towns, loaded with gold dust, ivory, and other marketable articles, which they exchanged for European goods and munitions of war. Even in Ashantidom, their interior wars had been settled satisfactorily, and they had celebrated a gala day in commemoration of their victories. The Ashantees, who are the life blood of the Gold Coast commerce, were now (being freed from internal commotions) bent on carrying on an extensive trade with the sea-coast towns. The Crobboes in the eastern district, through the influence of Governor Pine, were gladly paying their debt. There was a sort of happy lull in the political condition of the whole country, when, about the beginning of the year 1863, a misunderstanding arose between the British authorities and the King of Ashantee, which at first threatened the peace of the Protectorate, and which ultimately culminated in open hostilities between the two Governments.

The affair appeared at first to be very easy of amicable arrangement. It was reported to the King of Ashantee that one of his lieutenants or chiefs, Quacoo Gamin by name, had, contrary to the laws of the country, found and appropriated to his own use a quantity of gold nuggets. The King summoned him to appear in person at his Court in Coomassie (the

[1] *Ibid.*, p. 139, l. 1 ff.

capital) on a certain day. Gamin received the summons and promised to appear at the day and hour appointed; but being apprehensive of danger, he quietly fled with 80 of his adherents, subjects of Ashantee, to the British protected territory of Denkera. Quacoo Duah, King of Ashantee, one of the most peaceful rulers that has ever sat on the throne, sent a princely ambassador, accompanied by a numerous and richly-dressed retinue, to Her Majesty's representative, to give the necessary information of the case and demand the extradition of the runaways. At a meeting held at the Palaver Hall, in the Castle of Cape Coast, in which were assembled the Governor and Council, both executive and legislative, the Commodore of the station, the officer commanding the troops, the principal merchants (European and native), and the kings and chiefs principally of Cape Coast and its environs, the whole affair was warmly discussed. The case of the King of Ashantee was set forth in a speech by his war-axe bearer, which was remarkable for its fluency, rhetorical power, and argumentative clearness. There was a division amongst the members. Many of the merchants, with Commodore Wilmot, strongly urged the claim of the King of Ashantee, and recommended that Gamin should be delivered up; whilst the chiefs of Cape Coast, who had been bribed by Gamin and some of the merchants, were of a contrary opinion. Commodore Wilmot endeavoured to influence them, by showing them how prosperous the country then was and the evils of war, and clearly pointed out that, if they went to war with Ashantee, it would take fifty years to bring the country back to its then condition; but, *quot homines tot sententiae*, the voice of the multitude prevailed, the Gamin was quietly allowed to remain in the Protectorate. War was declared by the King of Ashantee, who made extensive preparations to invade the Gold Coast territory.

Viewing the state of affairs at this peculiar crisis of the country, an impartial witness cannot help justifying both parties for the part they played in it—viz., Governor Pine in retaining Gamin, and the King of Ashantee in immediately declaring war; but the balance of justification rests with the King of Ashantee. . . .

Governor Pine was justified, because, according to the British law, a refugee who cannot be proved to have committed any crime, and who claims protection from our Government, cannot legally be delivered up to a tyrant or a despotic government. It is well known that the lives of the refugees, if they had been delivered up, would have been sacrificed. No sooner would they have crossed the frontier, than their heads would have been taken off and sent to the King of Ashantee at Coomassie; and Gamin requested that his head should rather be cut off at the Castle-gate, than that he should be delivered to the king.

The King of Ashantee was justified in declaring war, because—First, the very throne on which he sat was in danger. If he had not acted promptly in this affair, his people would have branded him as a coward, and consequently unworthy to occupy the stool of the long-famed and brave kings of Ashantee. Second, if the refugees were allowed to remain quietly in the Protectorate, without any demonstration being made regarding them, more important men would also have followed their example, and sought protection and security in the quiet rule of the British Government. Third, before there was any commencement of actual hostilities between the two nations, the peaceful traders of the King of Ashantee were molested by the Fantees in the interior; their goods, consisting principally of munitions of war, were seized, and the men themselves put in irons. They were, however, released, but no compensation was given to them. Fourth, on such an occasion, the generals and captains of the King of Ashantee would swear the great oath—viz., that the king had received an unpardonable insult, and that they were determined to avenge it. After this oath, the king would be powerless to prevent them from marching an army against his enemies. It will therefore be seen that war was inevitable, since the runaways were detained; and as regards the author of the war, in defence of the King of Ashantee I leave Montesquieu to reply to it; he said, that 'the true author of war is not he who declares it, but he who renders it necessary.'

After collecting a force of about 30,000 men, the King of Ashantee made three grand divisions of his army, and placed them under an experienced general of royal blood—viz., Prince Owoosookorkor of Osoo Cokkor. The smallest division, consisting of about 2,000 men, was sent to the boundary of Wassaw on the west, with orders to avoid as much as possible any general engagement with the enemy, but to keep the Wassaws and Denkeras in check, and prevent them from joining the Fantee force. The second division, consisting of about 8,000 men, descended, after crossing the Praah, on the main road towards Cape Coast, and pushed rapidly into the middle of the country as far as it was safe, avoiding any engagement with superior forces. The third division and main body, under the personal command of Prince Osoo Cokkor, marched on the east of Fantee through Akim, the most powerful and warlike people in the Protectorate, forcing everything before them. This tactic was intended to prevent the Aquamboos and Accras from joining the kings in the eastern portion of Fantee.

Whilst these preparations were being made at Coomassie, the British force, consisting of small detachments of the 2nd and 3rd West India Regiments, and the late Gold Coast Artillery Corps, numbering about 400 men, were distributed in the eastern districts of the Protectorate—at James Town, Accra, Prampram, Quanti-nang, and Kpong—for the express purpose of effecting the early settlement of the long-standing Crobboe fine. His Excellency Richard Pine, Esq., Governor, had personally visited that province, and whilst in that district, he received a dispatch, confirming the rumour that three divisions of the Ashantee army had crossed the frontier and descended on British territory. Orders were immediately dispatched to recall the troops from the different outposts. Fortunately a detachment of the 2nd West India Regiment, from Lagos, arrived at Accra at this opportune moment, on board the transport, in which the other troops were embarked for Cape Coast. Preparations were rapidly pushed forward for taking the field. Most of the natives who were able to bear arms left their towns to form various encampments in opposition to the Ashantee forces. Great difficulty was experienced in obtaining transports for the guns, ammunition, and other stores for the regular troops, so that women and children were employed for that purpose. Captain Wood R.N., a revenue officer of the Government, received a commission as major of volunteers, and was ordered to proceed to Mansoo to organise the native force there, which comprises the inhabitants of Assin, Abrah, Denkera, Cape Coast, and Anamboe. The Cape Coast Volunteers were under the command of Captain Hutchinson, merchant; they were composed of the intelligent natives of that place.

Whilst these preparations were being made on our side, a report was received that a severe encounter had taken place in a considerable town of Agoonah, called Essicoomah. The Ashantees descending from Western Akim, whose king, Agiman, and subjects had fallen back as the Ashantees approached, met an army of the Agoonahs and Goomoors, who had posted themselves in the forest and roads to give them battle. The Fantees first opened fire, which was warmly replied to by the Ashantees; and after a severe engagement, which lasted for six hours, in which both armies fought bravely, and many men on both sides were placed *hors de combat*, the Ashantees became masters of the field, and the Fantee force made a rapid retreat to the camp of Ajimacoo. This victory was most important to the Ashantees, not only because it preserved their ancient *prestige*, but also because, whilst it struck terror to the enemy, it inspired courage amongst themselves. Again, it opened a direct line of communication between their army at Assin and the main body.

The British forces now hastened to the field. 400 regulars and about 70 volunteers, under the command of Major Cochrane, marched, on the 19th April, 1863, from the seaport town of Anamaboe to Mankessim. On their arrival, Captain Brownwell, with 100 men, was detailed to proceed to Winnebah, which was then threatened by a body of the enemy. The troops remained ten days at Mankessim, which is about twenty-two miles from Essicoomah, which latter place formed the headquarters of Prince Osoo Cokkor, the Ashantee commander-in-chief. They afterwards marched on to Bobecoomah, where a large native force (irregulars) were collected. The Ashantee army, after the battle of Essicoomah, marched proudly through the province of Akumfie into Goomar, and in the neighbourhood of Bobecoomah rashly advanced to a most dangerous position, where, if attacked with vigour and pertinacity, they would have been annihilated. The British force at Bobecoomah were now for the first time placed within a very short distance from their implacable foe. Scouts were sent out, which brought in positive evidence that the Ashantees were within a quarter of a mile of the camp. Some of them had been wounded by the enemy, many killed, and others escaped unhurt. Yet still, with all these postive proofs before him, the officer commanding both the British forces and the native irregulars (20,000 strong) did not, or rather would not, permit himself to believe them, but issued immediately an order to the effect that the regular troops, as well as the greater part of the native troops, should march on to a small village called Endume, which was some distance away from the enemy's camp, leaving only 5,000 at Bobecoomah. Some of the regular troops, with a great many of their officers, and the whole of the irregulars who had been told off, arrived the next day at Endume; the major commanding and staff, with the half of his regulars as body guard, marched in a tangent from Bobecoomah and Endume, and established his head-quarters at Mumford, on the sea-coast, twenty miles away from Endume. The officers of the 3rd West India Regiment, who had according to orders proceeded to Endume, were surprised not to find the officer commanding in the camp the next morning. The whole of the force which left Bobecoomah were dispersed in every direction; some were at Mumford, some at Endume, whilst a detachment found its way to Winnebah.

The Ashantees, flushed with the victory of Essicoomah, were determined now to try their whole force with the combined native and British troops. After driving in the pickets of the allied army, and whilst this crazy manoeuvre was being strategically performed, on Wednesday, the 12th May, 1863, at two o'clock, the Ashantees opened fire upon the native army of Bobecoomah, which had been so disgracefully deserted the day before. The battle lasted from two until five p.m., leaving the Ashantees masters of the town, with a large number of men killed, wounded, and prisoners. The town was razed to the ground; and had Prince Ossoo Cokkor pressed his victorious army further and marched on to Endume, he would have effected an easy victory over the panic-stricken host, which would have retaliated for their losses in Doodoowah, nearly forty years ago. But he was a man of vacillating character, and, although loudly advised by the several princes of the blood who held subordinate positions as commanders of divisions in his army, including two of the King's brothers, several of his sons, and the general's own elder brother, he refused to venture any further.

About this time a reinforcement of 180 men arrived from Sierra

Leone and Gambia in H.M. ships 'Dart' and 'Dover'. Forty were sent to Accra, and the rest (140) were ordered to Mansoo, under Captain, now Lieutenant-Colonel Harley, where a large native force had been remaining inactive in camp for more than one month.

Confusion now reigned within the ranks of the allied British and native forces, and nothing could be heard but loud discontent in the mouths of every one. The Ashantees having defeated the allied force in two actions, and having successfully maintained their footing in the most fertile province of the Gold Coast for eighty days, during which time they lived on the produce of the towns and villages, burnt or otherwise destroyed the cereals and other native food, razed to the ground about thirty-four towns and villages, and about double the number of plantations, fell back upon their own resources, or retired on towns bordering on the frontiers of Ashantee on the 24th May, unmolested by an equal number of the allied forces who were watching their movements.

Soon after the action at Bobecoomah, His Excellency R. Pine, under escort of a body of volunteers, organized by and in the pay of Mr., then Captain, William Charles Finlason, of Cape Coast, marched into the field, and pitched his camp at Denkare (Akumfie), a few miles from Ajimacoo, where a large body of native force had congregated. He endeavoured to inspire them with new spirit; and, in consultation with Major Cochrane, it was agreed to make a simultaneous attack on the Ashantee force, which was then at Akim Swadrue. At this time Prince Ossoo Cokkor sent by one of the captives (Fantees) a symbolical message to the Governor, consisting of two sticks, one short and the other long, and requested him to make his choice. If he took the short one, he was to give up the Ashantee runaways, and the war would be at once at an end; but if he retained the long one, he, the Prince, would continue the war for the next three years amidst all difficulties. Mr. Pine retained the *long stick*, and sent to inform the Ashantee general that he was prepared to prosecute the war for the next seven years, until the kingdom of Ashantee should be prostrated before the English Government.

The Ashantee general-in-chief, knowing from experience how disastrous it is to keep a large army in the field during the rainy season, principally from climatic affections, quietly withdrew into his own territory; and after disbanding most of his men, he quartered a few in the principal high roads to the kingdom.

Governor Pine, shocked at the unsatisfactory termination of the war, from which a great deal of good to the Protectorate had been expected, was seriously taken ill in the camp, and was brought down almost lifeless to Cape Coast. The regular troops returned to winter (rainy season) quarters within the forts on the sea-coast towns, and the native force returned each man to his own home.[1]

[1] *Ibid.*, p. 52, l. 9 ff.

75

6

Personal Experiences as Administrator and Soldier: *The Riots in Sekondi, Ghana, in 1873*

This chapter gives us a picture of Dr Horton as an administrator and a soldier. It shows that from both an administrative and a stylistic point of view, when under great pressure Horton could still write with controlled judgement. On the 16th January 1873, riots took place in and around the town of Sekondi in Ghana. During the whole day, with serious fighting going on, Horton wrote no less than four letters commenting on the events to Colonel Harley, the Governor, in Cape Coast.

Horton was the Acting Civil Commandant of Sekondi, the title of a post which was later changed in West Africa to that of District Commissioner or District Officer. Administratively, he was under Colonel R. W. Harley, who was Administrator (Governor) of the Gold Coast. Harley was under John Pope Hennessy, who was Administrator-in-Chief (or Governor-in-Chief) of the West African Settlements and stationed in Sierra Leone. The Governor-in-Chief was answerable to the Colonial Office and forwarded his despatches there, sometimes enclosing those of his subordinate officers. These despatches were all examined by senior civil servants in London—Under-Secretaries and Assistant Secretaries—before being presented to the Secretary-of-State for the Colonies, who was the final authority and who at that time was Lord Kimberley.

The incident of 16th January 1873 went through the whole process, from Dr Horton's despatches to Lord Kimberley's final decision, in nine weeks.

The background to the dispute arose from the exchange of territories in Ghana (then the Gold Coast) between the British and the Dutch Government in 1872. After the final transfer some of the local chiefs, who had been under the Dutch, still favoured them and acted defiantly towards the British Government, and sometimes particularly so towards those Ghanaians who had been previously under British protection.

In Sekondi, the position was even more complicated. The Dutch-favouring inhabitants and the British-favouring ones had had a long-standing dispute over a palm oil plantation. There had been some previous fighting over it.

In the following years, attempts had been made to settle the palaver. In 1868 when Sekondi was transferred to the Dutch, the British inhabitants (that is the Africans who had been under British protection) had left and gone to settle elsewhere; when finally the British took over the entire territory again, they returned once again to Sekondi. By then, the Dutch-favouring people had had full use of the disputed plantation for five years. Inevitably, quarrelling started again.

Andries was the name of the King, or Chief, of the Dutch territory. In 1873 he and his people were still known as the Dutch King and Dutch inhabitants. Fort Orange, the headquarters of the Civil Commandant, was in the middle of their town. Andries was also sometimes called the new British King, since he and his people had just come back under British influence. Inkatier, Chief of the British-favouring party, and his people were known as the old British King and the old British inhabitants, as they had been under the British before the transfer of 1868 to the Dutch and had come back in 1873 when Sekondi was transferred again to the British. They had thus remained British right through in their loyalties although their moving from Sekondi in 1868 had weakened some of their claims to the plantations when they came back. Andries and Inkatier began to quarrel violently again over the palm grove.

Dr Horton, as Acting Civil Commandant and the representative of the British Government, sent for them to settle the dispute. Andries was evasive but in the end agreed to come with his followers. Inkatier turned up with his own followers. They quarrelled in the presence of Horton, and Andries slapped Inkatier; the latter retaliated. Horton separated them and warned them. For some reason he then sent Andries away from the fort and kept Inkatier back for a short while. One can only surmise that Inkatier and his people, although in the right, had been unnecessarily aggravating and he had kept him back to warn him. Later he let him go, after arranging to see both of them the next day at six in the morning.

Fighting, however, broke out between both parties next morning; the Dutch party was overwhelmingly stronger, with about a thousand armed men. Dr Horton was in the fort with twenty-one men including a West Indian sergeant who had come from Cape Coast with the pay packets. Horton, almost surrounded on two and a half sides by the Dutch party, and with only a day's supply of firewood and half a day's supply of water, refused to risk the lives of his men by marching them out. However, he actively used three policemen and a jailer as intermediaries. He fired three rockets over the villages, although this, according to the sergeant who favoured more aggressive methods, had no effect. But a short while later, Inkatier's men hoisted a white flag, and Horton arranged a truce.

During this whole day of intensive activity Horton continued to write long despatches on the events going on. The West Indian sergeant on his return to Cape Coast reported that he felt that the disturbance would have been halted if Horton had shown more valour and marched his men out. Colonel Harley, the Governor, was of the same opinion. It seemed also that he resented the post of Civil Commandant being held by Horton, either on personal or racial grounds. He knew, in addition, that his immediate superior, Pope Hennessy, the Governor-in-Chief in Sierra Leone, who was greatly in favour of Africanisation, liked Horton. In fact, Pope Hennessy had mentioned Horton as a possible Governor of the Territory. Harley was afraid that Pope Hennessy would not take active disciplinary steps against Horton; he therefore embarked on a series of manœuvres aimed at ruining Horton's career as an administrator. He first gave the news of the Sekondi riots to the officers of the armed forces in Cape Coast, who made certain that it got to the ears of army headquarters in Sierra Leone and in Britain before Pope Hennessy could prevent it. Harley then ordered a local enquiry by the commanding officer in the Gold Coast and next demoted Horton, replacing him in his appointment as Acting Civil Commandant by a European officer. He sent for the two chiefs and jailed them, with some of their principal followers. After taking these steps he sent a report on the affair to Pope Hennessy in Freetown. Pope Hennessy in reply queried his actions and ordered that another, more properly constituted enquiry should be held into Horton's conduct before censuring him. Harley, to back his case, had got Inkatier and the sergeant as eyewitnesses to write damaging accounts of Horton's behaviour during the incident. He had not taken any evidence from any of the soldiers or policemen who were stationed in Sekondi, and who knew the local situation.

The Commission of Enquiry consisted of Colonel Foster-Foster, Acting Colonial Secretary and Collector of Customs in Cape Coast; D. P. Chalmers, the Chief Magistrate and Judicial Assessor, who became famous about thirty years later for his enquiry into the Hut Tax Rebellion in Sierra Leone; and George Blankson, a Fante who was then a member of the Legislative Council and who had, incidentally, been mentioned by Horton in his book *West African Countries and Peoples, British and Native . . . and a Vindication of the African Race,* as a possible King of the Fantees. All three, in fact, constituted the Legislative Council of the Gold Coast of that period. Blankson's position was a delicate one; he himself had difficulties of his own, and he was under suspicion for political intrigue against the British Government. This probably explained his extremely guarded but positive reply to the question asked each member during the enquiry on whether Dr Horton had behaved well. The general results of the enquiry were favourable to Dr Horton and exonerated him.

Harley persisted, however, in urging his removal when forwarding the results of the enquiry to the Governor-in-Chief in Freetown. By then the Governor-in-Chief had changed from Pope Hennessy to Keate, and Harley *probably hoped that the latter would side with him against the views of his own Legislative Council in Ghana. Keate, however, in forwarding the report of the Commission of Enquiry to the Colonial Office, recommended its findings, absolving Horton from blame. After some internal discussion in London, a letter was finally sent out by the Earl of Kimberley, Secretary of State for the Colonies, confirming the exoneration of Horton but rather lamely leaving a loophole for his removal if the local Government so desired.*

The Chiefs, Inkatier and Andries, who had both been arrested, were not tried for murder as Harley had suggested. They were instead fined heavily, warned and released. The whole affair was soon overshadowed by the gigantic events of the Ashanti War of 1873-4 which followed a few weeks later.

Horton was transferred to nearby Dixcove as a medical officer, from where, as Staff Assistant Surgeon (his substantive post), he later took part in the Ashanti campaign and was awarded the Ashanti medal.

Was Horton a coward as Harley had so cruelly hinted? The Commission of Enquiry and the Colonial Office did not think so. He could, however, have written less and acted more on that day. As a doctor and as a leader he was more concerned with trying to save the lives of the men under him and with trying, also, to bring about a speedy truce between the combatants. He averted the loss of many lives which would certainly have been incurred if he had sallied forth with reckless bravery. Other men might have acted differently with better results. A British officer with panache and a contempt for excitable natives might have marched his men out in a surprise movement and won the day; or might equally well have been cut down and his men massacred. Colonel Harley would have preferred marching out: Horton, by his temperament and training to save life, could not have been expected to do so.

Many incidents of this nature occurred in the history of imperial expansion and were sometimes of no great importance. This particular incident has been singled out, however, as one of the few recorded examples of an educated African who, as administrator in the nineteenth century, worked as part of the hierarchy of a European power. The official correspondence of this drama has therefore been reproduced in some detail, Horton's despatches particularly being quoted in full.

Most of its lessons would be lost if it were only treated as a case study in racial prejudice by a European Administrator against an African colleague. As we lean over Horton's shoulder at his desk in the beleaguered fort, watching him writing or dictating his despatches with the sound of shouting and gunfire around, and the cries nearby of his compatriots slaying each other, we are not simply watching a ghost of the distant past. We are witnessing the tests and trials of self-government in the first of the many

79

thousands of Africans young and old who now hold positions of lonely responsibility in their own countries, surrounded always by a critical audience —sometimes of their own people.

The Secretary of State in London, the Governor-in-Chief, the Governor, the Acting Civil Commandant and the warring Chiefs in Africa occupied the stage briefly in Sekondi in that fateful year. But the drama of which they were a part remains unending and universal. It will always continue to be played when men are called upon to exercise power and to govern others in situations like those in developing countries, which are yet unstable and fluid and which have not yet reached the firm stability of fixed conventions.

To His Honor   Orange Fort
Col. R. W. Harley C.B.   Secondee
Administrator   16th January, 1873
Gold Coast

(No. 10)

Sir,

I have the honor to report that there has been a matter of a very serious nature pending between the people lately transferred and the old Britishers who returned from Wassaw not very long ago.

The people of Ahyame in October last complained to me that since their return the people of Impintime had been in the habit of coming into their palm plantation and gather ripe nuts without their permission.

This plantation palaver has been a rich source of dispute between the two parties in the District. In 1856 there was a serious disturbance between the two parties of the town and Dr. Sawkins Commandant Dixcove and Mr. Bunckel Commandant of Secondee were commissioned by the British and Dutch Governments to examine the territory, make a division and place a land mark separating the territories of the two crooms, and on the 5th May 1856 the Kings and Chief attached their names to a document, giving their adherence to the land mark placed by the Commissioners.

The matter was again brought up in 1857 and Mr. Lazenby, Commandant of Dixcove and Mr. Kammerling, Commandant of that place were again appointed to settle the dispute, they confirmed the boundary set by Dr. Sawkins and warned all parties in each croom against trespassing on the plantation of the other.

The palaver seemed to have been settled and observed until the transfer in 1868, when the British inhabitants of Ahyame (Aggium) and other towns left Seccondee and went to reside at Wassaw and the Impintime people had the full use of it for the last five years.

I had to exercise the greatest patience and discretion in the matter, in order that the smothering misunderstanding between the two parties might not lead to an open row.

In November, soon after I paid certain money to King Andries (new British King) for fines levied by him on Inkatier and his people in May last, I informed him of the complaint made by the Chief of Ahyame, relative to the action of his Impintime people in his palm plantation, and requested that he should send for them in order that I might investigate the palaver, he promised to do so, but a few days after he sent to inform me that his child had died of small pox and consequently he was obliged to go to the bush to make Custom; he remained there for several weeks and when he informed me of his return to town early in December, I requested him to send for the Impintimes but he said that his wife had died and he would therefore beg to be allowed eight days according to the native custom before leaving his house, this was granted, but he left soon afterwards for his bush Crooms, sending to inform me that another relation of his had died in the bush. After a few days I insisted that he should send for them, offering to pay the messenger; The messenger on his return informed me that the whole of the Impintime Chiefs had been inoculated and were suffering from small pox, and consequently could not attend.

On the 6th inst I was informed that they all recovered and returned to their croom, I at once sent to King Andries informing him of what I had heard and requested that he should send at once for them; he said that his nephew had died, and begged to be allowed eight days; I thereupon wrote to both of the [Chiefs] Kings Andries and Inkatier fixing yesterday the 15th for hearing the case, and I further informed the former that should neither he nor his people appear, I shall give my decision in the matter, and that they would have to obey the orders of the Government.

On Wednesday at two o'clock the two Kings came to the Fort with a great number of their people; I welcomed the Impintime Chiefs as this was the first time I had seen them. Inkatier and his people made their statement and handed in the documents of Dr. Sawkins and Mr. Lazenby affirming their right to the plantation. Thus far every thing went on well; I then called upon King Andries and his Impintime people to make their statement, and as soon as Andries commenced he was repeatedly interrupted by Inkatier and his people and there was a severe altercation and uproar between both the Kings and their people. After a time I succeeded in stopping the row, and observing that both of them were

81

the worse for liquor, having been making Custom for a relative belonging to the two Kings who had just died, I told them that in consequence of the state they were in I dismiss the meeting until 6 a.m. of the 16th; King Andries rose up with his people to depart, some hot words passed between him and Inkatier, menacing language was used and he struck him on the face and there was a fearful uproar, but before it went further, I succeeded in separating the two parties. I sent King Andries away from the Fort with his people and detained Inkatier for some time; I called three of the principal Chiefs of Andries and requested them to keep their people quiet and that they were not to disturb the others when they are passing through their town. I then cautioned Inkatier and his people, not to create, either by word or deed a row in the place and sent them out of the Fort and sent a Constable to see that they pass through the old Dutch town unmolested.

At 10 p.m. the King of old British town (Inkatier) sent to inform me that the Impintimes, soon after the palaver, taking advantage of his people being here, left for the bush and attacked the village of Anno, and there is every likelihood of there being a row. I shall do my utmost to prevent it by quiet means.

For the last eight months I have been fencing between the two parties, and had it not been for the continued interruption of Inkatier and his party I believe that I would have been able to arrive at an amicable conclusion of the dispute; but however aggravated King Andries might have been, he had no business to strike Inkatier.

I have Your Honor, watched carefully the temper of the two parties in the District; they are always at feud with one another and it requires the greatest tact to keep them from coming frequently into collision with one another; I have studied their habits and temperament, and should the present misunderstanding be used as a plea for disturbing the peace of the District, I think the Government has a capital opportunity of preventing any future disturbance of the kind.

I should propose that King Andries and Inkatier should be summoned to appear before you at Elmina, and after the case is heard, each should be required to lodge a good sum of money in the chest at Elmina, as security that each party should keep the peace to the other, before they are allowed to leave Elmina Castle.

This I consider to be the best means to be adopted in preventing future rows; for it will be of no use settling the palaver at Secondee; a summons to Elmina will have a very good effect in the whole District from Adjuah to Chema.

On the 14th Ultimo I proceeded to the bush and examined the plantation in the disputed district and I confirm the decision arrived at by the two Commissioners; and for the future peace of the District, the Impintime Chiefs must be compelled to desist from trespassing in it.

I have &c.
J. A. B. Horton
Acting Civil Commandant.[1]

To His Honor   Orange Fort
Colonel R. W. Harley C.B.   Secondee
Administrator   16th January, 1873
Cape Coast

(No. 11)

Sir,

With reference to my letter No. 10 of this days date, I have the honor to report that King Inkatier and his Chiefs came to the Fort to-day and informed me that the people of Impintime, soon after the palaver in this Fort, went to the bush and attacked the villages of Anno, Ahyame and Cudjoecroom belonging to them whilst the men were at Secondee, they have pillaged the villages, seized some of the women and children; and I have also been informed that a woman in the last Croom had been killed, a boy was brought to me who had been shot in his posterior.

Up to 1 o'clock last night I had been endeavouring to get hold of King Andries' Chiefs, in order that I might induce them to prevent the Impintime people from committing any more depredation in the interior, but they could not be found. The whole of this morning I sent repeatedly to the houses of King Andries, his Chiefs and Captains but not one of them were to be found.

King Andries I am sorry to say has had a good deal to do with causing the Impintime Chiefs and people to act in the manner they have done thus causing such a serious breach of the peace and led to the destruction or pillage of several of the towns in the Interior.

I have succeeded in keeping the Chiefs and people of King Inkatier from proceeding into the bush and have placed my constables in such a manner as to enable them to give me timely notice, if there is any collision between the two parties.

I cannot close without bringing the fact to Your Honor, that this affair is urgent; my previous letters on the pacification of this part of the transferred territory has shewn the temperament of the people I have to deal

[1] Public Records Office, C.O. 96/96, pp. 412–18.

with; and this affair has given the Government an opportunity of acting vigorously and making the people to understand that the British Government is determined to keep peace in every part of the territory and that those who wish to create disturbances will be put down.

The two Kings are very near relatives and the ostensible cause of the action of the people of Impintime is that Inkatier slapped Andries before all his people in fact returning heavily the slaps that Andries first gave him.

I have &c.
J. A. B. Horton
Acting Civil Commandant.[1]

To His Honor   Secondee
Col. R. W. Harley C.B.   16th January, 1873
Administrator
Gold Coast

(No. 12)

Sir,

I have the honor to report that there is a terrible fighting going on between the old British and new British towns in this place, the latter attacking the former commencing at 10 o'clock. The old British town is burning and almost entirely razed to the ground.

I have fired three rockets over the towns to induce them to cease fighting, but they have continued and the few people in the old British towns are likely to be all killed.

Numerous people have been killed, but I have no means of giving any aid outside the fort.

I have &c.
J. A. B. Horton
Commandant.[2]

[1] *Ibid.*, pp. 419–21.   [2] *Ibid.*, p. 422.

To His Honor
Colonel R. W. Harley C.B.
Administrator
Cape Coast

Orange Fort
Secondee
16th January, 1873
6.30 p.m.

(No. 13)

Sir,

I have the honor to inform you that I have not had an opportunity either by land or sea to forward the letters which I wrote on the affairs of this place.

I have reported that during the fight, I fired off three rockets at intervals to induce the people to cease fighting; some time after the last shot, I saw a white flag hoisted from the top of one of Inkatier's houses, and sent to Andries to inform him that a white flag was hoisted by Inkatier and that he should at once cease fighting.

He sent to inform me that he would obey my orders should I induce him (Inkatier) to acknowledge himself vanquished. I sent a flag of truce with my three constables and Mr. John Crankiow, Gaoler, who went to Inkatier and his people; and they sent satisfactory reply to Andries and his Chiefs. Andries then sent to say that Inkatier should pay some thing to his army before they could retire, but I refused to allow it and informed him that he had promised to withdraw them; he agreed to my request; Inkatier however sent him two children as hostages, and I succeeded in getting them to withdraw from Inkatier's town; and the fighting terminated after the old British town with the exception of a few huts had been burnt to the ground; whilst writing (7 P.M.) the old Dutch inhabitants are dancing and firing in their town. Many returned from the old British town; and the whole of the people who came to join them from the bush from six to eight hundred people are now retiring.

Mr. Swanzy's store is burnt to the ground and pillaged.

I hope to have an opportunity late at night to forward these letters, as at present, Andries' people guard the road to Chema and would not allow any one to pass through from here, nor would they allow any canoe to be removed from the beach.

I have ascertained that only a few persons have been killed in the fight of to-day about 5 or 6 and the body of an old Britisher was exposed in the market place of the new British Town.

I have succeeded in thus far stopping the fight, and I do not think that it will be resumed in as much as Inkatier has humbled himself to Andries, I shall not call upon Andries for any explanations of his conduct but only await what steps Your Honour will think fit to take. I write in great haste.

I have, the honor to be
Sir,
Your Most Obedient Servant
J. A. B. Horton
Acting Civil Commandant.

P.S.
Several people have been killed in the Crooms of Cudjoecroom, Anno and Ahyame. I have not been able from morning until 6 P.M. to take my breakfast.

A.H.[1]

To His Honor   Orange Fort
Col. R. W. Harley C.B.   Secondee
Administrator   18th January, 1873
Gold Coast

(No. 14)

Sir,

I have the honor to repeat in confirmation of my letter No. 13, that no fighting has taken place since I got King Andries to withdraw his men from attacking Inkatier's Town.

On the morning of the 17th instant the King of Taccorady sent to inform Andries that should he require any Assistance he was ready to send his people to give him the necessary aid. The bush people of Chema on hearing of the fight without receiving any communication from their King came down armed, to the number of at least 300 men to assist King Andries, but some rum was served out to them and they were told that the fighting had ceased, and they left an hour after their arrival.

Early yesterday morning I was informed that Andries' people from the bush were determined to commence the fighting so as to burn down the few remaining huts in Inkatier's town, alleging that they had been informed that the Wassaws had come down to assist the people of Inkatier. This was an improbability in as much as it would take several days to reach Wapan; and the King of Wapan would not enter into action without first consulting the Government. I however sent a constable accompanied by messengers from Kings Andries and Inkatier

[1] *Ibid.*, pp. 423-4.

86

Dr J. A. B. Horton in the Full Dress Uniform of the Army Medical
Department, c. 1860

WEST AFRICAN

COUNTRIES AND PEOPLES,

BRITISH AND NATIVE.

WITH THE

REQUIREMENTS NECESSARY FOR ESTABLISHING THAT SELF
GOVERNMENT RECOMMENDED BY THE COMMITTEE OF
THE HOUSE OF COMMONS, 1865;

AND A

VINDICATION OF THE AFRICAN RACE.

BY

JAMES AFRICANUS B. HORTON, M.D.Edin., F.R.G.S.,

AUTHOR OF " PHYSICAL AND MEDICAL CLIMATE AND METEOROLOGY OF THE WEST COAST OF
AFRICA," " GUINEA WORM, OR DRACUNCULUS," ETC., ETC., ETC.

STAFF ASSISTANT-SURGEON OF H.M. FORCES IN WEST AFRICA; ASSOCIATE OF KING'S COLLEGE, LONDON;
FOREIGN FELLOW OF THE BOTANICAL SOCIETY OF EDINBURGH; CORRESPONDING MEMBER OF
THE MEDICAL SOCIETY OF KING'S COLLEGE, LONDON; MEMBER OF THE INSTITUTE
D'AFRIQUE OF PARIS, ETC., ETC., ETC.

" Africa ought to be allowed to have a fair chance of raising her character in the scale
of the civilized world."—EMPEROR OF RUSSIA.

LONDON:

W. J. JOHNSON, 121, FLEET STREET.

1868.

The title page of *West African Countries and Peoples*

and also one from the King of Chema to proceed to the interior to as far as Ahyame which is the last croom in the high road to Wapan, to prove that the report was false. At 7 P.M. they returned and informed me that there was not a trace of Wassaws in the District, and that the people in the different Crooms were hidden in the bush leaving their dead unburied.

This morning I visited the portion of the town burnt down and there is not the least doubt that had I not succeeded in putting a stop to the fighting a vast number of Inkatier's people would have been killed, as the attacking party had enclosed them within a small compass having completely surrounded them. I have sent a policeman with cane bearers from Andries and Inkatier to proceed to Cudjoe-Croom, Anno and Ahyame and beat gong-gong, so that the people in the bush may return to their villages and be informed that the fighting had ceased and every thing was quiet.

I have received great assistance in this affair from Chief Efferim of Chema who came here on his private affairs a day or two before the disturbance commenced and who represented both parties to me, and through his exertions we have been able to dismiss all the bush people, who came down and commenced the firing at the very time when Andries had sent to inform me that no fighting would take place in the town.

I have employed the few constables I have entirely to quell the disturbance and as Inkatier has acknowledged the superiority of Andries who is his Uncle, I have not the least fear of any more disturbance.

Good deal of property have been pillaged and destroyed by Andries' people and a signal example must be made of him so as to show to the people, lately transferred that disturbances of this serious nature will not be winked at by the Government.

Andries, with his Chiefs, and Inkatier with his Chiefs should appear before Your Honor at Elmina, and the case investigated and the former be made to pay all the property his people have stolen and to receive such punishment as Your Honor may think fit to inflict.

I have the honor to be
Sir,
Your Most Obedient Servant
J. A. B. Horton
Acting Civil Commandant.[1]

[1] *Ibid.*, pp. 425–9.

To His Honor
Col. R. W. Harley C.B.
Administrator
Gold Coast

Orange Fort
Secondee
January, 1873

(No. 16)

Sir,

In acknowledgement of the receipt of Your Honor's letter No. 20 dated the 17th inst I have the honor to state that the Rattlesnake steamed slowly into the roadstead on Saturday night the 18th inst. and on the morning of the 19th Col. Foster landed as Commissioner from Your Honor. I sent to both Kings Inkatier and Andries to appear with their Chiefs and headmen in the Fort at 12 o'clock which they did. After both parties had made their statement I selected the principal chiefs and headmen of importance among the crowd of both parties, handed them to Colonel Foster who issued out warrants against them on a charge of riot arson and plunder, they were detained in the fort and the rest of the people ordered to leave.

A search was made throughout the Dutch town for property belonging to the factory of Mr. Swanzy and with the aid of the police a large quantity has been recovered.

In my previous dispatches I have not stated that there were at least from 700 to 800 men of Andries' party attacking about 250 of Inkatier's people; the former fought under the Dutch flag and occupied all the bush path, and bush in the immediate neighbourhood of Inkatier's town and had I not succeeded in preventing them from continuing the fight, the whole of King Andries people from the bush would have come down and joined him. Taccorady also would have sent about 800 to 1,000 men to him and Chema about the same number.

Most of Mr. Swanzy's property were removed during the night after the fight and it must be stated that there was not a male representative, either in the form of a factor or laborer in the town to look after the property. The factor had unfortunately been ordered by the Agent of the firm to Boutry 15 miles from this place and a weak middle-aged woman was placed in charge. Under these circumstances the plunderers had every opportunity of doing just as they liked with the property whilst the three policemen I had at my disposal were performing the duties detailed in my previous letters; the landlord, ran away to the bush as soon as the fight became hot and only returned when the Rattlesnake was reported to be on the Roads.

On the 20th Inkatier reported to me that the people of Impintime had a number of children whom they had captured in . . . .[1] in their village in the bush; I sent a police constable up with other messengers and they were released and handed over to them. These people were brought down and delivered to Inkatier.

At the commencement of the search a very few only of the cotton goods of Mr. Swanzy was recovered and these were almost all cut up into remnants. Mr. Cleaver, Agent of Mess[rs] F. and A. Swanzy demurred receiving these goods but I informed him that it was the part of the Government to recover whatever property the people had plundered and deliver them up to him and it was his place to put whatever valuation he may think fit. I requested him also to leave a responsible person at Secondee to receive all such property and this was agreed upon.

On the morning of 21st Captain Hoare called in the Fort and received certain quantity of miscellaneous articles which were recovered, and he was told that a vast lot had been received from the bush Croom which was about to be brought into the fort. Capt Hoare refused to have any thing to do with them and although I requested him to leave an agent with me to receive whatever property the Government may recover he took away every person belonging to the firm from the place and sailed on board the Alligator for Adjuah.

Not ten minutes after the departure of Captain Hoare, a large quantity of his property which was recovered from the bush towns, were brought into the Fort, there was no representative of Mess[rs] F. & A. Swanzy's firm in the town.

Under these circumstances, having no stores to keep them I have put them in puncheons, headed them and await further instructions from your Honor.

On the morning of the 21st inst a warrant was signed by Colonel Foster J.P. and myself for the seizure of all guns and muskets found in the town, and about 54 were seized and destroyed.

I have, the honor to be
Sir,
Your most obedient Servant
J. A. B. Horton
Acting Civil Commandant.[2]

[1] Indecipherable (Ed.).　　[2] *Ibid.*, pp. 430–4.

To Captain Turton
2 West I. Regiment
Commanding Troops
Cape Coast Castle

Government House
21 January, 1873

(No. 24, Military)

Sir,

As events of very serious importance have occurred at Secondee, and as it would appear that the officer in charge of the Detachment of Troops stationed there did not employ them for the protection of life and property during the riots which took place on the 16 instant, and which I regret to inform you has been considerable, but as the reason for their inaction (if any can exist) is not before me.

I abstain at present from offering my opinion upon it but in the meantime I have to request that Captain Mathews who has been temporarily sent to Secondee may be kept there and that he may receive such instructions from you (should he not have already done so) as may be necessary for him to act with the civil power upon so great and urgent an emergency as that which has so unhappily taken place without receiving such assistance as the Military could have rendered and which if promptly afforded might probably have averted the results which have now to be lamented.

I am aware the Officer Acting as Civil Commandant is also the Staff Assistant Surgeon in Charge of the Troops and may be supposed to possess no executive authority as a Military man but he could in his capacity as Magistrate have called out the Detachment, in aid of the civil power to prevent the riot and have given his instructions and see them carried out, that he did not do so must of course under the circumstances lead to an Official Enquiry, but I beg you will understand that I am not reflecting in any way on the conduct of the Detachment, but rather upon the inaction which was adopted.

I am &c.
R. W. Harley, Col. Administrator.[1]

To The Officer Commanding The Troops
Gold Coast

Secondee
January 23, 1873

Sir,

In answer to your letter of the 21st Instant, I have the honor to enclose a letter from Staff Assistant Surgeon Horton giving full particulars of all

[1] *Ibid.*, p. 277.

that took place at this Station on the 15th and 16th of the present month between the English and Dutch portions of this Settlement.

I have &c.
F. L. Mathews. Capt
Commanding Detachment 2^d W.I. Reg.[1]

Dr Horton wrote a full report, summarising all the events and again defending his actions. He was forced to reveal what he had chivalrously omitted at first, that his predecessor, a British military officer, Lieut. Hopkins, had faced the same situation a year earlier and had decided on the same action that he himself took, to remain within the fort and defend it from there. At that time the Government had taken up an attitude of appeasement to Chief Andries, the Dutch-favoured King, and had publicly censured Lieut. Hopkins. Dr Horton, who had succeeded the latter, had been put in a position where the authority of his office had already been considerably weakened.

Staff Assistant Surgeon Horton's Report to Captain Mathews—

Secondee
Gold Coast
25th January, 1873

Sir,

In acknowledgement of the receipt of your letter of the 22nd Instant, I have the honor to state for the information of the Officer Commanding the Troops that there has been a long standing dispute between the two portions of the town respectively called Dutch and English Secondee, governed by two separate Kings. viz:—

Andries and Inkatier.

On Wednesday the 15th instant I called upon the two Kings with their Chiefs to settle the palm plantation question (all other vexatious disputes having previously been settled by me) and they appeared in the Fort at the hour appointed. I opened the case but soon found that the Kings who had been making Customs for a deceased relative were under the influence of liquor. And I at once requested that the case should be adjourned until 6 a.m. on the 16th. The Kings got into high words, and Andries struck Inkatier, who heavily returned the same. I separated them and warned them that should they disturb the peace, the Government would punish them and make an example of them for the future good behaviour of the inhabitants who have lately been transferred.

On the evening of the 15th (the day of palaver) a report was brought

[1] *Ibid.*, p. 278.

to me that Andries' people in the bush had attacked the villages of Inkatier's people and had committed a severe breach of the peace. I endeavoured up to 1 a.m. in the night to get either Andries or his Chiefs into the Fort, but I was unsuccessful as not one of them could be found in their houses or in any part of the town.

On the morning of the 16th instant after many futile attempts to see Andries and his Chiefs, an unimportant Chief was seen at about 11 o'clock, through whom I communicated with Andries in his hiding place, who sent to inform me that there would be no disturbance in the town. I was at this time engaged writing my despatches to His Honor the Administrator and at 10 o'clock as soon as I went into my bath I heard the firing commenced.

Both the Dutch and English towns are in close proximity with one another, there being not even twenty feet of space dividing them, and each town has its separate King. The Fort is situated in the Dutch town surrounded on two and a half sides by huts belonging to the Dutch inhabitants and on the other side partly by the sea with inaccessible cliffs and a fetish bush belonging to the Dutch town.

In leaving the Fort with the men I had under my Command, I should have had in the first instance to contend with the difficulty of passing through the narrow lanes of the Dutch town (filled with armed men) which as I have said surrounded the Fort on two and a half sides and intervenes between it and the English town, which latter place was being attacked on all sides by the late Dutch inhabitants who were in open insurrection and revolt. Even had I gained access to the English town, in order to endeavour to protect property, I should have then placed myself between the fires of the Dutch portion of the town who were attacking the English portion and in fact the Fort which I would have to relinquish proper military possession of for this purpose, would have been opened to the attack and seizure of the inhabitants of the Dutch town.

King Andries collected during the fight an armed force of about 700 or 800 men and I am certain that he could have mustered from his people above about 1500 armed men. He held full possession of the bush paths leading to both towns; of the beach and bush path leading to 'Cape Coast' or 'Elmina'.

Although the Fort is situated at the portion of the Dutch town away from the English town, yet still several shots were fired directly into the Fort and these men who revolted fought under the Dutch flag.

There has been brooding smothering discontent on the part of the Dutch portion of the District since the transfer although the Colonial Government has done every thing to remove it. I have during the last eight months fenced between the two parties and kept the old Dutch inhabitants from committing any breach of the peace against the old

English inhabitants of the place. And although by instructions of His Honor the Acting Administrator I delivered the English flag to both Kings on the 26th September last, Inkatier alone hoisted his from that date until now. Andries who was in the habit previously to hoist the Dutch flag never put up the flag given to him by the Government until two days after the fighting when the 'Rattlesnake' steamed into the roads.

On the evening of the fight the King of Taccorady sent to inform Andries that he was ready to send his people to give him assistance and 300 armed men from the bush towns of Chema flying the Dutch flag marched into Secondee on the morning of the 17th to join Andries.

During the fight I made several attempts to send my despatches on this affair to His Honor the Administrator by the employment of Elmina canoe men, no other men being available, and there is no Government canoe or canoemen in the place, but the armed men of the old Dutch King would not allow the canoe to be removed from the beach, I was therefore obliged to take quiet possession of a canoe in the night after dark to report the circumstances to His Honor the Administrator.

The mud pond from which the supply of water is obtained for the use of the troops is situated about a quarter of a mile from the Fort and the insurrection came on [so] suddenly that there was only half a day's supply of water for the Troops. There is a tank in the Fort, but it has several holes and cracks in it, which circumstances had been reported to both the Officer Commanding the troops and the Officer Administering the Government of the Gold Coast. I made attempts to repair it during the rainy season but without any success.

The supply of wood for the use of the troops is made daily by contractors in the Dutch town and there was only a day's supply when the riot took place.

So soon as I found that fighting had commenced, and noticed the hostile disposition of the armed men of the Dutch King Andries, I assembled the few men under my Command consisting of one sergeant one corporal and nineteen privates as well as the escort which brought the pay of the Detachment and ordered them to be served with twenty rounds of ball ammunition each & placed piquets of two men in various positions on the battery of the Fort, with orders to lie low whilst bullets were flying over our heads.

I placed the rocket tube in position and fired three rockets at intervals so as to induce the belligerents to cease fighting.

The first rocket was fired over both towns and over the heads of the attacking party. The rocket tube was then lowered a little and the second rocket fell on the last house of the attacking party and set two of them on fire.

After a certain interval observing that they had commenced fighting I sent another rocket over the two towns in the bush where Andries and people were in ambush and a short time afterwards Inkatier shewed a white flag, and I sent by the Gaoler one of the people lately transferred to inform Andries who was in the bush in the neighbourhood of Inkatier's town to stop fighting as Inkatier had shown a white flag who replied that he would if Inkatier considered himself conquered. I then sent the Police, who during the whole of the morning had been employed in endeavouring to arrest the disturbance, with an interpreter to carry messages between the two Kings which finally led to the dispersion of Andries' bush people.

In May last when King Andries' people took up arms against the old British King ......[1] and the matter was settled with just conciliation by the Government the Dutch inhabitants under and around the fort whilst Lt Hopkins 2 W.I. Regt was in command put up the Dutch flag in various parts of the town and defiantly beckoned to the soldiers on the Fort to come and remove it.

Placed as I was under the circumstances above detailed to expose the few men under my command between two hostile fires to be shot down without the chance of defending themselves and without the slightest opportunity of communicating with either the Civil or Military authorities at headquarters, as Civil and Military Commandant, I consider would have been the height of folly.

I have, the honor to be,
Sir,
Your most obedient Servant
J. A. B. Horton, M.D.
Staff Assistant Surgeon.[2]

[1] Indecipherable (Ed.).   [2] *Ibid.*, pp. 279–86.

7

Education

Horton's interest in education was great, and he held advanced views for his time. His insistence on the importance of female education was echoed half a century later by another great African educationist, Dr Kwegyir Aggrey, who wrote 'Educate a man and you educate an individual; educate a woman and you educate a nation.'

His interest in education was spread over the whole field of primary, secondary and higher education. He advocated a system of Inspectorates of schools for all West Africa, and he also made a detailed draft of an educational system for Ghana.

His major interest, however, was in higher education, and for many years he was foremost in trying to establish a University of Western Africa based on the only seminary of higher education then available, which was Fourah Bay College in Sierra Leone. He envisaged a Teacher Training College with a leaning towards Science Teaching which would lead to the University where again, Science would form an important part of the curriculum to enable Africans to tap the vast potential resources of their continent.

Another particular interest of his was the founding of a Medical School in West Africa. All his letters, petitions, and schemes were, however, opposed—mainly by European officials in West Africa.

It was not until 1878 that the affiliation of Fourah Bay College to Durham University produced a partial fulfilment of the aspirations of Horton and his friends. The Medical and Engineering schools which he proposed did not come into being until 70 years later, when a medical and engineering school in abbreviated form was founded at the Higher College, Yaba, in Nigeria, and when Achimota College in Ghana started preparing students for the external degrees in Engineering of London University.

It was only after the end of the second world war in 1945 that a serious beginning was made in higher education of the type that Horton and other African intellectuals had advocated as long ago as the 1860's.

Education should be made compulsory, by a convention, signed by all the chiefs, that every child between the ages of seven and fourteen should attend school. This would materially improve, not only the present, but particularly the future generation. From the very commencement, great attention should be paid to the education and civilisation of the female population. Their position in society should be well defined and no arbitrary infringement on their rights should be tolerated; for it is they who, in their respective spheres, would become the best expounders of civilisation to the subsequent generation, and by their immense influence on the growing population, would greatly assist in advancing education and in breaking down the barrier of ignorance between the different masses of the population. In every town there should be one or more schools, according to its extent and amount of population, and every facility should be given to teachers and scholars.[1]

In the coast towns, such as Cape Coast, Anamaboe, and Accra, there is comparatively a great advance in civilisation although there is vast room for improvement. The principal portion of the inhabitants, who are educated men, are hard-working, pushing, and in many cases thriving; they possess considerable enlightenment of manner. Agriculture forms no part of their occupation, but they are merchants, traders, and agents for English firms. They build and live in large houses, which possess all the air and comforts of civilization; they dress in European costumes, speak English, some can even speak four or five European languages; a great many have received sound education in England and Scotland; and even some of those who are educated in the old schools of the Coast are by any means inferior to them; those who have received a middling education, and could read and write letters in English, are called among themselves 'scholars'.[2]

There should be established all over the country [Gambia], Government schools with a uniform system of discipline and instruction regulated by schemes planned by the Government. They should have 'the same books, the same rotation of lessons, the same method of communicating instruction, the same hours.' Besides the ordinary course of instruction, Arabic should be made a part of the studies of the pupil; and Arabic teachers from Senegal should be engaged for that express purpose. The necessity for this is obvious, since the Governor frequently gets letters in Arabic from the Marabout chieftains in the neighbourhood, and he has to go about the town to get them interpreted; whilst in Senegal, the French Governor receives from the independent kings letters in Arabic, and communicates with them in the same language. The Government should make it compulsory for every child above and under certain ages, to attend in one or other of the schools in the Colony. An inspector of

[1] *West African Countries*, p. 193, l. 18 ff.
[2] *Ibid.*, p. 107, l. 31 ff.

schools should be appointed, whose duty would be to see that strict uniformity is observed in all the schools, and that the masters and teachers attend properly to their work. The parents should be made to pay a certain amount, however small, as 'education, like other objects of attainment, is not to be duly valued, especially by those who are unable to comprehend its ultimate uses, until it has the price of money put upon it; until some sacrifice is made to obtain it; and the party making this sacrifice thereby acquires, as it were, a property in it. Given for nothing, it is regarded as little more than nothing, and as what may be had at any time; but so soon as a payment is made, the regular attendance of the children becomes a question of profit and loss, and the parent takes care to enforce it.'[1]

General Improvement in the Educational and Ecclesiastical Department of Sierra Leone

It cannot be denied that the greatest regenerative influence in this department is the Church Missionary Society. They support at present a college at Fourah Bay, a grammar school in Freetown, and a large female educational institution, besides several village schools. They have, infinitely more than the Government and than any other religious body, laboured earnestly for the diffusion of useful knowledge in the Colony, and to their untiring exertion is due that degree of improvement which is now to be observed in the Colony of Sierra Leone. It is evident from their yearly report that they could not continue this support for a much longer period, whilst the Colony has grown to be self-supporting, and a large field is open to them elsewhere to do good; and therefore it is necessary that the people and the Local Government should take up the work they have so admirably done.

We want a University for Western Africa, and the Church Missionary Society has long ago taken the initiative and built an expensive college, which should now be made the focus of learning for all Western Africa. The yearly expenses of that Society for education are now £4,700, which falls short of their former expenditure, whilst the total sum expended by the Local Government for this purpose is not far above £400. The result is that the educational department of the Colony is greatly on the decline every year, and more support is consequently required; but the local authorities refuse to give this, although they liberally spend £14,000 yearly merely for police.

A superficial consideration of the theory of the Local Government for the limitation of its efforts in this important direction—viz., that extensive funds have long been, and still are being appropriated for that

Ibid., p. 234, l. 12 ff.

97

object from other sources, and, consequently, it could not be so until the aid is withdrawn, as reported by Colonel Ord—is so alluring and attractive that it requires a long residence in the Colony to prove that it is most unsound; and should the recommendation of the Chamber of Commerce, that a portion of the revenue be yearly voted for general education, not be adopted, it will be one of the greatest barriers to the general improvement contemplated by the Imperial Government.

Fourah Bay College should henceforth be made the University of Western Africa, and endowed by the Local Government, which should guarantee its privileges, and cherish the interests of literature and science in the Colony. A systematic course of instruction should be given to the students, and regius professors appointed; for it is high time to abolish that system of Lancastrian school-boy teaching, and a professor should be appointed to one or two subjects, and should give lectures on the results of extensive reading and research. The subjects will be better mastered by the teachers themselves, and the students would reap largely the benefit. Lectures should be given in the theory and practice of education, classics, mathematics, natural philosophy, mensuration, and book-keeping; English language and literature; French, German, Hebrew, history in general, mineralogy, physiology, zoology, botany, chemistry, moral and political philosophy, civil and commercial law, drawing and music, besides the various subjects which might be included under the term of theology.

But the study of the physical sciences, which are closely connected with our daily wants and conveniences, should form an essential part of the curriculum, as they cultivate the reasoning faculties. Algebra, arithmetic, differential calculus, trigonometry, and geometry, besides being useful in every day life, remedy and cure many defects in the wit and intellectual faculties; 'for if the wit,' as remarked by Lord Bacon, 'be too dull, they sharpen it; if too wandering, they fix it; if too inherent in the sense, they abstract it. So that, as tennis is a game of no use of itself, but of great use in respect it maketh a quick eye, and a body ready to put itself into all positions, so with mathematics, that use which is collateral and intervenient is no less worthy than that which is principal and intended'. The Commissioners of Public Schools in England, referring to the study of physical science, justly remarked in their report that 'it quickens and cultivates directly the faculty of observation which in very many persons lies almost dormant through life, the power of accurate and rapid generalization, and the mental habit of method and arrangement; it familiarises them with a kind of reasoning which interests them, and which they can promptly comprehend; and it is, perhaps, the best corrective for that indolence which is the vice of half-awakened minds, and which shrinks from any exertion that is not like an effort of memory, merely mechanical.'

In fact, the whole Colony should be divided into educational districts. In each there should be a free grammar school where scholars should be prepared either for a foundation school, to be established in the city, or for the University. Each district should tax itself according to its capabilities for the support of these free schools; and boys who have shown a good degree of intellectual progress in a parochial school should be sent there.

In every village there should be a parochial establishment, assisted by the Government, and not dependent entirely on the paltry sums collected at the school. The schoolmasters should be better paid, so that a better class of men might be obtained as teachers, and the schools visited yearly by Government agents, to see that the rules and regulations are properly carried out.

The Government should also establish a preparatory school at Freetown for the express purpose of training up teachers, or forming a corps of well-trained teachers, who should give instruction both in the theory and in the practical application of the sciences; if very proficient in studies some might be transferred to the University. But before admittance as Government or gratuitous pupils, they must bind themselves to remain in the preparatory school for a stated time and pass a rigid examination. This school could be made to receive paying pupils also, the Government only supporting those who are intended for teachers in the public schools, and who should undertake to devote themselves for ten years at least to public instruction; and thus a set of well trained and educated teachers would be obtained, which should supply the schools of the whole of Western Africa. It will not be out of place if a Minister or officer of public instruction be created, with suitable councils, to regulate and improve the educational branch, not only of the Colony of Sierra Leone, but also of the other Colonies of Western Africa; he should form one system of education for all the public schools, and should see that the instructions for the guidance of teachers are properly carried out. In these schools prizes and certificates of honour should be offered to the most meritorious and deserving students.[1]

Want of time must be my plea for not having fully replied to your valuable communications[2] relative to the formation of a University for Western Africa. I was delighted to find that the promoters have been so far successful as to obtain the support and strong recommendation of one of the most enlightened, unbiased, high-minded and liberal Governors

[1] *Ibid.*, p. 201, l. 10 ff.
[2] Addressed to the Editor of a local African newspaper, *The Negro*, in Sierra Leone (Ed.).

that has ever held the reins of Government on the coast. I mean Governor Pope Hennessy; who to make his views on the subject beyond the cavil of those who possess a thousand lynx eyes ready to find fault on every occasion, has placed at their disposal for the projected University a number of most valuable volumes as the nucleus for a library, which we hope will be of intrinsic worth to Western Africa.

The vast field which a University will open to the grasp of the at present undeveloped minds of Africa for general study and improvement, is so fertile with useful results that I fail to comprehend the grounds on which an attempt has been made to oppose its establishment. Where are the schools for the study of Botany, of Mineralogy, of Physiology, of Chemistry, of Engineering, of Architecture, and of other kindred subjects which are the fundamental sciences which elevate the mind and develop the intellectual growth of any race which aims at occupying a high status in the human nationality. Is it, may I ask, in the Grammar School, the Fourah Bay College, or the Wesleyan Institution? I view every movement by which the native population can be placed in an advancing position in education as a right movement towards the permanent elevation of the race, and I consider that any obstruction thrown in the way of carrying out a better system of education on the coast of Africa, aims at sapping the healthy growth of a vigorous African Community.

In no country of the British Empire is there such a lack of scientific development and study as in the West Coast of Africa. Australia, India, the West Indies, Canada and Cape of Good Hope, if not possessing Universities based on solid foundations, have Colleges where Arts and Sciences flourish. The time has come that we Africans will stand no retrograde movement, and every means must be adopted, and no stones left unturned to carry out the all-important undertaking against all oppositions.

The Church Missionary Society, the foremost amongst the Missionary bodies on the Coast in advancing the educational development of the native population, go silently and solidly to work, and the fruits of their labours are broadcast throughout the length and breadth of Western Africa.

I admire the indomitable perseverance of yourself, Professor Blyden and others in heedlessly pursuing your cause against the so-called opposition, and I hope the crowning of your efforts will be a flourishing University for Western Africa. Ever since 1862, I have, in my printed works advocated the establishment of a University for Western Africa, and I have corresponded from 1861 to 1864 with the first Ministers of Her Majesty's Government, relative to the establishment of an advanced educational seminary at Sierra Leone. At first my proposals were very favourably received by the Secretary of State, but were afterwards squashed by oppositions from the Coast.

You have most rightly argued that Sierra Leone of all the Colonies in Western Africa is the most central and the best place for the University of Western Africa; there are unfortunately a manifest prejudice among a few little-minded persons in the various Colonies against Sierra Leone but this cannot be helped as it must be expected among such variety of community; our objection, however, in which there is some grounds for complaint is the patois, or Sierra Leone 'Noang'; this is undoubtedly to be found amongst the lower class, for in the higher class, along the coast a far different tale is told. It should be remembered that a low class cockney and a high class Londoner both speak the English language, but with what difference!

Let me now state what I think is necessary to be done to make the University a success—

FIRST. It should have adequate support from the Government from the beginning; Professional Chairs formed and the Professors well paid and provided for by the Government, so that they can devote their whole time to the work. A leaf should be taken from the German State Universities where the Professors are lodged in the Universities and so paid as to make them entirely independent, and devoted to the work in which they are engaged.

SECOND. The Governments of the Gambia, Lagos and Gold Coast, should contribute yearly a fixed sum for the support of the University; consequently the administrators should have the privilege of nominating certain number of scholars, not less than eight from each of the Colonies to be educated and maintained in the University without any cost whatsoever to themselves and family. This will at once give to each Settlement the means of opening high Government Schools in each of the Colonies which may hereafter become affiliated to the University.

THIRD. The position of the University is to be as central as possible, if it is to be successful, neither Fourah Bay, nor King Tom's Point, will at all be suited for a University of Western Africa; these places are out of the way and therefore would only do when an educational establishment is intended for boarders only; but where the Alumni may be boarders, and have to reside in lodgings and attend the lectures of the University—these two places are not adaptable for it. A central position for the University would encourage far more pupils from far and wide, would give an opportunity to the business man to attend one or two lectures at the appointed hours as he may require, and would be accommodating to all those who would like to watch carefully the working of so vast an undertaking.

I must close now, and in doing so, you will first excuse me, for being only able to give you a brief sketch of my opinion of the question of the day; and secondly permit me to express my earnest desire that you would continue to press onward against all opposition this great West African problem the intrinsic worth of which is its universality for the vital regeneration of the Negro race.[1]

Medical Education

In West African Countries Dr Horton gives the following account of his efforts to persuade the War Office of the desirability of instituting a Medical School in Sierra Leone:

The Author feeling certain of the immense advantage which Africa will derive from so important an establishment, and knowing that for the population to rise they require some tangible stimulus, proposed the following scheme to the Home Government for a Medical School in Sierra Leone, the Central Government of Western Africa, in a letter to the Secretary of State for War (a portion of which is here quoted), dated 13th July, 1861, Dixcove Fort [the Gold Coast]:—

My Lord and Sirs,—It is an important and universally acknowledged fact, that the greatest friends of the Africans are the philanthropic sons of Britain; and that the Government under whose sway they obtained liberty, and can consider themselves perfect free-men, and from whom also they have received paramount blessings, both temporal and spiritual, is the English Government. Africa, therefore, has everything to gain whilst Britannia rules the world. By her squadron she keeps a watchful eye on all those nations who would follow that nefarious practice—the slave trade; her adventurous sons, the missionaries, pierce through the very den of barbarism to become pioneers of civilisation. The consequence therefore is that the Africans have a natural attachment for the Government that espouses their cause, and also for the philanthropic sons of that Government, who always take advantage of every opportunity to better their condition. Many have been the means which the English Government has used to raise the condition of the African. This is universally known by every nation, and the African also thoroughly knows and feels it.

The last act which is of great importance to the scientific world, to the rising generation of Africa, and to the whole population of Western Africa, is that which the Government has lately taken, and which was so strongly argued by the late Minister of War, Lord Panmure—viz. of

[1] *The Jubilee and Centenary Volume of Fourah Bay College*, p. 54, l. 25 ff.

ducating young sons of Africa in the medical profession, and placing them in the Army to serve principally in Western Africa. This in the very face of it, carries advantages with it which no other Government has thought of; and we in Africa are certain that when the Government has undertaken a subject of such intrinsic importance, and of so great utility to the country under their Government, they will be the last to stop short when the work is in an embryonic state and with nothing to prevent its germination.

The system of educating African surgeons for the Army stationed on the Coast of Africa has manifold advantages:—

1st, as to the Government and its officers on the Coast; 2nd, as to the country and the people who inhabit it; 3rd, as to the scientific world.

Of all the British possessions, the Coast of Africa is rightly considered the most unhealthy and deadly, in consequence of which the best educated professional men are required to take care of those who are sent out to govern and keep order in it. It is a well-known fact, that practical experience and a thorough investigation of certain diseases make a man become acquainted with the different phases which those diseases may take, as well as the best remedies to combat them. The perfection of this truism cannot be accomplished unless some years be spent where the disease is rife, and its pathology and treatment carefully investigated.

The Coast is so prejudical to European constitutions, that the Government has been pleased to allow medical officers to remain only one year in it. During that short period it is impossible for them to take any vital interest in the diseases of the Coast, and beyond the ordinary routine of business, the fatigue from the heat of the sun prevents them from a study which some would be only too happy to follow; and after the lapse of twelve months, their tour of duties being pro tem, expired, they are relieved; or, even before the end of the year, some are invalided home from disease contracted through the baneful influence of the climate.

But an African properly educated in Medicine, is in his native soil; there he remains (not that he is never ill—no—but in the majority of cases it is generally slight); he has the advantage, by his long stay there, of being able to investigate the causes, effects, and pathology of the diseases belonging to the Coast; he in time becomes acquainted with the different types in which the diseases may present themselves, and therefore is able to combat them, and even prevent them in time, before any injurious effect is produced in the system; when, on the other hand, a neophyte will be puzzled what to do. This is no mere imagination; for there have been cases where, by judicious treatment, many valuable lives might have been saved.

The Government then will be the gainer, as they will have on the Coast of Africa, professional men in their service, who are perfectly acquainted with the diseases of the Coast and who may lessen the percentage of mortality among the officers and officials employed on the Coast.

2nd, as to the country and the people who inhabit it.

The immortal Sir Fowell Buxton has truly affirmed that if Africa is to be civilised and evangelized it must be by her progeny. For reasons before stated—viz. the injurious influence of the climate on European constitutions, as well as the slow and gradual pace with which civilisation and improvement find their way amongst a population who are adverse to anything that appears to destroy the customs of their forefathers; and also, the soil not being native to Europeans, and that they, therefore, cannot fraternise with the people who are not highly educated in the same degree as with persons from their own native country; it is impossible for the surgeon, employed for such a short and temporary time on the Coast, to take any deep interest in examining and developing the scientific resources of the country.

The Government look forward to the improvement of the country, and that improvement can never be properly accomplished, unless by the aid of the educated native portion of the community. It is the African who can take a deep and vital interest in the rise of the country; it is he who when placed in a position to raise the standard of his countrymen, will never give up on slight disappointment, but will continue on, till he has accomplished his end. It will, therefore, be of very great importance to the country and to the people should the Government continue to send to the Coast of Africa, well-educated natives, scientific and professional men to serve in it, for the country will be largely benefited by it.

3rd, as to the scientific world.

The scientific resources of Western Africa are entirely in embryo; and we can literally and truly state that we are perfectly ignorant of them. There are vast treasures in the bowels of this extensive continent, potent medicines in its picturesque field, and objects of great importance to the naturalist, as yet unknown to the scientific world. Here then are subjects which the short stay of a European on the Coast will not permit him to investigate; but the African Surgeon, stationed in one place at first, say the Gold Coast, and then removed to the other stations say, Sierra Leone and the Gambia, has ample opportunity of investigating these subjects; and medicine and science generally, will be greatly benefited by it.

In every respect, then, the Government has begun an excellent and praiseworthy undertaking and which will make every African invoke blessing on her efforts, as it is one of intrinsic value to the country, the people of Africa, as well as the Government.

Two out of the three who were first sent to be educated in the medical profession for the Army, have now finished their studies, and are attached to the Army stationed on the Coast; the other, unfortunately, succumbed to the influence of the cold climate. The testimony, received through the Church Missionary Society by the Government, as to the efficiency and behaviour of the three African Students, who were educated through the instrumentality of the Government, from the Dean of the Medical Faculty of King's College, London, the College where they were educated, was of a nature, I believe, to encourage further trial, and to prove that the African, when placed in a proper position, employs his time to the best advantage; and all the Africans on the Coast, and the friends of African improvement, consider it a misfortune to the country that the wish of the Government and of the Church Missionary Society, that seven more Africans should be sent to receive education in Medicine, has not been carried out.

It may be asked what would be the best means of effectually carrying out this excellent plan of educating young Africans in the science of medicine? Having had ample opportunity of carefully studying all the various bearings of the subject, I hope that the following suggestions will meet with your approbation.

That a small Government Medical Establishment be made at Sierra Leone, and that certain young men, not above the age of twenty, be selected from those in the Church Missionary College or Schools, who have made some proficiency in Latin, Greek, and Mathematics.[1] That they should be prepared in the preliminaries of Medicine—viz. Anatomy, Physiology, Chemistry, Botany (of Africa), Natural History, Hospital Practice and Pharmacy, for a certain period, from one year and a half to two years. That they should continue during that time their classical studies, limited to those books required by the Colleges, in the way the Master of the establishment might think best. That the Master be an African, since, as we have endeavoured to prove, he will take a far greater interest in performing what will tend to elevate his country. That he should have his full power and credentials for selecting young men and managing the establishment from the Home Government, and that he should in any case of doubt consult the Church Missionary Society at Sierra Leone. Should it be left to the local power, I am certain that his efforts would be paralysed. That a few wax-works and books be sent for the establishment according to the application of the Master, who should also keep a laboratory for his chemical class. That the students be allowed a certain amount, according to the discretion of the Government, for their board, clothing, and other expenses, which I am certain would not be too costly.

For anatomy and dissection, monkeys may be advantageously used,

---

[1] In a subsequent letter the Author proposed that selection should be made from the four Colonies and settlements—viz. Gambia, Sierra Leone, Lagos and Cape Coast (Ed.).

as well as the wax-work. The botany of Western Africa as well as the natural history should be studied, and the Master, therefore, must be acquainted with these subjects. For hospital practice and pharmacy, abundant opportunities are offered at Sierra Leone.

It is a very difficult thing for the student unacquainted with anything in Medicine to begin in England, and compete with students who generally have had preliminary education in some of the subjects before they enter the proper colleges; and I am certain that by these means the Government would have their wishes fulfilled, and the country and people be greatly benefited—&c., &c., &c.

James Africanus B. Horton, M.D.

The Author received a most favourable reply from the Secretary of State for War, who said that the subject should have his full attention and consideration. At the same time, communications were forwarded to the principal Medical Officer and to the Officer Commanding on the Gold Coast, for information bearing on the subjects, so as to know how far the 'intended substitution, either wholly or in part, of native African for European Medical officers, is likely to be successful'. The subject received a combined and warm opposition, which nipped it in the bud.[1]

Horton did not give up his cause easily. Ten months after the letter to the Secretary of State for War, quoted above, and well knowing the nature of the opposition, he wrote again:

To the President and Members of the Educational Committee, War Office, London.

Cape Coast Castle
13th May, 1862

My Lord and Sirs,

I have the honor to return you my warmest thanks for the kind consideration and attention which you have hitherto given to my letter of the 13th July last relative to the appointment and training of African Surgeons In Service on the Coast of Africa.

It is an acknowledged fact that the benevolent cause which you are now favouring has for its grand object, not only to raise the standards of a race which only requires the stimulus to exert themselves for advancing their country's welfare but also to enable them to show to the world what England could do for a people that it espouses; and every African

[1] *West African Countries*, p. 46, footnote.

on the Coast of Africa as well as in every part of the globe who are duly informed of the same will always show their deep thankfulness to you.

It will be untrue were I to say that every individual on the Coast both European and African would advocate so noble a cause, as it is a natural thing that there must be some foreigners, but unfortunately as in this particular case not a few, who are opposed to the African race and who would not in any way favour any plan that tend[ed] to better their condition.

Many Europeans who are or have been on the Coast have argued that the Africans should be left exactly as they are in their native state and many a time have I been told that Missionaries ought never to be sent out to preach to the people as *it is the worst thing that the people of England could do.*

If we can find men here who oppose the preaching of the Gospel, how much more must we expect to find men strongly in opposition to matters that will raise the African to a people.

You may, My Lord and Sirs, perhaps meet discouragement from those whom you may expect to be the men to promote your plans but be assured that in a few years this plan so admirably begun will be pregnant with numerous advantages to the Government.

Already we have been told that a 4th West Indian Regt. is being formed to serve principally on the West Coast of Africa, whose headquarters should be at Sierra Leone. The new acquisitions of our government along this coast could now be conveniently occupied, such as the fertile regions of Quiah, the Slave [Limits?] of Bulama, the flourishing islands of Lagos and the different stations connected with it; besides several stations along the Gold Coast.

In the event these places are occupied by our troops, how profitable will it be to the government should native medical officers be employed; I am sure the advantages pointed out in my last letter will certainly be obtained by the government and more also that the government will save and apply to a better purpose the enormous yearly expense of sending out and relieving European medical officers.

It will not in the present state of affairs viz. the novelty of the undertaking be very advisable to have the Coast at once supplied wholly with native officers but only in part, from the fact that it will require a little time for the European officers on the Coast to realize the advantages that will accrue from it. It is generally known and believed that many of those who come out are *opposed to anything that will raise the African* and therefore it will require time for them to conform themselves with any such plans; but I am certain that the government will not allow individual prejudices to prevent them from continuing in this most noble undertaking. I only pray that we who have first received the benefit will so conduct themselves that you may regard us as worthy of the honour you have conferred on us.

In conclusion I must again state that I have no doubt that your endeavours will be crowned by greater success should young Africans have the advantage of preliminary education at Sierra Leone by *an African* before they be sent to England.

I have the honour to be
My Lord and Sirs,
Your most obedient humble servant,
Africanus Horton M.D.
Staff Asst. Surgeon.[1]

To this letter he received the following reply:

To A. Horton Esqr M.D.   War Office
Staff Asst Surgeon   19th June, 1862
Cape Coast Castle
Gold Coast

Sir,

I am directed by the Secretary Sir George C. Lewis to acknowledge the receipt of your letter of the 13th ultimo, and to acquaint you in reply that as it is not intended for the present to train any further candidates natives of Africa for Army surgeonries, Sir George Lewis does not consider it necessary to enter into the scheme proposed by you.

I am,
Sir,
Your obedient servant
Edward Lugard.[2, 3]

[1] C.M.S. Library CA1/0117.
[2] General the Rt. Hon. Sir Edward Lugard, P.C., G.C.B., was Permanent Under-Secretary of State for War 1861–71. He was the uncle of Frederick Lugard (later Lord Lugard of Abinger). See Perham, Dame M.: *Lugard*, I, p. 36 (Ed.).
[3] C.M.S. Library CA1/0117.

8

Banking and Currency

After his retirement from the Army Medical Service and about fourteen years after writing these extracts, Dr Horton opened the Commercial Bank of West Africa. He died, however, about a year after its establishment. His notes on the currency of Ghana are of considerable interest. The archi (sometimes spelt ackie or ackey), a silver coin, was in circulation during part of the first half of the nineteenth century but is now no longer used. The pessua (nowadays called the pesewa) is now in use again as a small coin after being displaced for almost a century by the penny.

The Formation of a National Bank at Freetown

The growing wealth of the city of Freetown necessitates the formation of a Government, and consequently a responsible bank in it. A bank at Sierra Leone, formed and supported by the Local Government, and placed in connexion with a safe bank in England, will furnish a most important lever to the merchants and small traders in the Colony; which benefit would ultimately extend to the other Colonies on the Coast. In commercial circles the importance of a good, reliable banking establishment is well known and appreciated. Even in this Colony, where there are only small private banks, so greatly are they appreciated that, at the approach of the mail steamers, the banks have sometimes to close their doors against business men.

It would be a very important savings bank for the poor, who now bury their small savings in the ground; they would thus obtain good security and a premium. It would supply the merchants and traders with money during the trading season, when ready cash is much required; and, by some arrangement, it might be made to supply the military and naval department on the Coast at a certain rate of premium. So that whilst it will be advantageous to the commercial and other inhabitants of the Colony, it would also be serviceable to the local authorities and the Imperial Government.[1]

[1] *West African Countries*, p. 226, l. 16 ff.

For the raising of a sufficient amount of money for rapidly carrying out those improvements which are essential to the health and industrial development of the Colony, a large amount of money will be required at once to carry out these useful improvements, over and above the present revenue. A loan has been suggested by many, but the Colony will be obliged to pay a large interest until the capital is paid; and this will necessitate an increase in the taxes. In my opinion this can at present be dispensed with if the amount required be not far over 100,000 *l.*, and let the Colony be her own debtor.

Let a colonial paper currency to that amount be issued, and made equal in value to the specie in circulation, and redeemable in ten or more years; let the Legislature be stringent in preventing any depreciation of its value; let the large mercantile establishments take it up and have it circulated, and let the Government redeem every year from two to four thousand pounds; and in a few years those large improvements indicated will be made, which, in the course of a short time, will pay their own expenses without any outlay from the colonial chest. A similar plan was, some years ago, adopted in the building of a large wharf (if my memory be correct) in Jersey with great success. . . .

Sierra Leone has a large revenue, which is above her expenses, and a few years ago she had in her chest about 15,000 *l.* over and above her expenditure. The paper currency, if adopted, will be for building public works, which will be made to pay their own expenses, without costing a farthing to the Government. Thus, if water be conveyed to the town and supplied to the different houses, the people will be taxed for it, and the money derived from it will go towards reclaiming the paper currency, until it becomes an independent source of revenue. I shall therefore recommend the adoption of this measure as the most practical that could be found suited for the Colony of Sierra Leone, and not to venture at present on a loan for these improvements.[1]

The currency of the Gold Coast is gold-dust, an ounce of which is sold for 3 *l.* 12*s.* The smallest quantity recognised in trade or for general use is a pessua, or 1½*d.*, which is regarded by a Fantee man in the same light as we regard a farthing. Thus, when a thing is considered worthless, a Fantee man will say that it is not worth a *pessua*. The sum is equal in weight to a small bead, or the seed of the *Aviculum*, or bird's-eye. The next in value is *Simpoir*, 3*d.*; and then *Teycoophan*, or Teycoo, 6*d.* A compound is used to denote higher value thus, 9*d.* is called *Simpoir na Teycoophan*, or, *Teycoo na Simpoir*. The most general calculation is one dollar, which in gold is called *Archi*, and equal to 4*s.* 6*d.* These conventional names were not originally native, but given probably by the Old

[1] *Ibid.*, p 224, l. 10 ff.

African Trading Company, so as to produce a uniformity of the currency of the country with the English coin. In the Eastern District, besides a small quantity of gold-dust, *cowries*, a small shell, the *Cypress moneta*, is extensively used in the interior, and is much employed for buying palm-oil. It is a cumbrous circulating medium, and fluctuates greatly in value. One head is supposed to be equal to half-a-dollar, being 50 strings, each string containing 40 cowries. For silver coin, I have known more than 60 strings given for half-a-dollar, or 2s. 3d. Besides cowries and gold-dust, which are purely native currency, English coin, dollars (American, Mexican, and Spanish) are found in large quantity; but for general use the natives prefer the English, from its standing value and convenience; it is very much sought after. The dollars are principally used to buy oil with from the people in the bush. The star, or Mexican dollars, are preferred, as their value is always 4s. 6d., while the others are subject to great fluctuation. The currency value of a dollar is 5s.; but the sterling value, 4s. 6d. This sometimes leads to great confusion among novices; four dollars are always spoken of as a pound, *i.e.*, a pound currency although its real value is 18s. sterling.[1]

[1] *Ibid.*, p. 113, l. 23 ff.

9

An Autobiographical Account of Dr Horton's Medical and Scientific Career

After qualifying as a doctor from King's College, London and Edinburgh University, Africanus Horton was commissioned as a British Army Medical Officer and left Britain for Africa. The reception he received from some of the British authorities there was not cordial and his presence at a senior level was obviously resented. He remembered, however, the advice which his patron and guardian, the great Englishman, Henry Venn of the Church Missionary Society in London, had given him and he wrote back to him touchingly as 'My dear Father' to tell him of his troubles.

Within a few years of qualifying, Horton had started proposing to the authorities in Britain the necessity of having a pre-medical school in West Africa and of training more Africans as doctors (see Chapter 7). His senior European colleagues in West Africa refused to support this, commenting that although professionally able, Horton, as an African, did not have the confidence either of Africans or of Europeans.

Horton set out vigorously to refute this by asking his prominent patients for testimonials. Reproduced in this chapter is one of two letters from the far-sighted and sympathetic Governor of the Gold Coast, Richard Pine, to Horton on this matter and on that of the medical school. It represents the best of the progressive side of British colonial policy in the nineteenth and twentieth centuries.

The later excerpts in this chapter are from Horton's prefaces to his scientific and medical books and give us a few details of his medical and scientific experience.

To the Revd. Henry Venn   Slave Coast
Church Missionary Society   Quittah Fort
London   3rd Feb., 1860

My dear Father,

Little did I think that I will be compelled at such an early period of my entrance into the Army to represent to you the unbearable treatment I have received from one of Her Majesty's officers. I have borne in mind & thank God able to carry out your last admirable advice to us, viz. Never to stand out too much for your right;—Be patient & time will bring it to you'; in consequence of this I have endured with silence, the un-gentlemanly & I almost say brutal treatment of the officer who com-manded the twenty soldiers station[ed] at Anamaboe Fort, viz. Capt de Rurigues; but silence seemed only to encourage him in his acts.

From the very first time I arrived here he has treated me with loath-some coldness for no cause whatever; he has trampled under foot all the privileges that my position as a Staff: Asst: Surgeon entails & as a govern-ment officer entailed. He has done all in his power to do every thing that will lead to my discomfort; more over he took no notice of those things which are highly necessary & practicable to prevent me from suffering from the climatorial effect of the country, although I duly laid it before him. He set such an example to the soldiers that would lead them to disrespect me but on the contrary I *received the greatest respect from them.* Men in the town and some officers in Head Quarters wonder at the idea that I have not represented his treatment to me to the Officer Commanding the Troops—His Excellency Lieut. Col. Bird. So that it went the round of table talk that I am too easy—that was the reason he was imposing on me. My reply was only this—that there was a time for every thing—slow & steady with firmness carries a man further than being too hasty & quick in representing matters—I said that I know perfectly well that I have friends in England who anxiously regard my Course; friends who will not suffer me to be unjustly impinged upon and who are ready to seek my right and obtain due satisfaction & that it is my greatest endeavour not to blast their hopes by being too hasty and rash, or mar my future prospect, and those of my countrymen who may here-after join the army by following the dictates of temper.

Full three months have I been tormented, annoyed, disturbed & vexed; scarcely three days can elapse without new devices, sought out & put into execution. Many a time have I been obliged like a school boy to go without my food. Many a time have I been obliged to ask friends for food out of the Fort in the town; many a time have I been left alone—without a servant, without a cook, many a time has the dinner which my cook was preparing for me been made to be left half cooked & myself deprived of my dinner. All these through the action of one man. The enigma then is; why have I not represented this ungentlemanly treat-ment to the Governor & had a redress.

It is a matter of paramount necessity that as I am amongst the first of the native Africans who have been educated by H.M. Government in the medical profession and sent out in the army as staff asst: Surgeon to practise that noble art amongst my own countrymen & those of the

Europeans who may require our attendance, that I should not be too hasty in whatever I am about to undertake—not to give in to the dictates of passion, or to take rash measures which the nature of the trials that I was suffering merited. I felt that it was the keystone of the continuance of that noble plan of educating young Africans & sending them in the Coast. Should I give way thousands of those here who are hostile to the plan will have grounds to complain, they will use every means to dissuade you and the Government from going on in that noble cause which is fraught with blessings for Africa. Truly it requires a good deal of patience, a good deal of self-possession & well might it be asked what prevents him from representing it to Head Quarters & so check it.

To be prevented from doing one's rightful duty—to be received with the utmost coldness—to salute & don't receive a reply—To be deprived of Quarter comforts—To have one's boy threatened to be flogged every day without any just cause—to be prevented from cooking in half the fireplace in the officer's kitchen—to have one's boy tied & flogged on the guns with the 'Cat o' nine tails' before his master without any cause and then turned out of the Fort whilst his master was calling him so as to ascertain the cause—To be deprived of one's dinner—to be totally prevented from cooking in the officer's kitchen—to be told to go & cook where 8 to 12 *half naked* soldiers' wives are preparing their husbands' meals—no kitchen whatever but a kind of tripod invented by themselves —to be prevented from using the filtered water provided by H. Majesty for her officers in the Fort—To employ harsh language to Her Majesty's Officer—stamping the feet on the ground—These are in brief language the sufferings I had to undergo since my arrival here. These are the trials I had to pass through. I am compelled not to allow this to pass unnoticed else an advantage will be taken of every African who joins the Army. I defy Capt. de Rurigues or anyone in the Coast to charge me of neglect of duty—I can obtain testimonials from the merchants and inhabitants of Anamaboe—rich & poor amongst whom I have laboured of their satisfaction at my attendance on them. In fact I had under my treatment, patients from nearly all parts in the Gold Coast coming down to Anamaboe, even from Cape Coast where there are two doctors.

It is a generally known fact amongst all the officers & some of the natives that as soon as we arrived in the Coast, they wrote to England to say that the Government should not send native doctors in the Coast, that it is a very bad step—alleging as a cause that the soldiers will not respect them—this is the very reverse of the case, for we receive the greatest respect from the soldiers—even the people in the town considered it as an harbinger of blessing to the Country.

The conduct of Capt. de Rurigues may be explained from the fact that they determined to annoy us until we commit ourselves & lose our commission but thanks that there is a Providence who thwarts the untoward designs of men.

I am very glad that Dr. Davies[1] at Dix Cove is placed under a person of a different temperament an old Captain—Capt. Brownwell, who loves the Africans & is beloved by them.

Certainly I did expect a degree of prejudice against us but not to such an extent.

It came to the knowledge of the Governor, who called me up to Cape Coast. He admitted that I had been badly treated by Capt. de R. without my having told him anything, but after I had read two items to him he said that it was sufficient:— that he settles it quietly & that I should leave things as they are—that he called me particularly to tell me that as Dr. Zeevan has been invalided & sent to England, I should get myself ready to leave by the Leeward steamer for Quittah. Afterwards he asked me through the Fort adjutant to destroy the notes that I had kept of his treatment—else that may ultimately bring him to Court Martial. Unfortunately I had all my things capsize whilst landing in the surf at Quittah. With my affectionate regards to Miss Venn & Master Venn.

Accept the same from
Yours ever
Jas. Africanus B. Horton[2]

*   *   *

From Richard Pine, Governor.

J. A. B. Horton Esquire M.D.   Government House
Staff Assistant Surgeon   Cape Coast
Anamaboe   7th December, 1863

Sir,

. . . I confess that I am surprised to perceive [from your last letter] the strongly expressed opinions of Captain Brownwell and Dr. O'Callaghan with respect to the alleged prejudice existing in this Protectorate against yourself and Dr. Davies, and their consequent report that the system introduced by Her Majesty's Government of educating young Africans as Surgeons cannot be pursued with advantage—I am especially struck with Dr. O'Callaghan's assertion 'that the inhabitants of the Gold Coast

---

[1] Another African army doctor trained under the same scheme as Dr Horton (Ed.).
[2] C.M.S. Library CA1/0117.

regard the natives of Sierra Leone especially with a distrust and barbaric aversion of which but a faint conception can be entertained in England.'

My experience does not warrant such a statement for I am aware that many of the inhabitants of this territory have intermarried with those of Sierra Leone, and there are and have been several government employees from the last-named colony, amongst whom I would mention Mr Coker, the first writer in the Secretary's office, and who enjoys certainly as much respect as if he were a native of the Gold Coast, if not more.

I am well acquainted with Captain Brownwell and Mr O'Callaghan and I venture to express a conviction that were these gentlemen now asked to confirm the opinions which they expressed two years since, they would hesitate to do so: nay I will go farther and state my belief that Mr O'Callaghan holds a different opinion on the same subject now.

I have already expressed in my note to you my knowledge of the position here of yourself and Dr Davies; and I unhesitatingly express a hope that Her Majesty's Government will reconsider and adopt your proposition, if it is not prepared to abandon its philanthropic objects with regard to the Civilization of Africa.

I will not disguise the fact of there being a prejudice and objection on the part of European medical officers to the introduction of men of Colour who may become their Seniors on the Coast; but I cannot for one moment imagine that a high and important principle is to be abandoned only on account of a prejudice which must be admitted on all hands to be unchristianlike, unreasonable, unjust and inconvenient, and which must, I contend, give way should Her Majesty's Government consider the fact established of the competency of the African for the medical profession.

I say this prejudice must give way, because it is within my recollection that the late Staff Surgeon Ferguson was held in the highest esteem and respect as principal medical officer on the Coast for years, and eventually became Governor of Sierra Leone, and I never yet heard of any surgeon junior to himself raising an objection to serving under him or of any officer, Civil or Military, having been permitted to protest against his rule on account of his Colour—and again the appointment of Mr Carr as Chief Justice of Sierra Leone upwards of twenty years ago is a proof that English Barristers have not thought it beneath their dignity to hold the office of Queen's advocate under him and practice in his courts. Mr Smyth, Mr Nicol, Mr Commissiong, have all held high positions in that Colony and European Gentlemen have served under them for years, and many a young Gentleman have I seen cheerfully serving under Coloured employers. Why then should the medical profession alone be permitted to retain and indulge in a mischievous prejudice against the man of Colour? Unless then the British Government permits it; the system of educating African Surgeons for service on the Coast should, instead of being abandoned, be pursued with vigour, so that the intellectual equality of the African Scholar may together with other considerations combat against and essentially dissipate narrow-minded prejudice.

I would suggest that the candidates selected for medical training should not be exclusively from Sierra Leone, but that a fair proportion should be taken from the Gold Coast and the Gambia; and that the only other remedy for the hardships complained of by *European* Surgeons is the formation of a strong African Medical Corps for continued service on the Coast.

In conclusion I would say that however erroneous my views may appear, I am willing to test them by a prolonged residence on the Coast with which I have been officially for many years connected.

I am
Sir,
Your most obedient servant,
Rich. Pine
Governor.[1]

*   *   *

1867

My opportunities of observation have been such as to enable me, from personal experience, to make accurate statements with regard to the climate from the Bight of Benin to Senegal. I was stationed for nearly a year at Quittah, in the Bights, and visited Lagos. I served from time to time, during several years, at all the military posts on the Gold Coast. I am a native of Sierra Leone, where, fifteen years ago, I made thermometrical and pluviametrical observations; and I was for two years and a half stationed in the interior and on the sea coast of the Gambia, the climate of which is almost identical with that of Senegal on the north, and the Casamanza on the south. . . .[2]

1874

More than fifteen years ago, on leaving the University of Edinburgh in 1859 for the Tropics, I formed a resolution to examine carefully and record faithfully the various symptoms and etiology of those Diseases of Tropical Climates which might come under my notice, noting them down in as ready and comprehensive a manner as possible; to record the various *post-mortem* examinations which I might chance to make; to examine and make personal observations of the effects on the system of the different

[1] *Ibid.*   [2] *Physical and Medical Climate*, p. x, l. 11 ff.

modes of treatment recommended by various writers; and then to draw my own conclusions from the whole.

Having served with troops in some of the most deadly intertropical climates, in charge of and attached to military forces in the field, on several occasions—on one of which, out of a force of 200 rank and file, I had no less than 103 men at once in hospital, suffering from Scorbutic Dysentery of the worst possible type, Diarrhoea, Malignant Remittent and Intermittent Fevers, Abscesses and other Diseases of the Liver and Spleen—I had ample opportunities of carrying my resolution into full practice, during fifteen years in which I was continually in the vortex of the Tropical Diseases, both among the military and civil population. . . .

In collecting together my notes, and arranging them in the form in which I now present them to the Profession, I have endeavoured to bring in also the opinions and experiences of the most able writers on the subjects of which I have treated, comparing them with one another, as well as with my own observations; and although I am painfully aware of the fact that there are many deficiencies and shortcomings in the work (more especially as the printers' proofs had to be sent out to the Coast of Africa for correction, a great number of which were revised whilst busily engaged in the field in the recent Ashantee Campaign), yet still I will crave their indulgence in stating that, in thus placing the accumulated facts before them, I have endeavoured to describe the diseases faithfully, both from my personal observations and from which I have obtained from the writings of others; and I hope that I have succeeded in giving much useful information on Tropical Diseases generally, and placing in the hands of young tropical practitioners a handbook of practical importance and utility in their early career. . . .[1]

[1] *Diseases of Tropical Climates*, p. vii, l. 1 ff.

Gloucester Street, Freetown, c. 1892; *Horton Hall is on the left, with portico and bay window. Opposite it is the Court of the Mixed Commission. Both these historic buildings have been demolished.*

Embarkation at Cape Coast Castle of the troops from the Ashanti War of 1864. From an engraving in *The Illustrated London News*

10

The Effects of Heat on Energy, Intelligence, Skin Pigmentation, Fertility and Longevity

The observations made in this chapter are of interest, especially when they were derived from Horton's own personal experience. The explanations given for them were not, however, always correct.

Most of the changes which he attributed to the effect of heat are really not due to heat alone, but also to humidity and the effects of solar radiation.

It is true that high temperature and humidity decrease human efficiency. It has been shown, for example, that the performance of complex tasks of mental arithmetic deteriorates when the body temperature is raised above normal. The mechanism, however, is still not properly understood.

Horton was not correct in writing that inhabitants of tropical climates do not show the same active development of the intellectual faculties, especially of the reasoning processes, as natives of a temperate climate. He was more correct when he followed this up by pointing out that the lack of educational opportunities at school and at home was partly responsible for their being left behind their contemporaries of other races who lived in temperate climates.

The increased deposits of black pigmentary matter (known as melanin) in the skin in the tropics is not due to the heat, but to the effect of certain rays of the sun.

The question of the inheritance of acquired characteristics remains a highly debatable one, and is not as simple as Horton and many others considered it.

In discussing the effects of heat on fertility, Horton does not differentiate between virility (sexual power) and fecundity (fertility). Virility may be impaired during the great heat of the day. The infertility or high sterility rate in women in tropical Africa may be due to poor health conditions, social customs such as a long weaning period, and polygyny. There is no firm reason to believe that the high sterility rate is due only to a high temperature. The virility of domestic animals which Horton mentioned again refers more to their fertility. In this case, there is evidence that the reduced fertility of animals in hot weather is partially explained by the direct heating of the scrotum rather than by a general increase in body heat.

The shortened life-span of human beings in the tropics is not due to excess work by the eliminating organs such as the kidneys and the sweat glands, as these adjust themselves to the climate. Malnutrition, poverty and deficient medical care are more likely causes.

Two facts must be borne in mind in reading this chapter: the first is that many non-scientists still believe, erroneously, in some of the explanations given a hundred years ago by Horton and his contemporaries on these matters. The second is that in spite of the many scientific advances of this century, their true causes are still imperfectly understood, and they still offer a challenge to medical schools and universities in Africa where Horton prophesied that the answers would eventually be found.

The effects of great tropical heat on the intellectual faculties of man is indeed very marked, especially when continuous; it seems, in the first place, to interfere with the regular nutrition of the cerebrum, producing a modification in the associative connections of ideational consciousness, and consequently interferes in some degree with the transmission of external expression made on that organ to the sensorium—the centre of consciousness.

One great example may be adduced from the want of success with which, in tropical climates, individuals in many cases attempt to exert the will to the recall of events which had previously been before their consciousness, but which do not at the time automatically or spontaneously present themselves in it. We very often hear the complaint, that 'The heat has destroyed my memory. I cannot recollect anything'. The individual fixes his attention upon ideas which had already been present in his consciousness, and places the full weight of his mind to it so as to intensify these ideas, and thus suggest and strengthen those associations which were connected with the circumstances under consideration, and yet he hesitates and bungles, and cannot give a positive and direct statement as to the facts.

The effect of this *modified nutrition*, occasioned by the constant exposure to heat, is to produce a species of absent state of the mind, a weakness of the 'bond of direct association', whereby the thoughts do not as quickly develop themselves when we attempt to recall events which at some past period had produced impressions of sensational consciousness.

But this state of absent consciousness is not permanent, since there are lucid intervals when the mind appears to be in perfect activity, and when the process of aggregating and collocating ideas, of decomposing complex ideas into simple ones, and of combining simple ideas into general expressions, is performed to a great extent automatically; and thus many philosophers believe that the same amount of mental and bodily application which is shown in temperate climates can be performed in the tropics—that the same vivid train of thought, the same mental consciousness and reasoning faculties, can be there exercised—in a word, they believe that there exists the same central activity, which, when our attention is fixed upon a certain class of ideas, suggests to our consciousness the same train of thought, in continuous and rapid succession, independently of our will, or without any purposed direction of our will to it, as is met with every day in temperate climates. This condition when duly considered and examined, it will be admitted, forms an *a priori* argument, which cannot possibly be attained in tropical climates.

The foregoing statement exhibits, without a doubt, the reasons why natives of tropical climates do not show the same active development of the intellectual faculties, especially of the reasoning processes, as natives of a temperate climate. Thus, with the former, the combination of suggestive ideas so as to produce important results in a material form, can only with great difficulty be obtained; and since this alone is the great source of improvement in knowledge, it is no wonder that the natives of tropical climates are deficient in the fundamental principle of education, whilst, on the other hand, those of temperate climates have every facility offered them. The young native inhabitants of the tropics do not undergo any proper mental cultivation; the fixation of the attention to certain objects, exclusively of many others, is not made the constant study of their parents, who do not instruct them to call into their understanding the relation and connection which exists between different ideas, nor how to isolate ideas and recognise their common properties. They do not withdraw their minds from those noxious influences which may occupy their mental activity—from what is sensual and debasing—and thus bring in appropriate ideas or fertile and productive faculties which will direct and invigorate, cultivate, and chasten their youthful consciousness.

Again, in tropical climates, the uninterrupted application of the intellectual or reasoning faculties for a few hours on any particular subject produces great mental fatigue; the automatic or attractive power, after a very short time, becomes incapable or finds it difficult, to rivet the attention on the class of ideas under consideration; and the thoughts, in consequence, either wander from the subject or do not 'develop themselves consecutively in the mind'; and very often the individual complains of severe headaches or vertigo. In temperate climates the case is very different; the author, whilst at college in England, frequently occupied fourteen out of the twenty-four hours in hard study without any evil result, but since his return to the tropics he finds six hours to be his utmost limit of continuous application without producing severe mental fatigue; and even this period he finds to diminish the longer he remains in the tropics.

In the northern portions of Western intertropical Africa, viz. Senegal and Gambia, the temperature, as has been demonstrated in the preceding chapter, is at certain seasons extreme, being continuous for several days from 102° to 110°; and the effects of this heat, *per se*, independently of any local condition, have decidedly ulterior influences in the reproduction and development of the inhabitants occupying these regions. The heat has of itself a great influence in increasing the deposits of black pigmentary matter in the coloured cells of the epidermis or true skin; in consequence of which the Jolloff and Mandingo inhabitants of these regions, but especially the former, are of a jet or lamp-black colour; whilst the Sarra Wollies and Footah Foolahs, who years ago migrated into these countries, become darker than the Moors of the interior, from whose stock they are descendants. It is common to characterise a very dark individual as 'Jolloff black', since the Jolloffs, as a nation, present a more perfect black tint in their pigment cells than any other nation, I think, on the globe, at least that I have ever met with, which seems to prove most convincingly that to the temperature, exclusive of any other condition, we have to trace the colour of the skin.

I must state the fact, that the offspring of inhabitants of other parts of the coast, after residing for some time in this region, become as jet black in successive generations as any Jolloff, although they themselves present no change, or very little, in the complexion. The converse of this I have noticed to be equally correct; for Jolloffs who remain for a long time in other parts of Africa of a more equable and limited temperature, all things being equal, have offspring of a lighter complexion. Jolloffs, in whatever favourable condition they may be as regards food, habitation, attention to bodily cleanliness when resident in their own country, retain that colour of their skin for which they are remarkable, and transmit the same to their offspring.

The heat also interferes with the general nutrition and vital operations of the body, either by disturbing the chylopoetic assimilation, or by acting indirectly through the nerve centres; but one thing is certain, that the inhabitants are much more attenuated than in any other parts, and although generally tall, their muscles are ill-developed, and they are incapable of severe muscular exertion, however short; their virile powers are quickly exhausted, and fecundity in the females is very limited. The Mandingo, especially, leads a sort of migratory life.

Even amongst some of the lower animals, which are expected to be very hardy in their habits, such as goats and pigs, virility is very much interrupted. I observed, in many instances, that a goat, which, as a general rule, brings forth two or three kids, if impregnated during the hot weather and exposed to the full effect of the heat for two or three months, gives only one kid; evidently showing that the heat interferes with the full results of fecundation.

Through the heat the eliminating organs of the body are called upon to perform more work, while the formative organs are retarded in their elaboration. The kidneys during the hot weather are much more loaded with solid matter, much lithates and uric acid, showing increased degeneration and destruction of tissues; the sudorific glands increase in activity, and the perspiration contains an increased proportion of chlorides and other salts; whilst, on the other hand, we find a decrease in performance of the functions of respiration, digestion, and sanguinification. The operation of these causes tends to diminish the 'span of life'; and the average of three-score years and ten is seldom attained by the inhabitants occupying these regions.

Besides being short-lived, the inhabitants in this hot region grow early old; they appear in most cases about ten years older than they really are. A Mandingo or Jolloff sixty years of age will have a long white beard, with grey hairs, and will give the appearance of a man of seventy years or more, which is not the case in other parts of the coast; and the natives themselves attribute it to the effects of the heat.[1]

[1] *Physical and Medical Climate*, p. 66, l. 5 ff.

II

The Importance of Agriculture: *A Forecast of the Value of Cocoa Cultivation in West Africa*

Horton's interest in Agriculture had been manifest since his childhood days in the agricultural mountain village of Gloucester in Sierra Leone. It was maintained by his tutors through his student days at Fourah Bay College, Freetown, and at King's College, London, and Edinburgh University. His thesis for the doctorate degree of Medicine at Edinburgh University included a chapter on food plants. In this excerpt, he mentioned that the Basel missionaries were trying to naturalise the cocoa plant in Ghana, particularly at Akropong. Horton advocated its introduction to West Africa, describing cocoa as 'an article of high commercial value, and also the richest and most nutritive kind of vegetable food'.

It was left, however, to another African, Tetteh Quarshie, who brought cocoa seeds from Fernando Po to Mampong Akwapim in 1879, to popularise a crop on the economy of which much of the wealth of Ghana and Western Nigeria is now based.

The Curator of the Kew Gardens, the late Sir W. Hooker, had always urged the necessity of introducing new plants in Africa, and was ready, and so his son also now is, to supply the specimens; but, there is no record of any such attempts on the part of the Government to develop the natural resources of Africa, although the native races are in that stage of civilization in which helps are most needed, and they have proved themselves apt to take immediate advantage of new sources of profit. The Government should therefore introduce such new plants, and encourage the cultivation of the best specimens of such native plants, as would, in course of time, be remunerative to the planters.

The following plants might be amongst those which, if introduced, would be beneficial to the country and inhabitants:—

Theobroma Cacao, or the chocolate plant, which grows spontaneously in the West Indies and in the central regions of America, and which has been introduced and cultivated in the Mauritius and the French Island of Bourbon, as well as lately in the Aquapim Mountains of the Eastern District of the Gold Coast by the Basle Missionaries, should certainly be one of the first plants introduced by the Government, as the climate and soil of the Mountain District is well adapted for its cultivation. This will at once bring into the market an article of high commercial value, and also the richest and most nutritive kind of vegetable food for the inhabitants of the Colony.[1]

Proper measures for the Encouragement of Agriculture should be introduced.

It is true, as remarks Mr. Venn, that although the Parliamentary Commitee of 1842 pointed out the neglect of the Colonial Government in not promoting agriculture and establishing model farms, yet up to this day it has never been attempted. 'The neglect of agriculture in these Colonies,' he says, 'is the great drawback upon their prosperity, and is often alleged against them as a flagrant reproach. . . . This neglect of agriculture arises chiefly from the taint of African slavery. Agriculture in other parts of Africa is carried on by slave labour. The free men of the British Colonies, therefore, prefer any kind of trade or barter to agricultural labour. Here, then, the Colonial Governments should have supplied the remedy by establishing model farms, by prizes to successful producers of agricultural produce, by public warehouses, where small farmers might store their goods for shipment and by various other modes of instruction and encouragement.'[2]

Coffee was first introduced by the Basle missionaries, who planted a large quantity in their station at Accrapong. At present they have in their plantation 60,000 trees, 30,000 of which are yielding fruit. Not only this, the Christian and heathen population about their stations are following their examples, and have their own plantations of coffee. The native merchants have also taken the initiative; Mr. Freeman has about 30,000 trees; Messrs. Leutrot, Hesse, Briandt, Bruce, and Dodo have all coffee plantations more or less large.

The same missionaries have commenced the planting of Virginian and Kentucky tobacco; they thus supply all that is required for their own use. Already they have sent specimens to Bremen, where it was considered good, but required improvement in the preparation. Besides this they are endeavouring to naturalise the Mexican cocoa or chocolate plant in this part of the Coast. They have a few trees growing at Accrapong which have borne very large fruit, and hopes are entertained that it will be a complete success. The natural advancement of this country is therefore being vastly increased by these Basle missionaries, who call themselves Germano-Africans.

[1] *West African Countries*, p. 216, l. 36 ff.
[2] *Ibid.*, p. 218, l. 10ff.

India-rubber and gutta-percha trees exist in the interior of this district; the inhabitants (women) use it principally for repairing earthenware pots. A small quantity was shipped to Bremen by Mr. Hillginbergh, clerk to Mr. Julius Ungar, who is connected with the German missionaries. It was in great request and remunerative, but the mode adopted for collecting it by the natives is very extravagant and destructive. They cut down the tree, burn one end, and allow the gum to exude from the other; the tree is therefore destroyed. The mode to be adopted should be to make fissures on the thick bark of the trunk of the tree, and the gum would easily flow out; when collected and exposed to the air, it gradually coagulates.

The Indigo plant is abundant in the fields of the Eastern district, and the natives use it for dyeing their native-made clothes. Ebony is also found in the woods of the interior, especially in a place called Pallimah, or Adapalmah, where the trees are said to grow in large numbers. A few sticks have been obtained on the Coast from individuals in this district.[1]

I have stated above that this neglect of agriculture has been alleged against the African peasant as a flagrant reproach by many Europeans who visit this Coast. These very calumniators of the African peasantry, who have closely observed how laboriously the peasantry of their country are obliged to work for their livelihood, always forget that the position, wants and requirements of the two classes are extremely different. Their general saying runs thus: 'At home a peasant would labour for a whole day and would do ten times the work these lazy fellows do. Your people are too lazy; they have lands in abundance which would soon make them rich if properly cultivated'. It is a fact which cannot be doubted by anyone, that European peasants do by far more work than the African peasant, but the conditions of the two people are vastly different. In England, for example, the lands are most unequally divided; the aristocrats are masters, and peasants more like mitigated serfs; in Africa the peasants are masters of the lands, and can cultivate any extent for their own private purpose without restriction. In England the number of the labouring class exceeds the number of workmen required to occupy the various necessary callings, and, consequently, those who have secured an employment are obliged to work hard to keep their place and credit; in Africa the contrary is just the case, the population is insufficient to cultivate the vast extent of lands by which they are surrounded, and they have no credit to keep up nor place to lose. In England the labouring class is compelled to work hard before they can be supplied with the necessaries of life, if not they must starve; in Africa if a labouring man is unable to work, his neighbours supply him with food, or go out and work the field gratuitously for him, or if well, he goes for a few weeks to his

[1] *Ibid.*, p. 147, l. 11 ff.

plantation, and without much labour obtains in a few months from the fertile soil his year's stock of provision. In fact, in England the labouring class has always great external pressure to bear upon them, demanding both their moral and their physical strength; whilst the same class in Africa has little or no external pressure to bear on them. In England the food of the peasant is compound, expensive, and very scarce; in Africa the food is simple, cheap, and plentiful. In England the peasant is compelled by the state of civilization and the necessity of the climate to procure clothing, which entails a greater outlay and a necessity for increased labour; but in Africa the climate is so hot and uniform that the peasants go about half-naked, and therefore have little or no expense for clothing.

Now with all these local advantages on the side of the African peasantry, can it be a matter of surprise that they confine themselves almost entirely to the cultivation of produce sufficient for their yearly consumption? Can it be a matter of surprise, I say, that the English peasant labours infinitely more than the African peasant? In the one case, the land supplies the peasant abundantly, whether he works hard or not; in the other, starvation awaits him if he does not work hard, and should he not pay dearly with his strength and skill he is sure to fall to utter destitution. To the English peasant the words of Mr. Thomas Carlyle, in his inaugural address as Lord Rector of Edinburgh University, echo loudly: 'If a man', says he, 'gets meat and clothes, what matters it whether he have ten thousand pounds or ten million pounds, or seventy pounds a year? He can get meat and clothes for that and he will find very little real difference intrinsically, *if he is a wise man*'.[1]

To the Editor, **The African Times**

I have often thought of giving you a short notice on this most important subject, [Agriculture] which lies necessarily at the very root of African improvement, and consequent civilisation. Circumstances have hitherto prevented my doing so, and I should perhaps have deferred writing about it at present, from the conviction that the materials at my command are insufficient to enable me to give you a report such as a matter of so great importance demands. Considering, however, that you have always more articles for your valuable journal than your space will allow you to publish, I shall try to give you *multum in parvo*. It has been one of the great aims of *The African Times*, from its formation, to point out to the rising generation of Africa the fact that the great wealth of a country depends upon the amount of its agricultural products; and that the immense riches of Africa can never be developed

[1] *Ibid.*, p. 219, l. 14 ff.

unless its people put their shoulders to the wheel, and perform their part. You have seized upon every occasion to point out the immense advantages to be derived from a systematic pursuit of agriculture, and you have also particularised important and fertile soils at points which might be taken as nuclei, for operation. For instance, you have thus singled out Quiah, at Sierra Leone; the interior countries of the Gold Coast; the lands on the banks of the several rivers in the country of Yoruba, as well as those of the Niger, the mother river of Western Africa, and the great high roads to its central territories. At Sierra Leone, the yearly burning of its fields; the excessive amount of iron in the composition of its soil—especially the peroxide; the practice of upturning that soil yearly from the time of the formation of the colony for sowing purposes, without any external assistance by manure; the imperfect knowledge of the science of agriculture and of chemistry by the farmers, which teaches that the difference in the inorganic ingredients of plants leads them to select different inorganic materials from the soil, and therefore that rotation of crops is essential where manures cannot be obtained—have led its soil to be rightly pronounced as not the most fit for agricultural pursuits. It is therefore highly pleasing to find that his Excellency Governor Blackall is using his influence to popularise the subject amongst the young men of Sierra Leone, and to point out to them the fertile region of Quiah. The lecture lately delivered by the Rev. George Nicol, on the agriculture of that colony, ought to be regarded as a *vade mecum* for every one. The lands bordering the sea on the Gold Coast are dry and arid, and contain throughout the year but very little moisture. They are rich in sulphate and other inorganic matters, but the uncertainty of rain consequent on the geographic position of the lands forms, in the absence of irrigation, a great barrier to planters. It is to the interior we must therefore look for a field of effectual agricultural operations. The inhabitants of the Eastern Districts, through the indefatigable exertions of the Basle missionaries and Mr. Freeman, are now becoming alive to the advantages of agriculture, and every man of consequence is devoting the best portion of his time to it. In the interior of Cape Coast, or the central portion of the Gold Coast Government, the soil is admirably adapted for sowing any kind of crops. The best is to be found in the regions bordering on the Ashantee frontiers or that of the Prah. It is there excellent for almost every kind of vegetable, and is rich in inorganic ingredients. It is an argillaceous superficial loam, intermixed with a species of sand formed by the disintegration of quartzose and felspatic rocks. The river communication should make this part the fulcrum for agricultural pursuits. It is needless for me to say a word on the fertility of the Yoruba and Niger soils, as all history goes to prove that they are rich in productive materials.

128

I must now allude briefly to certain products which among others ought to be cultivated here. In doing which I shall leave unnoticed those which have been continuallly alluded to by writers on African products, and which are now furnishing staple articles of trade—viz., palm oil, cotton, benny seed, and palm kernels. There are certain new ones which recent investigation has established that this part of Africa is capable of producing.

First—COFFEE. This article is consumed in considerable quantities on the West Coast of Africa, from the Senegal to Cape St. Paul de Loango. The soil is well adapted for planting almost any species, and yet, alas! with the exception of Liberia and the Gold Coast, the larger portion of what is consumed is obtained from Europe. Formerly it was planted in some quantity at Sierra Leone, but at present the cultivation is almost wholly abandoned there. In the Eastern District of the Gold Coast, through the example set by the Basle missionaries, more than 40,000 trees have been planted, and not only is the daily consumption of the inhabitants supplied, but some is exported. Coffee planting is unknown amongst the industrious populations of Yoruba and the Niger, and it is most desirable that the missionaries in those countries should take the matter in hand and show the natives what great benefits may be derived from its cultivation.

Second—Homologous in the active principle of its composition, and by no means of less importance, is the TEA PLANT. The tea plant, I believe, has never been known to exist in Africa, and the species which has only been recently discovered I call *Thea Ridlia*. It answers exactly to the description of Bohea tea, and is a most common shrub scattered over the dry arid soils near the sea on the Gold Coast. It is found in vast numbers, flourishing in great luxuriance, at Anamaboe, Cape Coast, &c. Mr. Ridley has found it in great abundance at certain localities. In the interior of this coast, however, from Dunquah up to the Prah, not a trace of it is to be found. I cannot vouch for its existence at Sierra Leone or Lagos; *but being indigenous on the Gold Coast*, it is likely to be found in those two places, and a proper investigation might perhaps lead to its discovery. It is now established beyond dispute *that the tea plant is indigenous in Western Africa*. Why, then, should it not now be extensively planted, and form one of the staple articles of export? Mr. Ridley, I am happy to say, is endeavouring to prepare a certain quantity for exportation. It is to be hoped that he will succeed, and that this will lead to some attempt on a larger scale.

Third—The plant which yields the INDIGO of commerce, known to botanists as the *Indigo tincteria* and *Indigo caerulea*. It is one of the most common shrubs in Western Africa, from Senegal to the Gaboon, and is used extensively by the natives for dyeing purposes. I have found it the principal shrub in an extensive plain in the Bight of Benin, and I am certain that Africa will be able, if only proper means be adopted, to supply all England with indigo, as well as with tea, with greater ease and far cheaper than she can be supplied from the East Indies and from China. I succeeded in making the *deep blue* whilst stationed at Quittah, in appreciable quantities, from plants obtained there; and with very little pains and expense it can be prepared in any quantity.

Fourth—THE CHICORY PLANT, or the *Battayanna chyrsabalana* (African chicory). This plant, I think, has never before been noticed as existing in Western Africa. I only came across it lately while examining the flora in the vicinity of Mansoo. A short description will enable most or some of your readers to find the plant, should it exist in their neighbourhoods. It is an annual; a shrub of the natural order *Compositæ*; found principally in hedges and waysides, having a fibro-tuberous root-stem, and a soft, yielding cellular stem, which latter presents a tuber at the inferior portion of each node, occupying a fifth of the internode, observable more in the full-grown stem than in the younger ones. Each tuber is composed of a lot of cells, and when fractured yields a colourless fluid, which, exposed to the air, becomes of a deep blue colour. The leaves are sheathy at the base, opposite, exstipulate, oblong lanceolate, distantly serrated, and when pressed yield a light yellow fluid (which becomes deep blue on exposure to the air) and has a disagreeable odour. The *flowers* are collected, as in all the compositæ, into dense capitula on a common receptacle; the *florets* are tubular, and of a whitish colour, having four equal teeth. The *fruit* is an achene, with erect solitary seed. *The blue matter exists in every part of the plant, even in its liachs.*

I beg to call the notice of the Rev. George Nicol to the existence of this plant in West Africa.

This plant is distributed on this coast in an uncultivated form. Will it not be of great importance to the farmers and to the merchants if proper attention be paid to it? There would not only be the exportation of *chicory* made from the root, but a *useful commercial blue might be made from every part of the plant.*

Fifth—THE BLACK PEPPER; or, the *Piper Nigrum v. Africanum.* All the world has looked to the East Indies for the supply of this most important article, and it has almost been regarded as a plant exclusively belonging to that portion of the globe; yet it is quite as much West African. It abounds in extensive quantities in the forests of Sierra Leone and the Gold Coast. In the latter I have found it in the forest between Mansoo and the river Prah, but more especially in the vicinity of the latter. In the former place it is in the forest in the mountain district, and is known by the name of '*Bush pepper*'. Its leaves are used medicinally by the natives as a vermifuge. It has a very pointed stem, and grows wild, climbing principally on very tall trees. It requires but very little attention, and Western Africa will, sooner or later, become an exporter of great quantities. The specimen before me, obtained from the forest at Prahsoo, has an exquisite aroma, and if cultivated would surpass the East Indies in the freshness of its stimulant and aromatic properties.

Sixth—THE CLOVES OF COMMERCE, obtained from the *Caryophyllus aromaticus*, common in almost any part of Western Africa. I met with specimens lately in the bush between Mansoo and Prahsoo. It is indigenous on this part of the Coast, and like the other plants mentioned, with but very little trouble any quantity could be obtained for export.

I might also mention several medicinal plants, such as the *Senna acutifolia, Lanceolata and Obavata,* the Sarsaparilla plant, or *Smilax officinalis*, the Tobacco plant, &c., were I not convinced that I was occupying too much space in your valuable journal.

It is my earnest wish, as it is yours, that West Africa should be made an extensive field of commercial enterprise, as her civilisation must thus be promoted; and if you think that the few brief indications of her latent wealth here given will assist in hastening its development, you will, I am sure, give it a place in your columns.[1]

[1] 'African Products', *The African Times*, 23rd May 1864.

12

Iron in Sierra Leone and Diamonds in Ghana:
Accurate Forecasts in the 1860's

The presence of iron in Sierra Leone was known when Horton wrote his book, **Physical and Medical Climate**. *The most productive area now mined in the country is about 70 miles from Freetown, in the Marampa deposits, farther away than had been properly explored at that period.*

The site from which the Freetown samples mentioned by Horton came is of historic interest. Melville's Farm near Mount Oriel (now Aureol) belonged to Michael Melville, Registrar of the Mixed Court Commission, whose wife recorded their stay there in her book **A Residence at Sierra Leone, by a Lady** *published in London in 1849. The farm was later purchased by Charles Heddle, a wealthy mulatto merchant, and is now more commonly known as Heddle's Farm.*

The burial ground which Horton mentioned, below Melville's Farm and Mount Aureol, was the Circular Road Cemetery in which Horton himself was buried fifteen years later in the family vault of his first wife, Fanny Pratt. Although his name is not inscribed on the vault, its location was rediscovered, from the obituary notices, during the preparation of this book.

On Mount Aureol itself lies the new site of Horton's alma mater, Fourah Bay College, in the scientific laboratories of which geophysical readings are regularly influenced by the extensive layer of magnetic ironstone which he so accurately described.

Even more remarkable was Horton's forecast of the discovery of diamonds in Ghana, where they form, at the deposits in Akwatia, a substantial part of the country's economy and provide the third largest production in the world.

In Horton's day, diamonds had not been discovered anywhere in Africa; the main source was Brazil, and in the year Horton wrote his book, 1867, diamonds had just been discovered in South Africa. But it was not until 1919, fifty years after Horton's forecast, that the British Geological Survey discovered the first diamond in Ghana.

The soil of Sierra Leone is composed principally of red clay, having a large quantity of iron in its composition. This is characteristic of Freetown, the capital. In the mountains it is composed of the disintegration of dark and blue granitic rocks, which are found abundantly in their elevated hills. At Waterloo, Hastings, and Wellington, in some places the soil consists of black alluvial loam, which are deposits from the Sierra Leone River and the several rivulets which join it. Towards the Cape, Aberdeen, and the countries around, the soil is alluvial beneath, but covered with sand.

Specimens of soil from Sierra Leone, examined by the late Professor John Bowman, of King's College, London, prove that it contains large quantities of oxide of iron. The following is the result of the different specimens examined:

No. 1 contains   8.84 per cent of oxide of iron.
    2 ,, 26.00 ,, ,, ,, ,, ,, ,,
    3 ,, 11.48 ,, ,, ,, ,, ,, ,,
    4 ,, 23.20 ,, ,, ,, ,, ,, ,,
    5 ,, 29.00 ,, ,, ,, ,, ,, ,,
    6 ,, 46.12 ,, ,, ,, ,, ,, ,,
    8 ,,   6.92 ,, ,, ,, ,, ,, ,,
    9 ,, 11.56 ,, ,, ,, ,, ,, ,,
Another No. 9 ,, 12.48 ,, ,, ,, ,, ,, ,,

This last Professor Bowman describes as taken up at the rising of the hill below Mr. Melvilles farm, not far from the Regent Farm Road, and a fair specimen of the earth of the colony. That in the bottle, with no label, but which is probably No. 7, contains 11.00 per cent oxide of iron.

The rocks at the burial ground below Melville Farm on Mount Oriel are an extensive layer of the magnetic iron-stone, out-crops of which are found behind Government House or Fort Thornton; and by the disintegration of these iron rocks, by the constant action of the sun and other atmospheric influences, the soil is highly impregnated with iron. Besides the ferruginous rocks, there are the black and blue granite, which are extensively scattered in the lofty and conical hills behind Freetown, and in every part of the colony; they are hard and compact, composed of augite and felspar, with quantities of magnetic or titanic iron; they are excellent for building fortifications, and Fort Thornton, or Government House Battery, and East Street Battery, are constructed with them. We find next extensive strata of hard red sandstone in every part of Freetown, and of the colony generally. They are used principally for building purposes, and resist for a considerable time the action of the elements. Some of these red sandstones in certain localities are softer than others; they present different hues also, being very dark red or light red. In some localities a fine white sandstone, not of very compact texture is to be seen. A specimen exists now in the out-crop through the water-course at Kissy Road Bridge.

In 1845 the following replies to questions were sent through Sir Charles Trevelyan to Sir Ranald Martin, from the Medical Department of the colony:—

Question 1. What is the geological character of the soil in and round the settlement?

Answer: Above high-water mark, red earth; below high-water mark, black mud; flats and valleys, black earth.

Question 2. Does ferruginous or red sandstone prevail, or red earth?

Answer: Red earth; red sandstone in the strata (used for building) underneath. Occasionally large blocks and some strata of blue granite (now used in building).

Question 3. Is the soil of the most unhealthy stations of a ferruginous nature?

Answer: I have never heard any one station in this colony called less healthy than another.[1]

From considering and examining the geological structure of the district around Accra, I am under the impression that there are extensive coal-fields in the interior of the country and in the kingdom of Dahomey, and this view has been confirmed by circumstantial evidence. When the rainy season is very severe, and the streams of the Volta swell up and become very rapid, large masses of coal have been known to be brought down from the interior and left on its banks. The last seen was at a place called Kpong, in Crobboe.

Seven years ago, while examining the conchology (shells) of this part of the Coast, I was forcibly struck with their resemblance and identity with those on the coast of Brazil ... there is [also] great resemblance in the botany of the two countries. The geological structure of the two countries is almost identical. These facts led me to the belief that when the resources of the country are much more developed, diamonds will be found, not only in the Eastern District, but also in the rivers and lagoons of Awoonah and Dahomey. I made fruitless researches myself whilst stationed at Quittah and Addah, but it is my firm belief that in years to come, all things being equal, and development progressive, the diamond will ultimately be one of the exportable articles.[2]

[1] *Physical and Medical Climate*, p. 121, l. 4 ff.
[2] *West African Countries*, p. 148, l. 11 ff.

13

The Weather of West Africa

Horton's powers of description and meticulousness of observation are seen here at their best. The description of a tropical tornado was first published in his Medical Topography but this account was later amplified in his book on The Physical and Medical Climate of West Africa and particularised to two storms observed at Quittah (Keta).

He was fond of mathematical calculations and fascinated by figures as shown in his estimates of rainfall in Sierra Leone in 1829 and 1860 and in his estimates of the quantity of urine voided in a year by the inhabitants of a West African city given in Chapter 14 of this anthology.

His account of the fall of hailstones in Sierra Leone and the report of snowfall in Ghana must be accepted although they sound improbable. He records the occurrence of earthquakes in the 1860's in Ghana and Sierra Leone.

He also kept temperature records at various dates and in various places of West Africa of which an example is given.

The Rainy Season

The occurrence of a tornado is generally marked with premonitory symptoms. At first a cold breeze is felt, which is soon followed by a clear, white, heavenly canopy, giving the atmosphere a kind of light rusty appearance. At once a dusky white spot is observed, pointing E.S.E., or E., at a great altitude, which gradually descends, spreading at the same time until it reaches the horizon, forming sometimes a cone—the base on the horizon, and the apex above; this spreads laterally until a half or a quarter of the visible horizon is covered with impenetrable darkness. Nature now seems to lie in dormant vitality, and its functions to be seized with a paralytic stroke; the most profound quietness pervades the whole earth; the leaves are perfectly at a stand still, not a creature is to be seen about in the street; the whole system now becomes oppressed with a mingled sensation of awe and apprehension of some stupendous phenomena. At once a blast of lightning vividly flashes from sky to sky, and then darting on the negatively electrified ground is followed immediately by a distant tremendous reverberating explosion, which startles every terrene animated being. A slight whirlwind is afterwards observed whirling with some velocity the light ponderable material found in the streets. At length a vehement, irresistible gust of wind rushes from the gloomy horizon with immense impetuosity, sweeping every unsubstantially fixed substance before it, up-rooting trees, carrying away slates and bamboos from the tops of houses, and sometimes even the roofs and chimney tops, and filling the atmosphere with an immense quantity of *infusorial protozoa*; then follow thick pellets of rain, which as it were retreat for a time, returning and terminating with a furious deluge, which falls in one vast sheet rather than in drops.

The above is a general description of a tornado. It will be of some interest and of more practical value should I here particularise all the various changes, carefully observed and noted, of two tornadoes as they occurred on the West Coast of Africa. The observations were made whilst our troops were stationed at Quittah, on the Slave Coast, in the Bight of Benin.

At 4.14 p.m. there was a dark, bluish-black cloud on due E., which extended in the next quarter of an hour to E.N.E., and E.S.E.; at 5 o'clock it had extended to S.E. by S., and then to due S. The appearance of the cloud from the horizon to 1 °[1] above was dark bluish-black, above this it was white; the latter suddenly and rapidly descended and over-clouded the former. During this period there was a dead calm all over the atmosphere; not the least movement was traceable in the most fragile branch; the sky towards S.W. by S. to N.N.E. was perfectly clear. At last the pent-up wind seemed, as it were, to overcome the difficulty, and the cloud was thrown all over the canopy; the wind now rushed from E.N.E. accompanied with a deluge of rain.

It will be observed that, in this description of a tornado there was no lightning nor thunder, as is sometimes the case; the observation was made on the 1st of May.

The following are the particulars of another tornado, which took place about the latter part of March on the same coast:—Wind on the beginning of the tornado E.; darkness all over the heavens, and thunder towards the east. No rain at the beginning; haziness all over the canopy, especially towards the sea, with heavy fog drifting from east to west. A pleasant light rain now fell in small drops, and lasted for a short time, which was followed by a violent gust of wind, and a clearness over the whole atmosphere from E. to S.E. The wind now stopped for a short time, but immediately returned with great force and velocity. A dense fog now covered the horizon, the greatest distance that could be seen around being

[1] Probably a misprint for '10°' (Ed.).

136

less than half a mile, more or less covered with fog. Twenty minutes after this the wind gradually decreased and the rain became more tense. Grumblings of thunder now began to be heard from S. to E., and increased in frequency and intensity; the wind became vehement, and the rain gradually ceased. About ten minutes after, the wind decreased, but the rain increased; the thunder became violent from the zenith, to S.W. by W.; then to E. by S. $\frac{1}{2}$ S., and then S.E. The wind now alternated with the rain; the thunder from N.W. to S; then heavy rain fell, with thunder to E. zenith S., and terminated in S.W. The sky began to get clear; the thunder continued in severity, with vivid flashes of lightning in various directions, and after a time all the phenomena ceased, and a most pleasant sensation was felt.[1]

The sum total of the rain which fell in the three months, June, July, and August of 1829, exceeds the sum total of the quantity which fell in the three months, May, June, July of 1858, and the six months, April, May, June, August, September, October of 1860, by 174.24 inches, or more than double the quantity by 44.48 inches.

What, most of my readers will ask, *is an inch of rain?* . . .

An inch deep of rain in one acre of land yields 22,622.5 gallons of water, since 277.274 cubic inches is equal to one gallon and an inch deep of rain in one acre of land is equal to 6,372,640 cubic inches of water, an acre, according to the English measurement, consists of 6,272,640 cubic inches[2].

Rain water must be considered as the purest of natural waters, especially when collected after a long continuance of rainy weather, and even then it will be found to contain an appreciable quantity of atmospheric air, together with some of the gases floating in it, to the extent of about $2\frac{1}{2}$ cubic inches of air in 100 of water. Distilled water, therefore, is the best material for experiment, a gallon of which weighs 10 lbs.; and one inch deep of rain being equal to 22,622.5 gallons of water, consequently the rain-fall on an acre of land is equal to 226,225 lbs. avoirdupois; but 2240 lbs. is equal to one ton, therefore an inch deep of rain weighs nearly 101 tons, or more correctly, 100.933 tons.

The quantity of rain, therefore, which fell in an acre of land at Freetown, Sierra Leone, in the months of June, July, and August of 1829, was not less than sixty-six millions six hundred and fifty-nine thousand five hundred and sixty pounds avoirdupois of water, or six millions six hundred and sixty-five thousand nine hundred and fifty-six gallons of water, or thirty thousand three hundred and ninety tons. Allowing Freetown to be about three miles square, it will contain one thousand

[1] *Physical and Medical Climate*, p. 184, l. **3** ff.
[2] A printer's error for 6,372,640 square inches (Ed.).

nine hundred and two acres; and, therefore, the quantity of rain which fell in all Freetown for the three months in 1829, if measured, will not be less than twelve billions six hundred and seventy-eight millions six hundred and forty-eight thousand three hundred and twelve gallons of water, or one hundred and twenty-six billions seven hundred and eighty-six millions four hundred and eighty-three thousand one hundred and twenty pounds weight of water, or fifty-seven millions eight hundred and one thousand seven hundred and eight tons of water. What an enormous quantity for only eighty days of rain ! ! ![1]

But there were 208.86 inches of rain in the three months of 1829, more than in the six months of 1860, i.e. there fell in an acre of land at Freetown forty-six millions seven hundred and eighty-four thousand six hundred and forty lbs. of water, or four millions six hundred and seventy-eight thousand four hundred and sixty-four gallons, or twenty thousand eight hundred and eighty-six tons of rain more than in the year 1860.

It might be doubted that so large a quantity of rain-fall could have taken place in 1829, whilst in 1860, and other years, so small a quantity is noted; but it must be remembered that the rain-fall is very irregular from year to year, especially in a mountainous place such as Sierra Leone, and this remarkable difference might be traced in other parts of the world:— Thus, in Bombay in 1824, the quantity of rain-fall was 34 inches, whilst just two years previously, viz., in 1822, the quantity was more than treble that, it being 112 inches.[2]

In the month of August I have frequently noticed the fall of hailstones in the mountainous district of Sierra Leone; they are generally of an inch or half an inch in size, and caused by drops of rain suddenly frozen on their passage to the earth. Snow, which is the visible aqueous vapour composing clouds in a frozen state, has also fallen in Western Africa. A writer in *The African Times*, August 1863, thus gives an account of one occurrence:—'On the morning of the 10th or 12th of May last the atmosphere was very heavy and there were signs of the approach of a great deal of rain; a thick cloud was observed towards the east, and a cold easterly wind was blowing. This was at Swadore, near to Winnebah. It drizzled a little, and then there followed a heavy fall of snow—real condensed snow—not like hailstones, but in small icicles. The natives, as well as the European officers, were struck with astonishment. This may be received as corroborative evidence of the statements of travellers in Eastern Africa, who reported that they found mountains covered with

[1] *Physical and Medical Climate*, p. 189, l. 19 ff.
[2] *Ibid.*, p. 191, l. 11 ff.

snow.' This statement was true, as I saw several officers who were present when the phenomenon took place.

When atmospheric electricity passes between the earth and a cloud, or between two clouds, lightning is produced; and the report that is occasioned through it forms thunder. In Western Africa lightning is very dangerous, and frequent observations corroborate the statement, that it generally strikes the south-east aspect of buildings, and never the northern.[1]

At the beginning of the rainy season and the autumn, several meteoric phenomena are observable in the evening—fireballs or shooting stars, flying in various directions in the atmosphere, or descending slantingly on the earth. I have many times seen the atmosphere lighted up in a most charming manner by these balls. These phenomena are connected with the stones fallen from the atmosphere described by ancient writers. They are meteoric stones or aerolites (aër, the air, and lithos, a stone); and when analysed, are found to consist of 54 parts of silica, 36 of oxide of iron, 9 of magnesia, 3 of oxide of nickel, 2 of sulphur, and 1 of lime.

During this season mosquitoes and sand-flies abound in Africa, and are very troublesome. In the Gambia region both of these are very annoying; at Sierra Leone, Liberia, and the Gold Coast, less so, there being but few mosquitoes, except at the swampy mouths of rivers, and no sand-flies. In the Bights of Benin and Biafra mosquitoes are plentiful.[2]

Harmattan or Cold Season

This season commences about the middle of November and terminates in the middle of February, occupying a period of three months. The name harmattan is derived from the Fantee *sharamanta*, a designation of the season when this wind blows, from *aharaman*, to blow, and *ta*, tallow or grease; since at this season the weather is so dry and parching that the inhabitants are obliged to keep their skin soft and moist by the use of grease. It blows along the whole Western Coast of Africa, extending from Cape de Verde, in lat. 15° N., and Cape Lopez, in lat. 0° 36′ 10″ S. and long. 8° 40′ E. Its intensity decreases as we leave the Gambia region to leeward. In Senegal, Gambia, and Casamanza it blows from E. and N.E., in Sierra Leone from E.S.E., on the Gold Coast from N.E., and at Lopez from N.N.E. The approach of the harmattan is generally indicated by the dropping of the leaves of trees, which do not putrefy as in the preceding season, but are dried up, so that they are prevented from being the source of malaria. Vegetation of every kind is affected; all the tender plants, and most of the productions of the garden, are destroyed; the grass withers

[1] *Ibid.*, p. 196, l. 9 ff. [2] *Ibid.*, p. 197, l. 6 ff.

and becomes dry like hay; vigorous evergreens suffer from its pernicious influence; 'branches of the lemon, orange, and lime trees drop; the leaves become flaccid, and so parched as to be easily rubbed to dust between the fingers, should the harmattan blow for several successive days.' It is generally accompanied by a thick fog or mist, extending out at sea in some cases to three leagues, which Baron Roussin considers to be sand in extreme fineness, and not inaptly compared with the characteristic London fog, differing, however, from it in its physical effect on the system. An idea of the nature of the fog may be obtained from the fact, that in the height of this season the sun at near noon might occasionally be seen through the fog as white as the moon.

One great peculiarity of this wind is that of extreme dryness. All nature seems to feel this effect. The ground is dry, parched, and cracked in various places; the grass withers, trees lose their green foliage; chinks are opened in the roofs of houses; the doors and windows become dried up, forcibly split, and cannot properly fit; the furniture made of the most seasoned wood loosens, warps, and cracks audibly; books bend concavely; wine-glasses or tumblers forcibly crack on the sideboard without the application of any violence. In the human body it produces great dryness of the throat, a sensation of thirst, which is to relieve the parched or dried up pharynx; the lips are chapped, and bleed occasionally; the surface of the body crisps, and the whole system suffers from great uneasiness. So early as in 1796, Mungo Park, the great African traveller, thus speaks of the harmattan wind:—'After the rains the wind sets in from the north-east and produces a wonderful change in the face of the country. The grass soon becomes dry and withered; the rivers subside very rapidly, and many of the trees shed their leaves. About this period is commonly felt the harmattan, a dry parching wind, blowing from the north-east, and accompanied by a thick smoky haze, through which the sun appears of a dull-red colour. This wind, in passing over the great desert of Sahara, acquires a strong attraction for humidity, and parches up everything exposed to its current. It is, however, reckoned very salutary, particularly to Europeans, who generally recover their health during its continuance. I experienced immediate relief from sickness, both at Dr Laidley's and at Kamadia during the harmattan. Indeed, the air during the rainy season is so loaded with moisture, that clothes, shoes, trunks, and everything that is not close to the fire, become damp and mouldy, and the inhabitants may be said to live in a sort of vapour-bath; but this dry wind braces up the solids which were before relaxed, gives a cheerful flow of spirits, and is even pleasant to respiration. Its ill effects are, that it produces chaps in the lips and afflicts many of the natives with sore eyes.'

I have sought in vain, from a great many English and French treatises on the harmattan wind, for an account of the origin of this strange wind.

Every one agrees that it is from the desert, but the proximate cause seems not as yet to have been discovered. To me it appears that its origin may be traced to the following causes. A large portion of the sandy desert of Sahara is within the tropics, and this sand has a special attraction for the sun. During the months of July, August, and September, little or no rain falls on it, it being within the region where the trade-wind is more or less constant. Towards the end of September, and during the whole of October, and sometimes the beginning of November, the atmosphere is hot and sultry, the heat oppressive, and the thermometer in some days rises beyond 100 °F. even in the West Coast towns. In the sandy desert the heat is excessive; the sand becomes perfectly dry and parched.

This sultry and heated period lasts until the end of October, when the wind shifts from the west, south-west, or north-west, towards east, north-east, or south-east, just as the winter or cold portion of autumn commences in the temperate zone. The cold winterly air travels exceedingly fast from the poles towards the equator to replace its heated sultry air which rapidly ascends. On passing through the sandy desert the cold winterly air is deprived of its moisture by the parched up sand, so that it arrives towards the coast on lands beyond the desert as a cold, dry, parching wind. In the northern portion the cold air blows for days continuously, and then shifts for a time to allow a heating process to take place. The air becomes heated, another rush takes place, and so it continues, alternating irregularly, until towards the close of the winter, when the air from the temperate and polar zones becomes warmed as it traverses Southern Europe before passing over the desert, where it receives additional heat, and arrives on the coast as a hot wind.

The cold atmosphere of the harmattan is, in reality, the cold air of the temperate zone passing rapidly into the tropics, slightly modified by local causes. The dry, parching character is acquired whilst passing through the desert of Sahara, the sands of which, yawning for moisture, quickly deprive it of its humidity, and thus we have it as a cold, dry atmosphere. The haze or fog, is obtained from the light sand of the desert wafted away by the cold breeze as it passes through it in fierce velocity to replace the heated air of the coast. All those places which lie on the west and south-west of the desert receive the harmattan wind more or less constantly and regularly for three months in the year, as it is in the Senegal, Gambia and Casamanza, and their interior countries; those south, or bordering on the south, more sparingly, as in Pongas, Nunez, Sierra Leone, and a part of Liberia; and those having but small connection with, and a great distance from it, have the wind occasionally and very sparingly, and their only chance of getting it at all depends entirely on physical causes, as on the Gold Coast and in the Bights. The light sand detached from the desert is carried to the regions where the wind blows, where it deposits a part as it goes along, and places where it continually blows receive more, and places where it sparingly blows receive less. The cold dry air abstracts from vegetation, from the surface of the earth, from the bodies of man and beast, and from all material substances, all the moisture that it possibly can get, and, consequently, at this season, as we have before said, the ground is parched and dry, the leaves of trees wither and fall, the frames of houses become loose, dry, and cracked, and a dry sensation felt.

During the blowing of the harmattan wind, the temperature of the atmosphere is more dry even than at any other period of the year, especially in the Gambia region. The variation which at other seasons ranges between 20° to 40°, is now reduced to only 7° in some days. This is when the harmattan breeze blows during the whole of the twenty-four hours. Sometimes it blows only in the morning, and then shifts to southeast, when the wind becomes hot in the afternoon, at which time the range of temperature becomes very great.

The thermometer at its maximum in the Gambia region averages 90°; medium, 86°; minimum, 76°: Gold Coast and Bights, maximum, 82.10°; medium, 79°; minimum, 76.5°. During the blowing of the harmattan wind the barometer rises to 31 inches, and keeps there for days, and then gradually falls until it assumes its normal standard.

It must be understood that the harmattan wind does not blow continuously during the whole of the season, but only for some days. In the intermediate days, in the *zone of calms*, the regular interchange of land and sea breezes takes place. In the *zone of the trade-winds* an easterly or southeasterly wind blows. It is sometimes so strong that the atmosphere, which is very hot outside, is very cold indoors, from the constant change in the general sentient surface. The wind is so strong that the dust flies about in every direction, and whirlwinds are frequent in squares. This wind does not produce the curvature of books and depredation to furniture which is the characteristic feature of the winds of the season. This easterly wind is very unhealthy, and when it blows individuals generally complain of uncomfortable feverish sensations, as well as of disease of the internal secreting organs.

During the blowing of the harmattan wind insensible perspiration is not entirely destroyed, for frequently on rubbing the forehead the surface is felt to be rough and gritty, and on removal small crystals are found at the end of the fingers. These consist of the salts which form the solids of the sudoriferous secretions, and are composed principally of chlorides of sodium and potassium. The cold, dry harmattan wind dries up the watery constituents of the perspiration so quickly that the salts become at once deposited.[1]

[1] *Ibid.*, p. 200, l. 8ᵣff.

Western Africa is subject to those subterranean disturbances which are connected with internal heat. In 1855 the colony of Sierra Leone was one evening put to confusion by the shock of an earthquake, which took a direction from east to west. In 1861, 1862, and 1863, Accra, on the Gold Coast, was subject to repeated shocks of earthquakes. In August 1862 a series of shocks were felt; the first was so severe that it destroyed the whole of the stone buildings and fortifications at Christiansborg Castle, Dutch Accra, and James Town; it was felt from below the River Volta to 300 miles along the sea coast, and far into the interior. I was present during this and several other convulsive movements. The noise was very astounding, stunned some of the weak nerved and even strong nerved inhabitants, and deprived some of their senses; it was like the noise of a powerful train passing under a tunnel, or the subterranean peals of thunder of the loudest echoes. Cape Coast suffered also in this subterranean agitation, but to a comparatively limited extent.

There are tangible evidences everywhere that the Gold Coast was the scene of repeated earthquakes and volcanic eruptions in ages long past. Volcanic scoriae are scattered in the high-ways and along the sides of the clumps of hills around which Cape Coast is built. I have picked up several of these so-called stones, which corroborated statements put forward by me some years ago in a small pamphlet, entitled 'Geological Constitution of Ahanta, Gold Coast,' wherein the volcanic origin of those parts was taken into consideration.[1]

Some Weather Observations and Measurements in the Gambia, Sierra Leone and Ghana in the 1860's

Thermometric Register, Christiansborg, Gold Coast, September, 1860
Maximum observations—Morning—23rd, 28th, and 29th, 76°; 6th, 11th, 24th, 26th, and 27th, 75°; Noon—25th, and 29th, 79°; 22nd, 23rd, 26th, and 28th, 78°. Evening—24th, 26th, and 29th, 76°.
Medium observations—Morning—7th, 13th, 16th, and 18th, 74°; Noon—5th, 77.3°. Evening 12th, 73°.
Minimum observations—Morning—12th, 15th, and 17th, 72°. Noon—4th, 74°. Evening 12th, 72°.

Remarks—Lightning on the 10th, N. and N.E.; 17th, W.N.W.; 18th, N.N.W.; 24th, W. to N.W.; 27th, N.E.; 28th, W.N.W. Thundered on the afternoon of the 23rd, N.N.E. and zenith. Wind, W. and S.W. most prevalent; on the 3rd, W. all day; 5th, W. in the morning, S.W. by W. afterwards; 6th, morning, S.W. by W.; 7th very still morning—afternoon, strong S.; 8th, N.W.; 9th, N.E. Drizzled at noon on 1st; in the morning

[1] *Ibid.*, p. 75, l. 9 ff.

of the 22nd and 27th. Morning and evening of the 15th and 20th very foggy; and evening of the 19th.

River Gambia, September 1864

Maximum observations—Morning—15th, 81.5°; 3rd, 5th, 7th, 9th, and 18th, 81°. Noon—5th, 92°; 15th, 91°. Evening—5th, 93°; 9th and 10th, 92°.

Medium observations—Morning—2nd, 4th, 11th, 16th, 17th, and 30th, 78°. Noon—2nd, 19th, 21st, 25th, and 26th, 89°. Evening—17th, 23rd, and 26th, 89°.

Minimum observations—Morning—24th, 75°. Noon—12th and 29th, 85°. Evening—12th, 16th and 30th, 86°.

Remarks—Heavy tornado on the 5th, 11th, 15th, and 22nd. Rained, 8th, 12th, 21st, 24th, and 27th. The days were generally fine. The prevailing wind S.W.; on the 27th, N.E.[1]

Slave Coast, Bight of Benin—Quittah Station, February 1860

Maximum observations—Morning—3rd, 6th, 7th, 14th, 22nd, 23rd, and 29th, 84°; 1st, 7th, and 8th, 83°. Noon—17th, 90°; 7th, 9th, and 27th, 89°; 24th and 28th, 88°. Evening—16th, 23rd, and 26th, 86°; 4th, 85.25°.

Medium observations—Morning—15th, 80°. Noon—2nd and 25th, 87°. Evening—1st and 28th, 85°.

Minimum observations—Morning—16th, 78°. Noon—12th, 84°. Evening —9th, 79°.

Remarks—Thundered on the 10th; direction W.S.W. and N.W.; on the 17th slightly N.E.; and on the 26th, E.N.E. It was very hot and sultry on the 4th, 7th, 17th, 19th, 24th, and 27th. Cloudy during the day on the 3rd, 8th, 9th, 18th, 22nd, and 23rd; and during the evening, that is, from 7 p.m. to bedtime, or to 10 p.m. on the 7th, 10th, 14th, 16th, 17th, 19th, and 26th. Slight harmattan was felt on the morning of the 5th, there was in consequence a haze round the visible horizon. Severe lightning towards N.W. by N. on the evening of the 4th, 14th, 17th, and 18th; W. and S.W. on the nights of the 12th and 20th; E. during the day on the 22nd, 23rd, and 29th. Sea breeze blowing generally S.W. by W.; commences on the 1st, 2nd, 3rd, and 26th, at 9 a.m.; on the 6th, 8th, 9th, 10th, 13th, 16th, and 20th, at 10 a.m.; on the 5th, 7th, 17th, 18th, and 19th, at 1 noon; on the 4th, 13th, 14th, 21st, 23rd, and 24th, at 2 p.m.; on the 22nd, 27th, 28th, and 29th, at 3 p.m.

N.B.—In these observations I have not reckoned the fractions of an hour.[2]

[1] *Ibid.*, p. 45, l. 1 ff.   [2] *Ibid.*, p. 27, l. 20 ff.

Thermometrical Observations for the Gambia and Gold Coast (month of May)[1]

| DAYS. | River Gambia. | | | | | | | | | Gold Coast Command. | | |
| | 1863. | | | 1864. | | | 1865. | | | 1860. | | |
	7 A.M.	NOON.	4 P.M.	7 A.M.	NOON.	4 P.M.	7 A.M.	NOON.	4 P.M.	7 A.M.	NOON.	4 P.M
1	78	89	98	76	99	104	87	101	104	78	86	83
2	77	89	98	81	95	101	83	99	107	76	83	82
3	80	91	101	86	100	104	86	99	105	80	83	82
4	81	93	98	83	95	103	82	98	104	81	82	81
5	81	89	95	81	91	101	85	95	100	81	82	80
6	81	89.30	98	78	..	101.5	81	95	99	81.10	83	82.10
7	80	90	100	80	94	98	88	98	100	79	84	82
8	81	98	101	75	91	96	85	99	108	80	85	83
9	84	99	101	77	99	100.5	83	96	104	80	83	80
10	85	98	100	79	101	104.5	84	95	104	78	83.50	80
11	84	95	100	82	103	104	81	93	102	80	85	83
12	80	94	101	84	99	101	80	96	103	80	85	83.50
13	81	91	97	81	95	..	84	96	104	78	84	81
14	80	90	95	83	93	100	82	97	106	77	80	80
15	74	89	94	79	98	103	85	99	107	76	83	82
16	78	90	91	78	98	101	83	97	104	78	83	83
17	78	91	98	78	94	102	84	99	103	77	80	80
18	78	90	97	76	94	102	84	97	105	79	85	84
19	75	90	96	77	96	102.5	86	99	106	80	85	83
20	78	88	97	80	97	100	83	99	105	76	80	82
21	80	97	100	82	95	102	..	93	102	80	84	83
22	84	95	99	78	94	101	81	..	102	81	85	83
23	80	97	98	79	94	98	84	97	104	79	83	83
24	82	98	99	71	92	97	80	95	101	76.45	82	78
25	81	92	98	70	98	99	83	97	105	75	82	80
26	78	88	98	77	96	..	84	96	100	79	84	81
27	80	91	95	82	95	100	85	97	103	78.40	83	80
28	79	80	97	80	90	96	86	99	103	75	83	82
29	80	92	100	83	..	96	84	95	102	80	84	80
30	82	91	99	81	98	101	84	97	104	78	83	81
31	78	85	90	83	93	99	83	95	103	75	82	80

[1] *Ibid.*, p. 36.

14

Diseases of West Africa: *Seasonal Diseases; Alcoholism; Worms and Public Health*

*This chapter will be interesting to medical and non-medical readers alike. **It should, however, be stressed that many of the remedies and facts mentioned in it are now out of date and have only historical value.***

Africanus Horton had remarkable powers of observation in medical and scientific matters. Like his medical contemporaries, he paid a great deal of attention to the influence of diet and climate on disease. The detailed advice he gives on food (see Ch. 15) and his long discussion, given in this chapter, on the nature of the harmattan and the diseases prevalent during this season illustrate this. Many of his observations on diseases predominant during the different seasons of the tropical year are still true. Like a good scientist, he put down exactly what he had observed. His deductions were not always correct. He did not have the time or opportunity to carry out detailed research, although when he could, he tested out known hypotheses or did simple scientific and medical experiments. Similarly, his theories on the causes of various diseases were not always correct although his observed medical and scientific facts were. His limitations were those of time and opportunity, and the period. The microscope, for example, was not then used in tropical research as much as it was twenty years later, and he seldom mentioned it in all his writings.

*In the therapeutic sphere, Horton also noted in his book some African remedies which were used at that time: boa-constrictor fat for gout, rheumatism and consumptive diseases—the idea probably being that the qualities of elasticity and free movement of the body of the snake would be transferred to the stiff joints and tight consumptive chests of the human patient; the leaves of the 'sour-sour' plant (**Abutilon esculentum**) for fomentation of jigger lesions; and soaking raw fresh beef secretly in the favourite drink of an alcoholic to cure him of his addiction by the nausea and vomiting it produced.*

Seasonal Diseases in West Africa

(a) Diseases of the Harmattan or Cold Season

This season has been justly considered the most healthy on the coast; fever is of very rare occurrence. The harmattan, the cold, dry wind of the desert places a veto on animal and vegetable decomposition, and, consequently, on malarious exhalations, and consequently, malarious fever is uncommon in this season. Those suffering in convalescence are restored to their proper health; all malignant diseases, as if by magic, disappear; ulcers quickly cicatrise, and cutaneous eruptions are arrested. Even the most dreadful outbreak of small-pox cannot withstand it; the pustules soon heal up, and the disease disappears. If the best vaccine matter be used for inoculation whilst the harmattan wind is blowing its effect is nullified, and the system becomes perfectly exposed, as an unvaccinated patient, to the baneful influence of the epidemic. It has exactly the same effect with the exanthematous fevers, curing them by hastening the different stages or without allowing them to run their regular course.[1]

On the West Coast of Africa individuals of arthritic temperament suffer most severely from gout and rheumatism at certain seasons of the year, occasioned either by excessive debauchery, undue exposure, or hereditary predisposition; and in a great many cases we can only account for the cessation from meteoric circumstances. I have seen patients suffering most severely from the worst forms of gout and rheumatism, with flying pains all over the body, swollen joints, intense local pains, with a deposit of what is wrongly called chalk-stone, before the occurrence of the harmattan wind; and when it blows, all, like a spell, disappear; the swelling is greatly reduced, there is no pain, and the patient is able to move about with ease and comfort, and generally expresses himself to be 'jolly;' but no sooner does the harmattan cease, and the N., S., or N.W. winds begin to blow, than the symptoms gradually begin to reappear, much to his discomfort. The best remedy used by the natives in the Bight of Benin for gout and rheumatism is the fat of the boa-constrictor. I have never had an opportunity of examining its effects; but judging from the statements of the natives, it seems to possess a powerful penetrative action. It is employed also in consumptive pains in the chest, which, they say, it greatly relieves.

During the harmattan season pregnant females suffer a good deal from cold and coughs, which they describe as far exceeding any other time; and they also observe that the cold is less felt when in an unpregnated state, although the weather is of the same temperature. They, however,

[1] *Physical and Medical Climate*, p. 246, l. 6 ff.

feel lighter and more able to move about than previously, if they have suffered from great weight and heaviness. Labour during this season is very quick. It takes about three-fourths of the ordinary time. The patients generally complain of severe cold and trembling just before and after the commencement of labour pains. The pains then come on, and the uterus seems to act with double energy and force. The pains are principally dragging lumbar pains. After delivery, severe pains are felt all over the lumbar and pelvic regions, and in the hip joints; but they continue only for a short time, and then disappear. This wind has an invigorative effect on the galactophorous glands. A dry, scanty breast now secretes a large and abundant quantity of milk.

The young infant at this season of the year suffers much from cold, especially amongst the lower class. The babe is said to cry much more than at any other time, and is much more troublesome in nursing.[1]

(b) Diseases of the Hot Season
The months of February, March, and April, although the hottest in the year, especially in the Gambia region, are the most healthy. The heat is only uncomfortable, and produces great laxity of the constitution, yet it is the most healthy period; there is scarcely any record of deaths, especially in the interior countries, where the ground is parched and dried up, and no swamp is anywhere to be seen. It is the ground-nut season, and the time at which each merchant performs a great deal of labour, and yet there is scarcely any case of fever, dysentery, or diarrhoea; there may be now and then a little derangement of the liver, but otherwise there is very little necessity for a doctor. At M'Carthy's Island, where I acted as physician to the natives, the dispensary was generally crowded during the whole of the year, commencing in June, until the hot winds began to blow, when there was scarcely a case in for months. This proves without a doubt that the higher the temperature, unmixed with humidity, the more healthy is the climate; but if the temperature is high and surcharged with moisture, the climate becomes very deadly.

At Sierra Leone, Liberia, the Gold Coast, and Bights, the weather not being so hot, and being mixed with moisture from their close proximity to the sea, the season is not so very healthy as in the Gambia region, although in the two former places it is comparatively so; and in the latter places the inhabitants suffer much from diarrhoea and dysentery.[2]

The places where dysentery and diarrhoea are most prevalent in Western Africa, are at Accra and the Bight of Benin, principally Badagry and Lagos. In the month of October, in M'Carthy's Island, and St. Mary's, at Sierra Leone, and Liberia, diarrhoea and dysentery are of occasional

[1] *Ibid.*, p. 249, l. 10 ff.   [2] *Ibid.*, p. 210, l. 4 ff.

occurrence during the commencement of the rains, from the water being contaminated.[1]

Febris Intermittens—Ague

*Malaria was at the time considered by many doctors to be caused by bad air rising from marshes and stagnant water. Its name (**mal**—bad; **aria**—air) indicated this belief. We know now that it is the mosquitoes which breed in these localities which are responsible for carrying the malarial parasite from an ill and infected person to a healthy one. The malarial parasites were discovered about a quarter of a century after Horton wrote his books, by Laveran and Ross through microscopic examinations in malarial human blood and in infected mosquitoes respectively. The mode of their transmission from a malarial patient by mosquitoes to infect a healthy person was worked out after this in the closing years of the century by Professors Grassi and Bignami of Italy and Sir Patrick Manson of Great Britain.*

*Horton, like his contemporaries, had accepted the theory that bad air caused the disease. He was convinced in addition, however, that ozone, a gas naturally occurring in the atmosphere and belonging to the same family as oxygen, had a neutralising effect on the disease. With characteristic thoroughness he measured the quantity of ozone in the atmosphere and tried to correlate the rise and fall of the frequency of malaria with the diminution and increase of ozone in the atmosphere. He knew that quinine was the cure for malaria and used it, but he felt that ozone, if obtainable in sufficient quantities, would be better. Horton's experiments by the lagoons showed that malaria could be caught near them. It was then believed that this was impossible, because lagoons contained salt water. This belief was still generally held after the real cause of malaria had been discovered as it was felt that mosquitoes could not breed in salt water. Seventy years after Horton had decided from his experiments on himself that malaria could be caught near lagoons, it was discovered in West Africa that a species of mosquito, **Anopheles Gambiae melas,** could breed near the vegetation by the watery edges of estuarine salt water and could carry malaria. Horton had been right in the postulation, formed from his experimental approach and scientific method, of the existence of malaria near lagoons, but he had incorrectly deduced that the cause of lagoon malaria was a fall of ozone in the atmosphere near the lagoon, instead of a malaria-bearing mosquito in the lagoon.*

I should strongly recommend that persons who reside in malarious districts, or who in any way are exposed to the influence of malaria, should now and then take the sulphate of quinine, as it serves as a

[1] *Ibid.*, p. 211, l. 35 ff.

preventive; or should the person be attacked, he would have a milder and more manageable disease than another who has not been so protected. The best mode of giving quinine for such a purpose is in the form of quinine wine—four grains to every ounce of sherry; of which, especially during the fever season, one ounce should be taken every morning before going out, and repeated if required in the afternoon. . . .

Among other things that should be guarded against, is the too frequent use of drugs.[1]

It has sometimes been asserted by foreign inhabitants, residing south of the Volta, that the lagoon does not give out malaria, that, in fact, it is healthy—advancing, as a presumptive reason, that 'its water is a salt water, and salt water is opposed to malaria.' When we consider the number of cases of paludal fever which occur in the region, and that the only marsh is to be found in the lagoon, one could hardly account for it otherwise. I have always maintained, and I do still positively believe, that the lagoon is the source of this pestiferous poison.

1st, because it contains a less amount of salt than the water of the sea, the proportion being about one-fourth.

2nd, Because at its banks vegetable and animal putrescent matters are to be found, which, when washed of their salt by the rain, form an abundant source of malaria.

3rd, Because its banks, which extend about 250 to 300 feet (breadth), covered with low, rank grass, form generally several beds, which receive the rain-water, and become stagnant pools, which are prolific in the generation of littoral poison.

Paludal or littoral poison is given out in deadly quantity from these sources, drifted by the W., W.S.W., N. and N.E. winds; *cœteris paribus*, it becomes pernicious to individuals residing in those tracts of land lying on the border of the sea.

Ergo, the lagoon is undoubtedly the source of malaria. To prove more substantially that the lagoon is the *fons et origo mali*, on the evening of the 18th May I went down the banks of the lagoon, and walked slowly up and down for twenty minutes, exposing myself in every conceivable way to the effects of malaria. Every circumstance was favourable to its generation. The breeze was blowing from W.S.W., along a tract of the malarious beds for at least twenty miles; the vegetation near where I stood had been removed by farmers, and rank vegetation and pools of stagnant water were almost under my feet. On referring to the meteorological observation which I kept, I found the ozonometer to be as low as 0.5°; during the whole of the day the thermometer was 84°; dew-point, 73°; hygrometer, 9°; saturation of the atmosphere, 695.8°; tension of aqueous

[1] *Ibid.*, p. 290, l. 11 ff.

vapour, 1.104°. The quantity of ozone, which is nature's grand and stupendous neutraliser of malaria, was remarkably small. This is proved to be a positive fact by comparison with the corresponding day of the two preceding months, which we find to have been in March 6.4°, and in April 4.1°. The other observations on the same evening in April stood as follows—thermometer, 85°; dew-point, 78°; hygrometer, 7°; saturation of the atmosphere, 771.1°; tension of aqueous vapour, 1.241°.

I returned to the fort, and as a precaution, in order that, should I get the fever, it might not be too strong, I took one grain of the disulphate of quinine. I slept very sound that night; but in the morning I felt a little seedy, though I thought nothing of it. I lost my appetite, and began to feel a degree of lassitude, languor, and weariness, as the day advanced, and I felt that I could not apply my mental powers to anything. I therefore lay down quietly. At two o'clock I felt a burning sensation all over my body, commencing from my feet. I had a severe headache, and, in fact, all the symptoms of remittent fever in the form in which it generally attacks one. The sweating stage came on at half-past seven, and I was then relieved, but still suffered from severe headache. I now used the proper means for preventing its reappearance, which succeeded. The next day I felt much better, but rather weak, and suffered from slight headache, and in three days after the exposure I felt as well as before.

The facts to be gathered from this are, not only that malaria exists in the lagoon, but that it also exists in a very concentrated form; that its influence is speedily manifested in the system, although it is probable that in some individuals it may not show itself for some days.

The lagoon, therefore, or its banks, form several beds from which are generated certain deadly poisons, which, in contact with the human system, produce these phenomena known as fever, *quod erat demonstrandum*.[1, 2]

The Bights of Biafra and Benin are well watered with many rivers. The Ogun, Niger, Bonny, Calabar, Cameroon, &c., are to be found here; but we have more to do with stations at Biafra, which are situated on a narrow tract of land between the lagoon and the Atlantic; and although Lagos is a few miles inland, it still is near enough to receive its benefit. The banks of the lagoon are low and muddy, and covered with rank vegetation near the land. At the commencement of the rains, the extensive dried up banks are covered with small pools of stagnant water, which give out putrid exhalations. It is the great source of the unhealthiness of this part of the coast, and the only remedy would be to cover these banks with large trees.

[1] *Ibid.*, p. 225, l. 23 ff.   [2] Which was to be proved (Ed.)

That fens, bogs, lagoons, and such accumulations are the source of disease, the immortal Shakspeare has even told us thus:—

> Caliban: As wicked dew as e'er my mother brush'd
> With raven's feather from unwholesome fen
> Drop on you both.
>
> TEMPEST, Act I. Scene 2.
>
> Caliban: All the infections that the sun sucks up
> From bogs, fens, flats, on Prosper fall, and
> Make him by inch-meal a disease!
>
> TEMPEST, Act II. Scene 2.
>
> Coriolanus: Though I go alone
> Like to a lonely dragon, that his fen
> Makes fear'd, and talk'd of more than seen.
>
> CORIOLANUS, Act IV. Scene 1.

But we find that the natives have instinctively protected themselves from the results of these deadly emanations from the banks, by surrounding their towns with large lofty cocoa-nut trees, which are densely packed together. This has assisted a great deal in putting down the malaria evolved, and the inhabitants are comparatively healthy. Lagos, as has been described, is situated at the confluence of these rivers, and in some parts is below water-level. There are, unfortunately, not many large trees in the town, and it is not surrounded, as in the other towns, by lofty cocoa-nut trees.[1]

Alcoholism and Delirium Tremens

Horton's recognition of alcoholism as a disease was much ahead of his time. He resisted the temptation to leave it untreated or dismiss or castigate it simply as a sign of moral weakness or of sinful indulgence.

This is a form of delirium which is met with principally amongst drunkards, associated with imperfect and perverted nutrition of the brain, and consists in an abnormal condition of the blood, caused by the presence of alcohol. It is characterized by fantastic hallucinations, the horrors, tremors of the tendons and muscles of the hands and limbs, and a great want of sleep.

It is a disease which should be particularly guarded against in the tropics, as, unfortunately, Europeans—especially soldiers and sailors—in the tropics are not, as a rule, temperate in their habits. The effect of tropical heat on the nervous system is very depressing and exhausting, particularly when combined with humidity of the atmosphere, and,

[1] *Ibid.*, p. 104, l. 26 ff.

consequently, the same quantity of alcohol which could be indulged in with impunity in temperate climates cannot, without great risk, be so used in the tropics.

Symptoms and Progress

The disease might come on after long and continuous debauch, without any intimation, or it may occur after a sudden temporary withdrawal of the accustomed stimulants; in which latter case, as Dr. Gardiner has shown, the withdrawal might be only the result of the commencement of the disease. The premonitory symptoms are extreme nervous depression, or a feeling of sinking of the vital energies; a very anxious and agitated countenance, a slowness of the pulse, a cold and clammy skin, imperfect respiration, frightful dreams, impaired digestion, vicious appetite, furred tongue, and a disposition of the bowels to constipation. The pulse is feeble, easily compressed, varying from 90 to 120; the mind is weak and confused, the sleep much disturbed, and the individual rises with great agitation. Slight muscular exertion produces great fatigue and profuse perspiration; the hands tremble in the act of taking anything, and the person occasionally suffers from nausea and vomiting in the mornings. This state may continue for a longer or a shorter time—from twenty-four to forty-eight hours, when the delirium sets in with great fury.

In the young and robust, the symptoms show excessive irritability of the nervous system; the person becomes very violent, and wanders about with terrible weapons to defend himself from some imaginary foes; he mutters incessantly; uses foul language; sees dreadful objects before him (venomous serpents, leopards, or loathsome vermin), and he imagines himself the subject of attack; he also sees little hobgoblins of all possible shapes flying about his apartments; he becomes more and more violent; his tongue is very tremulous, and furred brown, or in many cases might be clean; his head is hot; respiration is but imperfectly performed; pulse ranges from 120 to 130, full and throbbing; the heart's action is violent, he is sleepless and restless, and hears voices at a great distance speaking to him; he replies, and then struggles and attempts to fly. In some cases the individual has some special object of terror which forms the prevailing idea of his delirium. 'One person is pursued by justice, another flies from a creditor or an avenging enemy, another is attacked by robbers or assassins. Voices are heard conspiring the destruction of the patient; he sees a gun pointed at him through the window, or a knife glittering in an imaginary hand within the curtains. He hides from pursuit; defends himself against assaults; struggles violently against persons aiming to seize or bind him; perhaps jumps out of a high window to escape; screams for aid, or implores pitifully to be spared; occasionally even seizes a pistol or a sword, and commits manslaughter in supposed self-defence.' I have met with cases where after a long march under noon-day sun, a debauch was indulged in, and Delirium Tremens was the result. In these cases there are excessive irritation of the nervous and engorgement of the vascular system; the delirium assumes the type of maniacal fury, and the patient dies very early of coma.

Amongst the old topers, who have been long in the tropics and whose constitutions seem to be seasoned with alcohol, the delirium in most cases is generally mild. The patient is quiet, sometimes melancholic, often hesitates when he speaks; his countenance is anxious and suspicious; he is not violent, but has vague delusions, is more easily managed, and takes his medicine without trouble, when offered him. He often imagines that he is considered mad by those who are about him, and endeavours in some cases to persuade them that he is not so, he might give rational answers when his attention is strongly fixed, but as soon as reference is made to the peculiar object of his delirium, he at once betrays himself.

There is a third kind of case, not often met with; the peculiarities are that the disease is seen amongst old drunkards, who are careful to take now and then small quantities of some sedative medicine. They generally avoid opium, but hyoscyamus seems to be the favourite prophylaxis. Of four cases which lately came under my notice after long and continuous hard drinking, the individuals were left in a semi-delirious, stupid state for weeks; they were not decidedly mad, but became so suddenly. They were very terrified at everything; very quiet, lying down as if endeavouring to sleep, they spoke quietly but much nonsense, and they were not furious; the pulse was feeble and frequent; there were tremors of the whole body, and the skin was cold and clammy. A small quantity of sedative medicine was sufficient to put them into a deep sleep, from which, when they awoke, they appeared feeble, pale, and hungry, quite recovered from their delirium, but not from their thirst after liquor. In the four cases, I had been watching for the disease, so that as soon as it manifested itself I was prepared to combat it. No doubt had the cases been allowed to remain any length of time, the delirium would have been furious.[1]

Ebriositas—Trembling or Drunkard's Insanity

Objects are far more vividly conceived, and produce a much stronger impression than they do in health. If your patient thinks he is going to be murdered, and that his nurse is in league with some one for this purpose, do not try to convince him to the contrary: you will only irritate him, and produce a conviction in his mind that you are in league with his enemies. Send away the nurse; put your patient in another room;

[1] *Diseases of Tropical Climates*, p. 558, l. 1 ff.

command absolute darkness and absolute silence; and in the majority of cases this will succeed. Beware of using force or of tying your patient down, by which means slightly delirious patients have been driven frantic. Patience, gentleness, and firmness will almost always succeed; but above all things gentleness. Remember you can never handle a sick person too gently, nor speak to one too softly. To a shattered or highly sensitive nervous system, the slightest sound, the faintest light, the gentlest touch are sometimes almost unbearable. If, therefore, a patient will get out of bed and walk about; will persist in throwing about his arms and legs, let him do so. It is far better that he should exhaust himself by himself, than by himself and one or more attendants. If suicide is attempted in any form, force must be used, but proper nursing will never give an opportunity for an attempt of this nature.

Prophylactic Treatment

This consists in the exhibition of such remedies in the potation as would induce nausea and vomiting; *tartar emetic* or *ipecacuanha* in doses sufficient to produce severe vomiting should be secretly added to the favourite liquor of the person. . . . It gradually produces such nausea, vomiting, and fear of death, as completely to frighten the person from going on in his drunken course of life, for that time at least; and much to the joy of friends, ultimately produces in many instances, when nothing else would effect it, a complete change of life; one from drunkenness to temperance. When ipecacuanha is used half a drachm may be given at once.

Natives of the tropics soak fresh beef secretly in the liquor the drunkard specially delights in, and when it is taken, it produces severe nausea and vomiting, and a general distaste for any spirituous liquor. I have employed this means, and found it efficacious for two or three months, even in persons who were confirmed drunkards; they could not face or endure the smell of their most favourite drink, but turned away from the sight of it with disgust. In one instance, the person, a confirmed drunkard, was unable to sit in the same room where gin was being drunk, without feeling a sensation of nausea and vomiting, although he had taken the remedy a month before.[1]

Causes of Guinea Worm

Horton's pamphlet on the guinea worm gave an accurate description of the symptoms and signs of the disease and of the locations in the body where the worm exhibited itself. He discussed the various theories of the transmission of the disease but rejected the one later discovered to be

[1] *Ibid.*, p. 576, l. 26 ff.

correct—that of transmission by drinking polluted water—because among other reasons, neither he nor others had observed guinea worms in the liver. He argued that if the worm had been absorbed through the stomach and gut by drinking water it should have later passed through the liver as usual. He was right: guinea worms are never found in the liver. But he did not realise that there was a second route of absorption from the stomach and gut which by-passed the liver and which went straight into the main bloodstream through the lymphatic system. This route of absorption was discovered much later by modern microscopic techniques. By a happy coincidence, the fact that the embryo guinea worms used this second route was discovered almost a hundred years afterwards by another African scientist, Sanya Onabamiro.

Horton's inconclusive experiments on trying to grow guinea worms in mud again illustrate his scientific approach. He was unsuccessful because the worm needed two hosts for full development. It was discovered much later that the embryo guinea worms were first swallowed by tiny freshwater cyclops in polluted water. When this was drunk by man, the cyclops died but its parasites —the developing guinea worms—emerged into the human gut, were absorbed through the lymphatic system and then started their development and wanderings in the human body. The adult female, pregnant and elongated, moved on to that part of the surface of the human body which was usually wet—the shoulder and back of the Indian water-carrier, and the bare feet in the case of Africans tramping on muddy ground and streams. It partially emerged through a preliminary blister after perhaps a day or two of fever and skin rashes and then spilled out its thousands of embryo guinea worms in a milky fluid which, on contaminating water, were swallowed by the freshwater cyclops beginning another cycle by the latter being swallowed later by man in contaminated water.

The excerpts from his treatise on the guinea worm show how near the truth he often came but how wrong he was in his conclusions through basing his deductions on incomplete evidence. He had assumed that the point of exit of the guniea worm was the same as the point of entry. The method of infection which he gave for guinea worm is now known to be that used by some other quite different organisms, such as the hookworm.

The causes of Guinea Worm have long been a disputed point amongst scientific men, and inhabitants of Guinea Worm districts. If the inhabitants of some districts where the disease is endemic are questioned as to the cause of the worm, they at once reply that it is not known for certain; but as the best view or the best hypothesis is that which embraces all known facts respecting the subject in question, so I shall here detail and review the different causes which have been alleged to have induced the disease, and then point out, from direct and circumstantial evidence, what is the most likely source of this pest.

I shall divide the causes into predisposing, or *causes which lead to the susceptibility of the system to the disease*; and exciting, or *immediate causation*. I shall, however, both on account of the importance of the latter, and also the bearing of the predisposing on the exciting cause, give the first consideration to the latter.

There are three views which have been maintained as the exciting causes of Guinea Worm—viz., that it is derived—

I.—From the drinking-water that is used by the inhabitants.

II.—From hereditary transmission.

III.—From direct contact with the earth.

We shall now consider the value of each of these causes. Those who maintain that drinking-water is the cause, support their argument by the following considerations:—

1.—*That Guinea Worm is only found where water is scarce—in fact, where the people use tank-water.*

This is not literally true, although it is principally found in places where water is not plentiful, as in Syria, Arabia, various parts of India and northern regions of Africa; but it is also found in the tropical regions of Asia and Africa, where water is also abundant. In great numbers we meet with it among the coloured population in the West Indies; and in Western Africa, where I made it a point of special observation, it is very common in regions below the River Volta, where the people obtain good water in abundance by only digging a well three or four feet in depth. It should also be remembered that the poor class of the population in some places where the disease is endemic, do not drink tank-water, but well-water, so that the argument of the drinking of tank-water being the cause falls to the ground, since the disease is more prevalent amongst the lower than the higher class.

2.—*That the embryo worm can be seen in a larval state in the water drawn from the tank, which may lead to the deduction that the embryo, being very minute and disseminated in the water, is taken into the system, and distributed amongst the chylopoetic viscera, and thus transmitted into the system.*

It is a positive fact that when water is drawn from a tank that has not been cleansed for a long time, several small species of worm are seen very active, and twisting about in the water. Some of these are the larval state of some insects; others are a peculiar worm known as Tank Worm. We meet with the larval state of the mosquitoes in great numbers. By being passed through the filter, the whole of these are removed. If we admit that the worm is taken up by the blood-vessels which form a network in the chylopoetic viscera, some of the embryo, at least, will first be distributed in the liver; and as this organ is composed of a number of very minute vessels, a few must be arrested, and thus undergo the different changes necessary for the development of the worm: but we have never heard of Guinea Worm in the liver. I have seen it attack the side, external wall of the thorax and abdomen, but never the internal organs.

Guinea Worm, therefore, in the system, cannot claim, as its original source of production, the tank-water which is drunk by the inhabitants.

3.—*That the Guinea Worm sometimes attacks far and distant, as well as important organs, which cannot be from actual contact—e.g., the eye, tongue, etc.*

When the Guinea Worm is found in the neighbourhood of the eyeball, it must have originally attacked the external surface of the parts near the organ, and cannot be said to be interrupted in the minute blood-vessels in the eyeball and then undergo development. The history of the case will always clear up this part of the question. That Guinea Worm has been found in the interior of the eye, lodged in beds made for itself, and only making periodical movements, at that time causing irritation and slight inflammation without destroying vision, can scarcely be believed, on account of the destructive character of the worm. It is most likely that many of those who detail such cases confound it with the entozoa peculiar to the eye, viz., the *Filaria oculi*; for the latter is perfectly harmless when compared with the former.

The tongue has also been the seat of Guinea Worm. According to Dr. Scott, the socket of the eye, the mouth, the cheeks, and the tongue have formed seats for it; and according to M. Dubois, the nose, ears, and eyelids.

4.—*That it invariably attacks the lower class of the inhabitants, who drink bad water.*

The lower class of the people in the Gold Coast drink water that is accumulated during the rainy season in stagnant pools, or that obtained by digging a well a few feet into the earth, and which is very brackish, muddy, and unhealthy; they very seldom use tank-water. On examining the well-water, we do not find so many embryo organisms as in the tank-water. More leeward, in the country of Awoonah or Aungla, the people obtain very good water from wells of the depth of from three to six feet, and yet they are affected with Guinea Worm. At Dix Cove, Apollonia and Axim, where the inhabitants live on river and spring water, Guinea Worm appears to be more common in the first of these places than in any other parts where the disease is endemic.

It cannot be urged, therefore, that the drinking of bad water is the source of the worm, since it has been shown that people who have very good water, either from well or from spring, suffer alike with those who drink bad water, where the disease is endemic.

The drinking water, therefore, is not the source of Guinea Worm, as it is prevalent in places where water is abundant, and where the inhabitants do not use tank-water.

II.—*Hereditary Transmission.*

In making observations on Guinea Worm, as it occurs amongst the inhabitants of the Gold Coast, one is sometimes told that it attacks children a few months or weeks after birth; and they account for it as being transmitted through the mother. This view, I am of opinion, is untenable, since the embryo worms are so large that they cannot be taken up by the absorbents, transmitted into the blood, and conveyed into the foetal and maternal system in utero. Hereditary transmission, therefore, is impossible.

III.—*Immediate Contact with the earth or with an Infected Individual.*

Every argument goes to prove that this is the direct source of Guinea Worm. That this is the case is proved:—

1. *It occurs only among those who walk barefooted, either constantly or occasionally.*

In discussing the subject with the educated natives, some generally object to immediate contact, on the ground that Guinea Worms occur on some who do not walk on their bare feet; but if we trace their minute actions we find that they either were accustomed in their youth to go without shoes, or only used them occasionally; that the disease was not engendered after they made shoes a constant part of their dress. Most of those in this class who have got Guinea Worm have travelled a good deal in the interior, and at seasons when the road is covered with mud and water. All authors agree that Guinea Worms exist in moist earth and mud; but the peculiar condition of the young worm before it attacks the system is as yet unknown. 'It is probable that the hair-like worms found by gardeners in India coiled up together, may be the *filaria* of the Guinea Worm in sexual congress, whose progeny, as *zoösperms* or a filiferous females (like the Tank Worm of Carter), make their way into the body. It is known that the *Gordius aquaticus*, when young, enters the bodies of large water-beetles; and at a certain stage of life, it leaves its abode in the beetle and goes into the water, where it becomes a variety of *Tank Worm*. It appears that there are white and brown Tank Worms —nay, that there are no fewer than seventeen species of minute *filaria*; and some say that all Tank Worms are white at first, but become black after a time in the water.' (Aitken.) But the difficulty is to determine the phase of existence of the young *filaria* after they have quitted the body of the parent, and lived an independent existence.

. . .

2. *That it occurs among Europeans who travel about.*

That Guinea Worm attacks some European residents in the tropics has been used by some as a strong argument against direct causation since Europeans are supposed to be always with, or very seldom without, their shoes. But Europeans who remain for a long time and whose occupations require them to travel from place to place, become after a time careless of themselves, and unwittingly expose their bodies to the influence of the disease. Many a time during their travels have they been obliged in some places to walk on bare feet, or with shoes perfectly saturated with mud and dirt, not knowing that the element of a most painful disease could be transmitted into the system through it. In no case have I known of careful European English officers having been attacked with Guinea Worm, although some have been for several years in places where the disease is endemic; and this is entirely due to the care they took of themselves. But merchants of long residence and free habits, and supercargoes of merchant vessels, have been attacked.

3. *That it occurs principally on the lower extremity.*

The part of the body in which this worm is most commonly found is in the lower extremities, the foot and ankle more particularly. Out of 300 cases noted, not less than 206 were on the foot; the next in frequency was the leg, then the testicle, and then the thigh; the face, back, breast, and tongue, being rarely affected in Africa.

The following statement, made from the observations of 300 cases, will show the frequency with which the different parts of the body are attacked:—

300 Cases

Foot, including the ankle	206 cases
Legs	38 ,,
Thighs	16 ,,
Testicle	19 ,,
Abdominal Walls	8 ,,
Breast	2 ,,
Face	2 ,,
Tongue	1 ,,
Back	1 ,,
Arms	7 ,,
TOTAL	300 cases

This is easily accounted for. In India it occurs in the lower extremities of those who are accustomed to go into tanks, or dried-up wells, which yield a very small quantity of water, where they remain till they can be supplied; they stir up the mud, which is the abode of the *filaria*, from which some make a lodgment in some part of their feet. In other parts, it is obtained from walking through mud and swamp, and also from washing in stagnant pools, disturbing the minute worms from the bottom of the water. Some length of residence is required for development. In the latter part of 1862, two companies of the 2nd West India Regiment landed at Cape Coast Castle, from Sierra Leone; not one had the Guinea

Worm. After remaining there for twenty months, most of the cases of admittance into hospital from that disease during the Ashantee Expedition of 1864, were entirely among that corps. In India it is exactly the same.

Dr. Forbes, whilst examining several tanks in India, in the neighbourhood of Dharwar, found numerous *filariae* on their banks, and in half-dried beds, 'some of them very much resembling those produced by the Guinea Worm when infesting the human limb. Their vermicular motion in the water is exactly the same; their general appearance is the same; and they are active and equally numerous. The point of a penknife inserted into the mud will raise up abundance for examination. They are most numerous where the water assumes a variegated appearance, with a pellicle floating on its ochry surface; the fine, soft, impalpable mud just above water-mark contains most, and the best time to find them is about three or four o'clock in the afternoon. Two kinds may generally be detected in the soft mud; one kind is seven or eight times the size of the Guinea Worm young *filariae*; the other exactly resembles them.'

4. *That when it occurs in the upper part of the body, it does so among those who sleep on the ground.*

Besides the lower part of the leg, Guinea Worm is sometimes met with in other parts of the body. We do not infrequently meet it in the thigh, testicle, walls of the abdomen, and sometimes in the upper extremity; this of course, is not likely to have been produced by Guinea Worm in the foot. It is easily accounted for when we consider the habits of the people. In some parts of the tropics, and where the disease is endemic among the lower class, we find they recline on small mats spread on the ground, which in many cases is very damp. Should the embryo worm be about the spot, which is not unlikely, especially where the worm has prevailed in the family for many years, its access to the most dependent part of the body is very easy; its entrance is insidious, and it does not show itself until it is about to make its exit. Again, this class of people, as a general rule, are not upright pillars of sobriety, and in some of their bacchanalian fits they sometimes lie for hours on damp ground, in almost perfect nudity, and on their face; so that the attack in the various parts of the body may easily be accounted for, and also shows that walking or standing in mud is not the only way an attack may be occasioned.

Washing in muddy tanks, or stagnant muddy pools, is another fruitful source. Mr. Mitchell, in the *Madras Times* (Supplement) of 18th December, 1861, and 18th January, 1862, relates cases where he could date the accession of Guinea Worm from gentlemen bathing in tanks contrary to his advice.

But it is not all mud worms that are the essential *filaria*; for in countries where it is not endemic, the inhabitants may walk in mud and swamp, may bathe in stagnant pools, without any ill effect, although there are several minute worms in them, but these are not that particular species of *zoösperm* which produces the Guinea Worm.

5. *That a similar worm, called in some parts of Western Africa, GROUND ITCH, but in the West Indies, CHIGA, attacks the body by actual contact, and produces severe but moderate inflammation, and an ulcer.* (The 'jigger'— Ed.)

At Sierra Leone and its neighbourhood, in Gambia, and in the West Indies, this disease occurs, but it is not very general. Like the Guinea Worm, it generally attacks the sole of the foot, especially between the toes, or at the groove in the plantar surface of the toes. It is a very small worm, which pierces through the skin unobserved. The period of its activity is in the rainy season, when every place is damp; in the dry season the worm could be discovered in some places, making a conical hollow in the ground, the small apex in the earth and the broad base on the surface. This opening is surrounded by very fine earth, and if care be taken in the search the worm could be detected in its recesses.

The period of attack is not generally known, but after a time the part itches a great deal, and becomes inflamed, and if hot fomentation and warm Soursour (*Abutilon esculentum*) leaves be applied to it, the inflammation soon subsides; a small ulcer opens, the worm escapes, the parts are healed, and the patient never suffers again from it. But if care be not taken from the beginning, it remains for a long time as a troublesome ulcer, and heals very slowly, interfering with the general health of the individual.[1]

Public Health

There is nothing so necessary for the healthy growth of a community as the drainage and sewerage of the towns they inhabit, and the inefficient mode in which this is done in Western Africa shows that the general population or their superiors have set a limit to their own existence. Yes. The air we breathe, loaded with carbonaceous matter, sulphurous and sulphuric acid, sulphate of ammonia, and sulphuretted hydrogen, is deprived, by the absence of vegetation, of the revivifying principle, oxygen, and is hence less fitted for the necessary changes of the blood effected during respiration. The earth which we tread under our feet, loaded with the ashes of our forefathers, and rich with the remains of animal and vegetable matter of ages long gone by, saturated with the putrefying contents of cesspools and leaking sewers of our own day, emits, at certain seasons of the year, the poisonous emanations which generate typhus, diarrhoea, dysentery, and cholera; whilst the waters

[1] *Guinea Worm*, p. 27, l. 1 ff.

162

of our principal tidal rivers, converted into open common sewers, teem with pestiferous exhalations charged with the germ of disease or the messenger of death. If under these favourable conditions a pestilential epidemic invade our shores, it finds us an unprepared and easy prey.'

This should be an important subject with the Governor-General of the Coast. An officer of public health should be appointed in the various colonies in the Coast Government, and ample means afforded him for the efficient performance of the duties which would devolve upon him. He should be made plainly and distinctly to know that his duties are—To examine and watch over the health of the population at large; to see that the water is pure and plentifully supplied; to ascertain that every public building and the dwelling-houses of the poor are properly ventilated; to prevent the committing of nuisances in the streets and lanes of towns and villages; or in their immediate neighbourhood, the burial of the dead in houses, and all noxious and unwholesome trade from being carried on within a given distance from the town and dwelling-houses; to establish public slaughtering-houses and burial-grounds; to make strict sanitary inspection of all trading vessels; and especially to 'lay down and carry out an effectual, efficient, complete, and common-sense plan of drainage and sewerage for every town and city.'

The sewage of towns and cities consists of the solid and fluid excreta of men and animals, which, if not continually removed from the dwelling-houses, or if inefficiently removed, forms one of the most prolific sources of disease.[1]

It is a question of life and death, and I, consequently, bring it prominently forward here for their notice and consideration. An organised system of sewage removal must be adopted; a legislative Act compelling the use of cheap deodorisers and disinfectants should be enforced; and not till the local Government condescend to think on these apparently small matters, will any real improvement in the healthiness of the climate of West Africa take place.

Say the population of a West African City were put down as 20,000. If the average daily quantity of urine of each individual (man, woman, and child), is 40 ounces of urine, these 20,000 people void every day 5,000 gallons of urine; or, in a year, 1,825,000 gallons of urine. These figures show only the quantity for a twelve-month period. The cesspools are far from being emptied yearly. Five, six, seven, eight years' accumulation, and even more, are continually found in the city, with little or no use of deodoriser or disinfectant; and do these increase the health of the town and country around? or do they not add immeasurably all the

---

[1] *Physical and Medical Climate*, p. 112, l. 27 ff.

causes already enumerated in making the place, 'a Golgotha and a Gehenna?'[1]

1. The first movement should be a legislative Act, making it compulsory on all owners or dwellers of houses to have their privy cesspools emptied once or twice every year, under the immediate supervision of the Government; and if once a-year, it should be done in the month of November.
2. That the faeces and urine, or the sewage, be removed from the privies, and collected in proper carts provided by the Government for that express purpose, under the superintendence of the Officer of Health or his subordinates.
3. That, as the water-closets are made as I have above described, the dry process shall be the only means employed for the removal of the sewage which they contain.

The contents of the cesspool should first be mixed, in sufficient quantity, with one of the disinfectants or deodorisers named above. Lime, charcoal, or M'Dougall's patent (carbonates of lime and magnesia), will be found very expensive, and consequently I should recommend that surface earth, consisting of clayey or marly soil, should be well dried and baked in an oven, and thrown into the water-closets in sufficient quantity to precipitate the solid constituents, and dry up the liquid. The hardened solid material should be removed into the Government cart, and thence into poudretta manufactories, or conveyed at once to the soil. Mixed with dried clay, the sewage becomes an excellent fertilising manure, which might be sold to farmers, or employed in the model-farm already recommended to the Government.
4. In process of time, the Government might recommend, and see carried out, especially in houses in the centre of the town, a standard form for water-closets, by which the sewage might be very easily removed —something like what was proposed in 1858 by the Bengal Government.
5. That owners of houses be made to pay a small tax, if found necessary, towards this cleaning, and the Government should principally employ the numerous prisoners who infest that jail of Freetown for this purpose.

That Sierra Leone is groaning under a want of material sanitary reforms, and that within the last few years the health of the colony has deteriorated in a marked degree, may be proved from the following quotation from the weekly paper, *The Observer*, of August 2, 1866:—

'This colony, we are sorry to state, has not improved with respect to its health. Fevers and dysentery are still known amongst us, but we employ little or no means to get rid of them. Unwholesome meat is still sold in butchers' stalls, and paraded about the town for sale; there is no

[1] *Ibid.*, p. 115, l. 3 ff.

inspector of stock, or of meat, or of markets. A board of health is unknown to us, and sanitary inspectors more so.'

With these facts before us, the editor asks, 'Can there be any surprise that fever and dysentery visit the colony?' 'The present state of the butchers' market,' he observes, 'is most disreputable; the building is quite dilapidated, and the stalls where the meat is exposed for sale are most filthy. There is not the slightest convenience in these stalls; and what is worse than all, water is not accessible.' The consequence is that they are never washed, and the quantity of dirt and filth accumulated in them is such as to shock the nerves. 'The malaria arising from the quantity of filth must, as a matter of course, not only infect the meat, but must be injurious to health.' The public have no guarantee that the animals killed are in good health and condition. The cattle plague has been busy amongst the herds in the colony, but 'there are no inspectors to inspect and look over the beasts slain. Why could not a diseased animal be imported into the market, killed, and sold? Again, in the butchers' market the stalls are quite exposed; there are no doors; and a butcher who cannot sell his meat during the day takes it home, or to any unwhole-some place for the night; carries it again next day to his stall, and exposes it for sale. It may be that at his residence yellow fever or any contagious disease reigns; it follows then that the meat becomes also infected, and passing into the possession of another, the disease, whatever it may be, is carried into another house, place, or locality.'

Dilating on the injurious effects of filthy dwellings, he continues:— 'What can be more pernicious to life than filthy dwellings and stagnant pools? The former are numerous in this town; indeed, even in the middle of the city the yards of several houses are in a most detestable condition. The latter are frequently seen in streets and roads not quite familiar to business men, and where the poor are in general congregated. Now, I ask, should there not be regular sanitary inspectors, not only to visit yards, and to see that they are kept clean, but also to inspect streets, roads, and lanes?' He predicts, without a question, that the health of the colony would be greatly improved if an inspector of markets and stock be also appointed.[1]

[1] *Ibid.*, p. 138, l. 24 ff.

15

Advice on how to keep Healthy in Nineteenth-Century Africa

Horton's 'Valuable Hints to Europeans for the Preservation of Health in the Tropics' were first included in his book, **The Physical and Medical Climate and Meteorology of the West Coast of Africa,** *(1867) and were also included in the first and second editions of his* **Diseases of Tropical Climates** *published in 1874 and 1879.*

They follow the pattern of similar advice given in books by other authors published for European residents in India which were popular in that period. Horton acknowledged his debt particularly to Sir James Ranald Martin, C.B., a distinguished London consultant in Tropical Medicine, who had seen service in India, and had played an important part in reorganising the Army Medical Services. He had also written extensively on diseases commonly suffered by Europeans in the tropics.

Horton, in addition, included his own advice gained from experience of the manner of living of some of the Europeans on the west coast at that period. He advised the newcomer from Europe to avoid, as much as possible, the company of those of their compatriots of licentious indulgences and of irritable and violent temper as such habits were peculiarly catching and had an injurious effect on the health. The newcomer was also advised to seek the company of 'real' ladies.

A strict moral principle is beneficial in the tropics.

The Christian religion has a more beneficial influence on the minds of men in the tropics, than either Mohammedanism or any other.

Slothful and squalid habits should be avoided. The saying is true that '*a slothful, squalid-looking population invariably characterizes an unhealthy country.*'

Every substance or circumstance which induces nervousness and excitability of the nervous system should be avoided.

Persons accustomed to licentious indulgences are to be avoided, especially on first arrival.

Always keep the mind occupied in doing something; never sit down and allow the thoughts to go astray.

Agreeable society should always be courted, as it relieves the mind a great deal. The society of real ladies will be found preferable to any other.

The occupation of lofty buildings, or buildings in elevated portions of a town or city, has a very beneficial effect on the mind. The converse is also true.

In order that the moral principles might be more easily kept, the new arrival should watch over and prevent any laxity in habit or principles acquired in his early religious training.

The companionship of persons of irritable and violent temper should, as much as possible, be avoided; as in the tropics such habits are peculiarly catching, and have an injurious effect on the health.

Too hot diet, or hot condiments taken in excess, have an injurious influence on the passions. . . .

A poor diet and a simple vegetable diet affect the passions injuriously, and therefore should be avoided.[1]

One cannot be too cautious, especially on his first arrival in tropical climates; he has to moderate all habits of life—drink, sleep, exercise, &c. —and gradually to adapt his constitution to the vicissitudes of the climate. A mistake at the commencement may lay the foundation of the most serious and complicated diseases in future years. What madness will it be considered if a native of a tropical climate, in residing in the temperate zone, carries there with him his tropical habits! A few days alone will suffice to bring him to the consciousness of his folly, and reduce him to the dust from whence he came. What is injurious in the one case is also injurious in the other. A native of a temperate climate, on making the tropics his abode, should gradually adapt himself to the climate, and should particularly observe the minute points in tropical hygiene.

Besides, the death of every new-comer tells very much against the climate of the country. The individuals themselves are seldom blamed for it; the deadly nature of the place receives all the blame which their bereaved friends can give; and the progress of the governing influence is checked. The country becomes the sufferer in another way. It is deprived of the civilising influence which radiates from them. It prevents others from attempting to reside in it; and generally only the most reckless and desperate will venture to do so.[2]

[1] *Physical and Medical Climate,* p. 287, l. 9 ff.
[2] *Ibid.,* p. 270, l. 25 ff.

Materials which keep up an equable temperature of the body are the best adapted for the tropics. Linen is very cold, and transmits heat through everything beneath it; and when wet by any source, either by perspiration or rain, communicates a cold sensation over the whole of the body. Woollen fabrics, being bad conductors of heat, feel very uncomfortable, when the temperature of the surrounding medium far exceeds that of the body; and when it is a little below, it will be found to be too slow a conductor of the heat of the body. Cotton is the material best suited for tropical climates. 'The cotton dress,' says Sir R. Martin, 'from its slowness of conducting heat, is admirably adapted for the tropics . . . but this, though a great advantage, is not the only one. When a *vicissitude* takes place, and the atmospheric temperature sinks suddenly far below that of the body, the cotton covering, faithful to its trust, abstracts more slowly the heat *from it*, and thus preserves to the wearer a more steady equilibrium. To all these advantages must be added the facility with which the cotton absorbs perspiration. . . .'

A cotton undershirt should always be used; and if drawers be worn, those made with cotton are best.

Cotton socks, as a general rule, should be always worn. If about to travel a long distance, and there is a probability of walking through swamp, woollen stockings, not very thick, are preferable.

Shirts made of cotton, with linen fronts, should be worn. The warm Crimean shirts (flannel) should only be used on special occasions—*i.e.* when travelling or in an expedition. When worn for every-day purposes, they look dirty, are rather too hot, and feel heavy. The wool irritates the skin and increases the perspiration, the converse of which being what we require.

Collars should, when we can socially do so, be avoided. The shirt band should be very free.

Chemises and night-gowns or shirts made of cotton material, should be preferred to linen. The rule is, cotton should always be next to the skin.

At night use cotton sheets for covering, or if linen, lie on cotton. When the temperature is high and the bed-linen hot, cover with a thin flannel blanket.

During the hot season at M'Carthy's Island, when the temperature at bed-time is 100°, I have found sleeping between linen sheets to be unhealthily warm, for the simple reason that linen easily conveys the heat to the body. Woollen and cotton are cooler, which is proved in the following experiments:—'Let two beds be placed in the same room during the day, when the thermometer stands at 90°, and let one be covered

with a pair of blankets, the other with a pair of linen sheets.' On remov-
ing both coverings in the evening, the bed with the blankets will be found
the cooler. Being non-conductors of heat, they prevent the external heat
from penetrating; whilst the linen bed and the linen being good conductors, transmit the heat to everything beneath them.

Whatever hat is worn, the crown should be well protected or covered
with several folds of white turban. It is best when ventilated.

An umbrella should always be used when obliged to go out doors
during the heat of the sun.

The boots should be provided with thick soles, especially during the
rainy season. When wet and damp, they should be immediately changed.

The body linen should not be changed too often; twice a day is quite
sufficient, especially amongst new arrivals. . . .

When caught in rain, and the linen becomes wet and damp, it should
be immediately changed, and the body sponged with hot water and
vinegar or lime juice.

In places where Dysentery or Diarrhoea is prevalent, a cotton or
flannel waistband should be worn, especially at night, to keep the bowels
from sudden impression of cold.

II Food

As it is necessary to change the food when one resides in the polar
regions, so as to increase the heat of the body, so it is necessary, when we
attempt to reside in a tropical climate, to moderate the quantity and
select the quality of our food. Since the heat predisposes to congestion
and the development of febrile excitement, we should so regulate our
diet as to moderate the former, whilst at the same time we neutralize the
latter.

Before getting out of bed, or before going out of doors, a cup of tea,
coffee, or chocolate should be taken.

The breakfast and dinner hours should be stated and regularly kept.

At breakfast the viands should be very simple and plain, especially
amongst first arrivals, consisting of eggs, either boiled or poached, a
little fish, unbuttered bread, tea or coffee, and rice and curry.

If the dinner be late, shortly after noon, about two o'clock, a little
bread and butter might be taken with a glass of porter, or still better,
draught ale. A glass of sherry or port wine might be taken for a change,
also fruits and easily digested food in small quantities.

The dinner should be at about four, or half-past four; but when this is
inconvenient, it should not be later than seven o'clock. It should be the
principal meal, and should not be too heavy, in order to ensure a natural
and refreshing rest.

Suppers ought always to be avoided in the tropics, where a good rest at night is essential for the preservation of the health and vigour of the mind and body.

When dinner is taken early, tea or coffee should be taken at seven or eight, and will be very much relished.

Excess in eating and drinking should be particularly avoided; excess will be known by a general feverish sensation after the meal. Dr. Clark truly states that much of the suffering of the Europeans on the Gold Coast is occasioned by over-feeding.

The sub-acid fruits—such as oranges, pine apples, and grenadillas—will be found very agreeable and refreshing. But the European on his first arrival should carefully watch the effects of the various delightful tropical fruits which he eats, as they act differently on different constitutions. He should gradually select those which best agree with him. Thus the mangrove [*sic*][1] is stimulating and heating, and might in an unseasoned European, bring out pustular eruptions or boils; the plantain, even when ripe, is astringent, and consequently not well adapted for those who are habitually constipated. Oranges (sweet) are always wholesome taken in the morning or afternoon, and so is the banana.

Unripe fruits should be avoided, especially in places where Dysentery, Diarrhoea, or Cholera is rife.

Condiments or spice should not be used by new comers in the tropics; they should not force their stomach with an already good appetite, to increased and unnecessary action. When, however, by long residence the tone of the general constitution and of the stomach begins to fail, then their use will be beneficial.

III Drink

It is a physiological fact that a man in good health does not require the use of wine or spirits, or any stimulating liquor. It produces no beneficial result in his constitution, and in the tropics acts rather injuriously, even in small quantity, by increasing that febrile state of excitement which is the consequence of the heated atmosphere. . . . It has become the habit of some men in the tropics, on opening their eyes in the morning, to have a 'good stiff shot of brandy' the first thing before rising; and I have seen cases where a bottle of brandy has been nearly consumed before breakfast. Nothing is so injurious to the constitution as this habit. It does not at all satisfy the thirst, but leaves a desperate degree of craving for the bottle —which, in many cases, never ends until delirium tremens supervenes.[2]

[1] Probably 'mango' (Ed.).
[2] *Diseases of Tropical Climates*, p. 662, l. 19 ff.

New arrivals in the tropics should refrain as long as possible from all heating drinks, especially in places where good water can be obtained.

If not subject to constipation, cold tea will be found agreeable and refreshing.

Where vegetables are not plentiful, weak lemon juice is necessary now and then; when taken in the afternoon it diffuses a coolness all over the body.

Sherbet will be found salutary, and any quantity may be taken, as it is wholesome and grateful.

Any quantity of ice might be taken; it is not only agreeable and salutary, but it revives the spirits, strengthens the body, and assists digestion.

When an aqueous regimen cannot be kept, the best and lightest wine that could be safely used is good claret, which should be taken with water.

For those of weak constitution a glass of porter in the afternoon is very strengthening, and in the tropics is better than bottled ale.

Brandy is unnecessary; it increases the febrile excitement of the body to a marked degree, which is followed by a corresponding depression of the vital functions. It should only be used when prescribed by the medical attendant.

When, after long exercise before dinner, or hard bodily exercise, it is found on sitting at the table that the appetite is gone, take a glass of sherry and bitters, and this will excite the action of the stomach.

Warm tea or coffee after severe marches in the sun will be found a refreshing beverage. (Martin.)

A newly-arrived European in the tropics should never attempt to imitate the old residents in the use of the magic bowl. He must always consider, that what the old topers can take with seeming advantage, will prove death to him.

During seasoning, when a course of [temperance] has been fully entered on, under no consideration must an occasional debauch be committed, as the system is very much subject to endemic and epidemic tropical diseases. (Martin.)

IV Exercise

Exercise to the extent in which it is taken in a temperate climate, is here to be avoided, as it will soon prove injurious to the constitution. The object of exercise in a cold climate is to keep up a just balance of the circulation, to support and maintain the functions of the skin, and to promote the different secretions of the body; but the perspiration, biliary, and other secretions, being already in excess in equatorial regions, a perseverance in 'the European habit of exercise' would prove highly injurious, and it often does so, by promoting and aggravating the ill effects of an unnatural climate. Debility follows, then diminished action of the skin and visceral secretions, and then an inequilibrium of the blood. Again, it is injurious to take no exercise at all; for it is equally necessary for the due performance of all the functions of the body, that a certain amount of exercise should be taken.

New arrivals, in places where there are good roads, should take gentle exercise on foot every evening. It should on no account be fatiguing.

In the damp and rainy season, exercise in the morning should never be taken. Due time should be allowed for the sun to disperse the malaria which accumulated on the surface of the earth.

In houses where there are long piazzas or verandahs, a walk within them in the morning will be found strengthening, agreeable, and not at all injurious.

Exercise on horseback is strengthening to the young; and with new arrivals will give a gentle impulse to the functions of the whole body.

Dancing, except for a short time in the cold months, is injurious. Every dancer in the tropics knows too well the feeling in the whole system, after a dance continued throughout the night.

Passive exercises, in carriages, palankeens or hammocks, is very serviceable to those who have long resided in the tropics, and whose circulation is very languid.

With children, hoop-racing is an agreeable and bracing exercise, as it exercises both the mind and the body.

Shampooing is both useful and salutary, it invigorates the circulation after fatigue or long inaction, and excites the insensibility of the cuticular secretion (Martin). It is of great advantage to those who have been a long time in the tropics, and whose liver is torpid.

Before dinner, one hour's repose is very salutary, and places the stomach in a condition most favourable for the reception of food.

On no account must exercise be taken under the rays of a noon-day sun, or when the sun's rays can be felt.

Walking out in the night should always be avoided; it is injurious in every respect.

. . .

The swing is an exercise which will be found grateful and salutary, especially if done in-doors when it is rainy. It will relax the cutaneous vessels, and produce a determination to the surface, and be consequently very beneficial, especially to those who are suffering from torpidity. (Martin.)

V Bathing

. . .

In no climate is there a greater necessity for the performance of good ablution than in intertropical countries. The enormous calls on the cutaneous vessels, which result in an excessive discharge of their secretion, lead to an accumulation of extraneous matter on the surface which, if not removed, produces a mischievous effect on health. The stomach is at first disturbed, and then a series of disturbances take place, which involve most of the viscera of the body. Regular ablution, therefore, is a necessity in the tropics; but there are certain rules which are laid down for the observance of those who live in the tropics.

In the tropics a bath should be taken once at least every day.

The best time for taking a bath is an hour or half-an-hour before breakfast; the body is then cool, and the stomach in excellent condition for the morning repast.

When a bath is taken twice a-day, the second bath, which must always be cold, should be taken an hour or half-an-hour before dinner. It is very refreshing, especially after a hard day's work; removes the sensation of thirst in the stomach through sympathy with the skin; and, in a great measure, mitigates nervousness.

With the *temperate* and *healthy*, the cold bath should always be taken. It is delightful and advantageous in keeping the skin cool and moist, and reducing the sense of internal fullness.

Amongst the *intemperate*, the cold bath is dangerous, and should not be indulged in. The tepid bath will be found more serviceable.

To persons suffering from visceral diseases, the tepid or warm bath is the only safe bath that could be used with advantage; and once a-day is quite sufficient.

During the cold weather, and at the blowing of the harmattan, to persons who have suffered from enlargement of the spleen and liver, from dysentery and chronic diarrhoea, a warm bath is a necessity.

The relative temperature of the baths should be as follows:—
Cold bath, from 60° to 75°; tepid bath, from 85° to 92°; warm bath, from 92° to 98°; hot bath from 98° to 112°.

During the hot weather, when the temperature in the sun ranges from 120° to 140°, the cold water should be kept in the sun for some time, and an agreeable tepid bath will be obtained.

Amongst habitual topers, and those who are in the habit of keeping late hours; whose abdominal viscera, in consequence, are in an irritable state, and the balance of whose circulation is disturbed, the cold bath immediately aggravates the symptoms, and leads to fearful congestion. The warm bath is a necessity.

Before using the cold bath, it is unnecessary to wait until one is *cooled down* first. Amongst the delicate it is beneficial to be first immersed in a warm bath before plunging into the cold, which will produce a healthy reaction. (Martin.)

We find it the habit of many to take a bath a few minutes after their meals. This is injurious, and should be avoided, as it interferes with the process of digestion, and might result in functional derangement of the stomach.

VI Sleep

Good sound sleep is necessary for the enjoyment of good health in the tropics. Those who have habituated themselves to going late to bed, predispose their constitution to every form of disease, and put a limit to their earthly existence. It must be remembered that temperament has a great influence in the extent and manner of our sleep.[1]

Regularity in the hours of going to sleep is very important in the tropics. Between nine and ten will be found the best time.

The apartment should be cool, and every means adopted to keep it so; but the individual should be completely kept from draught, and from the sudden changes of temperature and the humidity of the atmosphere which is peculiar to the tropics in early morning.

Every circumstance by which the sleep can be disturbed should be obviated. Thus, in places where mosquitoes and sandflies are prevalent, proper curtains should be used.

It is always most preferable and desirable to go to bed with a clear head. The habit of much drinking at night disturbs the sleep and renders it unrefreshing.

Those who are habituated to late hours and bacchanalian riots, will find themselves much relieved from the after consequences of the imprudent habit, by bathing their heads with cold water before going to sleep.

Reading late at night, in the tropics, is a habit not to be encouraged; for the nervous system has enough of excitement during the hot and busy hours of the day, and requires repose at night.

When there is a feeling of tension, heat, headache, throbbing, and other unpleasant sensations in the head, we should lie down quietly, and endeavour to get sleep; for it is certain that something wrong is going on in the brain, and rest and quietude are most likely to relieve it.

Sleeping until too late in the morning, when the sun has ascended to a great distance above the visible horizon, produces lassitude and want of energy in individuals in the tropics.

[1] *Ibid.*, p. 670, l. 8 ff.

Rising at daylight, and enjoying the fresh and cooling breeze of the morning, in a verandah, or beyond the reach of malaria, is very healthy and invigorating.

During the blowing of the hot simoon, in the hot season, in the tropics, or the sirocco of the east, when no dew falls, sleeping in open verandahs is not only safe but advantageous. On the other hand, during the rains, the harvest, and harmattan, such a habit will be found most destructive to life; in fact, there are many cases in the tropics where men, whose names I might mention, have continually exposed themselves in this way, contrary to all advice of their friends, and thus laid the foundation of acute diseases, which have proved their death-warrants.

The dyspeptic, namely, those who suffer from flatulency, heartburns, and griping pains, are occasionally troubled with nightmare, which disturbs their rest. They should take carbonate of soda and a little peppermint; and always keep their bowels regular.

Late suppers, cheese, and other flatulent food, and all indigestible fruits, should be avoided at night. This rule is particularly incumbent on the dyspeptic.[1]

[1] *Ibid.*, p. 677, l. 3 ff.

16

The Rapid and Progressive Development of Africa

The argument advanced in this short extract may seem to many to be self-evident and unnecessary. It must be seen, however, against the background of discussions—very prominent then, and which indeed have continued to our own day—about the nature and rate of African development.

Horton in succinct and condensed prose tried to impress on his readers that the state of 'barbarism' in which it was felt Africa then existed was not inherently a permanent one but only as transitory as that which had existed in ancient Britain, France and Germany. He stressed that development would take time and that there would be mistakes, but that the goal would eventually be reached. These arguments were essential in an era when racialists were trying to show, by biased scientific arguments, that the African would never attain the level of civilisation of contemporary Europe.

There are still many who believe that it ought to take the African as many centuries as it took Europeans to achieve their present state of civilisation. Horton felt otherwise and his belief has always been shared by most Africans. It is our view that the civilisation of a country or continent is built on the foundation of the more advanced civilisation of neighbouring countries; it never starts from the beginning. The essential factors in previous civilisations are always included in a condensed form in the most recent, and the rational point to begin is surely from there.

Should a child from a developing country be expected to invent the wheel before he is allowed to learn how to ride a bicycle or drive a motor-car? It is evident that life is too short. If possible, he should be introduced to the stages of the development of transport through playing with the appropriate toys as a child. If he misses this, he should begin with the simple forms of modern transport as a youth—but not forced to remain at that level. His country, similarly, should be expected to progress rapidly through the range of past inventions to modern ones. Those nations which are slow in adjusting themselves to more advanced civilisations to which they are exposed risk extinction.

A more significant factor than the rate of development is the manner in which the new civilisation is introduced. Unless its moral and fundamental aspects are stressed at the same time as its material and more superficial advantages, it might undermine and corrupt rather than strengthen and ennoble.

'ROME was not built in a day'; the proudest kingdom in Europe was once in a state of barbarism perhaps worse than now exists amongst the tribes chiefly inhabiting the West Coast of Africa; and it is an incontrovertible axiom that what has been done can again be done. If Europe, therefore, has been raised to her present pitch of civilisation by progressive advancement, Africa too, with a guarantee of the civilisation of the north, will rise into equal importance. The nucleus has been planted; it is just beginning to show signs of life and future vigour; it shoots out legitimate as well as extraneous buds. Political capital is made of the latter by narrow-minded persons; whilst the liberal-minded, with more philosophy and generosity, make ample allowances for these defects, and encourage the legitimate growth. We may well say that the present state of Western Africa is, in fact, the history of the world repeating itself.

The civilisation of France and England, and even of Germany, dates from the time when Rome, agitated by social contentions, made Julius Caesar proconsul of Transalpine Gaul; the brilliant conquest which he made over the then savage tribes who lived in caves and miserable huts, and the wise but rigid government which he enforced, led in eleven hundred years to the gigantic discoveries and improvements which now startle the denizens of less favoured climes.

But I argue that modern inventions, such as printing, steam agency (both as regards railways and navigation), and the electric telegraph, which facilitate rapid communication in a most wonderful degree, leave not a shadow of doubt in my mind that, although it took eleven hundred years to bring France and England to the high standard of civilisation which they now occupy, it will take far less time to bring a portion at least of Western Africa to vie with Europe in progressive development.[1]

[1] *Letters on the Political Condition of the Gold Coast*, p. i.

17

Obituary Notices and Excerpts from the Last Will and Testament of Dr Horton

The last Will and Testament of Dr Horton showed his passionate interest in Education and the wide sweep of his affection for Africans of different backgrounds.

He provided for the founding of a School or College for the teaching of Science and he left money for scholarships for students from all over West Africa.

Much of his wealth was tied up in mining concessions, particularly in Ghana.

Unfortunately, his will was challenged in court, and went through many years of litigation. During this period, especially between 1897 and 1901, there was a boom in some of the concessions held in his estate brought about both by the uncertainties of the South African War and the opening at last of his cherished railway to Tacquah (Tarkwa). Had his estate been realised then, it would have resulted in a vast fortune, more than enough to cover his educational bequests. However, litigation continued and by the time a final settlement had been reached there was a slump in the shares and his estate depreciated badly in value. Some of it, however, was used for the furtherance of technical education in Sierra Leone.

Horton Hall in Gloucester Street, opposite the Central Post Office, Freetown, was sold to the Government and the site used, appropriately enough, for the building of official quarters for Government Medical Officers.

Horton's immediate material wishes thus ended in an anticlimax. The ideas, however, which he put forward towards the realisation of nationalism and independence and his intense interest in education, have inspired, and will continue to inspire, thousands of Africans for many years to come.

The Late Dr. Horton

Now, alas!, it is our melancholy task to register the death of Dr. Horton. Although he had been greatly suffering during his visit to England last year, we had cherished the hope that his restoration to health had been perfect, and that many years of honourable usefulness were still before him. We give in another column an extract from the *Christian Observer*, of Sierra Leone, which will give some slight idea of the high estimation in which he was held in his native city. He fully merited that esteem. As a sincere and attached friend of many years, we deeply deplore his loss. No man has more successfully vindicated the just claim of the African race to mental equality with the more favoured portions of mankind. The son of liberated Africans—that is, of Africans who had been rescued from on board slave-ships by cruisers of Her Majesty's Navy—he had the disadvantage of being of the first generation of his family in the ranks of civilisation. He had none of the advantages possessed by Europeans of hereditary culture. What he affected was all his own—all the fruit of his own labour utilising the elements placed at his disposal by the Christian philanthropy of Great Britain. The Church Missionary Society may record his name with pride as among the fruit of their persistent labours in West Africa and Her Majesty's Government had certainly no cause to regret having taken him into the medical ranks of the Army, in which he attained to the high position of Surgeon-Major, and from which he retired last year, after a full period of service, but without receiving the decoration of St. Michael and St. George (C.M.G.), which could only have been withheld because he was an African. It is scarcely necessary to say that we deeply sympathise with his bereaved family.

Obituary Notice *The Christian Observer* (Sierra Leone)

Surgeon-Major J. A. B. Horton, M.D., F.R.G.S.

Death, the common enemy of man, has snatched from our midst one who had reached the acme of fame and fortune by dint of that indomitable perseverance, energy, and fortitude by which men have always risen from the ranks to the highest position in the circle of their profession. Prince Surgeon-Major Horton, of the 'Commercial Bank of West Africa' is no more. Alas! . . . 'what dying worms are we!' He quickly passed away at about 9 o'clock p.m., of October 15th, after a short illness of about eight days, in the 49th year of his age. Truly, 'in the midst of life we are in death'!

In his death Sierra Leone has lost another of its great men—a class not so common amongst us that we can afford to be indifferent to those we have or are losing. He would be a rash prophet indeed who will undertake to say when Providence will again vouchsafe us such men as the late M. P. Horton, W. Grant, H. Quaker and Prince Horton, and their compeers of active, pushing, and aspiring talent and genius. The interest he recently manifested in the welfare of the Church Native Pastorate, his recent election on the Church Council, and the position he held as Treasurer of the Institute, and the warm interest he displayed in going about to collect for the Church Endowment Fund, are indications that he was not wholly engaged in the things of time and sense, but that whilst 'not slothful in business, he was diligent in spirit, serving the Lord'.

Dr Horton was one of the only two Africans that have the privilege of holding Her Majesty's commission to serve on the Army Medical Staff, and by their exemplary conduct and capacity for the position they hold, have demonstrated the capacity of the Negro to hold any important position. After a successful career of twenty-four years in the Army, he retired on a well-earned pension, with the rank of Surgeon-Major. His recent efforts to establish a Bank at Sierra Leone, though of yesterday, and yet in its infancy, had begun to make steady progress and to become appreciated, though the establishment is scarcely a year old.

Dr. Horton's work on 'Political Economy for Western Africa' and his other work on the medical aspect of diseases peculiar to the African climate, are matters of history, and require no brushing up at our hands. Viewed from many standpoints, his death is an irreparable loss, and more so to his widow and two daughters, and a large circle of friends and acquaintances. We truly sympathise with his bereaved family, and hope his end was peace.

> 'Lives of great men all remind us,
>   We should make our lives sublime;
> And departing, leave behind us
>   Footprints on the sands of time.'

Dr J. A. B. Horton's Trusts

(A) *Bequests to Fourah Bay College and the Sierra Leone Grammar School*
. . .
The balance of the cash receipts of the second Company and the cash receipts of every new Company that may hereafter be formed are to be divided into ten equal parts of these:—
. . .

59. I give and bequeath to the Wesleyan Mission Society for Africa the half of one part of the remaining one part.
60. I give and bequeath to the Sierra Leone Fourah Bay College Fund two-fourths.
61. I give and bequeath one-fourth to the Sierra Leone Grammar School Fund.
    . . .
79. It is my desire that the remaining shares and all shares in Companies that may hereinafter be formed to work the different mining Concessions shall be divided into ten parts as each Company formed and shall be disposed of in the following manner.
    . . .
87. I give to be divided towards the maintenance of the Fourah Bay College, Grammar School and the Wesleyan High School at Sierra Leone one part in these proportions—two-fifths to the first—two-fifths to the second, and one-fifth to the third.

(B) *Horton's Collegiate High School*

I give and bequeath to the hands of trustees to be hereinafter appointed under conditions hereinafter to be named my house, lands, tenements and real estate in Gloster Street, Freetown, Sierra Leone and known under the name of Horton Hall which shall only be taken over after the death of my dear wife or the occurrence of the circumstances already named for the purpose of conversion into a superior school for giving general education to youths of Western Africa; the school to receive the name of Horton's Collegiate High School. It is my desire that the aim of this School should be the introduction of high Scientific Classes of study (Mineralogy, Geology, Botany and Allied Science) and that every effort should be made to advance the standard of education in the school and to cause the said school to be affiliated to an English University.
11. I give and bequeath in the hands of the Trustees (Committee of Management) of Horton Collegiate School the whole of my present and future shares in the Gold Coast Mining Company the interest when paid should every year be invested in substantial stock for the benefit of the said High School.
12. I give and bequeath in the hands of the Trustees of the said High School £3,000 (Three thousand pounds) Peruvian Bonds invested by my agents Messrs. Sir C. McGrigor Bart. and Company of London; the principal is not to be sold but the interest to be employed for the use of the school but during the time that operations in the school

are in abeyance the interest accumulated should every year be invested for its future benefit.

...

I hereby appoint the Bishop of Sierra Leone and for the time being Two Lay Gentlemen at present William Grant and Mr. Bull of Wilberforce Street Sierra Leone and Two Clergymen of the Sierra Leone Native Pastorate, Trustees of all the property left by me now and to become due to Horton Collegiate High School hereinbefore mentioned subject to the conditions contained in the Schedule attached to this my said will.

Schedule

The schedule referred to on the above written will is:—

1st. That the school should be known under the designation of Horton's Collegiate School.

2nd. That it shall be competent for the Trustees to change the name to Horton's College, Sierra Leone—and affiliate it to a University.

3rd. That high scientific subjects should be the basis of its teaching.

4th. That two students from the Niger Mission (one at least shall invariably be from the Eboe district) two students from the Colony of Sierra Leone (one to be of the Eboe race) and one student from the Cape Coast Wesleyan High School shall be educated or kept continually in the school gratuitously.

5th. That the instructions in the school shall be based on the religious principles of the Church of England.[1]

Dated 2nd December 1880
Died 15th day of October 1883 (Ed.)

[1] *The Jubilee and Centenary Volume of Fourah Bay College,* p. 149, l. 11 ff.

Works of Dr Horton

The titles of books written by Dr Horton and from which most of these extracts have been taken are as follows:

The Medical Topography of the West Coast of Africa; with Sketches of its Botany. (Thesis for the Doctorate of Medicine, Edinburgh University) London, 1859.

Physical and Medical Climate and Meteorology of the West Coast of Africa. With Valuable Hints to Europeans for the Preservation of Health in the Tropics.
London, 1867.

West African Countries and Peoples, British and Native. With the Requirements necessary for Establishing that Self-Government recommended by the Committee of the House of Commons 1865; and a Vindication of the African Race.
London, 1868.

Guinea Worm, or Dracunculus: Its Symptoms and Progress, Causes, Pathological Anatomy, Results, and Radical Cure.
London, 1868.

Letters on the Political Condition of the Gold Coast since the Exchange of Territory between the English and Dutch Governments, on January 1, 1868. Together with a Short Account of the Ashantee War, 1862–4, and the Awoonah War, 1866; Addressed to The Right Hon. E. Cardwell, D.C.L., Secretary of State for War; and The Right Hon. Earl Granville, K.G., D.C.L., Secretary of State for the Colonies.
London, 1870.

The Diseases of Tropical Climates and their Treatment with Hints for the Preservation of Health in the Tropics.
London, 1874.

Other works by Dr Horton either referred to or later incorporated by him into his major works above:

Political Economy of British Western Africa: with the Requirements of the

several Colonies and Settlements. (The African View of the Negro's Place in Nature.)
London, 1865.

The Geological Constitution of Ahanta, Gold Coast.
London (before 1867).

Letters and articles in *The African Times* (London), in particular

(a) 'African Products', 23rd May 1864.
(b) 'The Negro's Place in Nature', 23rd April 1866.

The ideas and arguments in these two letters were later incorporated in the books *Physical and Medical Climate, and Meteorology of the West Coast of Africa* and *West African Countries and Peoples* respectively.

Selected References

Books

Ajayi, J. F. A. *Christian Missions in Nigeria 1841–1891*. London, 1965.
Ayandele, E. A. *The Missionary Impact on Modern Nigeria 1842–1914*. London, 1966.
Blyden, E. W. *Christianity, Islam and the Negro Race*. London, 1887.
Burton, R. *Wanderings in West Africa from Liverpool to Fernando Po*. London, 1863.
Curtin, P. *The Image of Africa*. Madison, Wisconsin, 1964.
Fyfe, C. *A History of Sierra Leone*. London, 1962.
Fyfe, C. *Sierra Leone Inheritance*. London, 1964.
Gailey, H. A. *A History of the Gambia*. London, 1964.
Gore, A. A. (M.D., Surgeon-Major). *Medical History of West African Campaigns*. London, 1876.
Gray, John M. *A History of the Gambia*. Cambridge, 1940.
Hargreaves, J. D. *A Life of Sir Samuel Lewis*. London, 1958.
Hargreaves, J. D. *Prelude to the Partition of West Africa*. London, 1963.
Hearnshaw, F. J. C. *The Centenary History of King's College, London (1828–1929)*. London, 1929.
Kimble, D. *A Political History of Ghana—The Rise of Gold Coast Nationalism, 1850–1928*. Oxford, 1963.
Kopytoff, J. H. *A Preface to Modern Nigeria: the 'Sierra Leoneans' in Yoruba, 1830–1890*. Madison, Wisconsin, 1965.
Page, J. *The Black Bishop, Samuel Adjai Crowther*, London, 1908.
Parliamentary Papers, 1865, Vol. V, p. 2. Report of the Select Committee on the State of the British Settlement in West Africa.
Pope-Hennessy, James. The John Pope Hennessy Family Papers. Donated to Fourah Bay College, Freetown, Sierra Leone.
Pope-Hennessy, James. *Verandah*. London, 1964.
Porter, A. T. *Creoledom*. London, 1963.
Robinson, R., Gallagher, J. and Denny, A. *Africa and the Victorians; the official mind of imperialism*. London, 1961.
Thompson, T. J. *The Jubilee and Centenary Volume of Fourah Bay College*. Freetown, Sierra Leone, 1930.

Vogt, Carl. *Vorlesungen über den Menschen, Seine Stellung in der Schöpfung und in der Geschichte der Erde.* Geissen, 1863.

Winterbottom, T., M.D. (Physician to the Colony of Sierra Leone). *An Account of the Native Africans in the Neighbourhood of Sierra Leone; to which is added An Account of the Present State of Medicine among Them,* 2 vols., London, 1803.

Articles

Agbodeka, F. 'The Fantee Confederacy, 1865–1869; an enquiry into the origins, nature and extent of an early West African protest movement'. *Transactions Historical Society of Ghana*, Vol. VII, 1964, p. 82.

Gwam, L. C. 'The Social and Political Ideas of Dr. James Africanus Beale Horton M.D., M.R.C.S., F.R.A.S., F.R.G.S., 1835–1883'. *Ibadan*, No. 19, June 1964, p. 10.

July, Robert. 'Africanus Horton and the Idea of Independence in West Africa'. *Sierra Leone Studies*, New Series No. 18, January 1966.

Nicol, Davidson. 'A Far-Sighted Sierra Leone Doctor'. In *Eminent Sierra Leoneans (in the Nineteenth Century)*, ed. M. C. F. Easmon, Freetown, 1961.

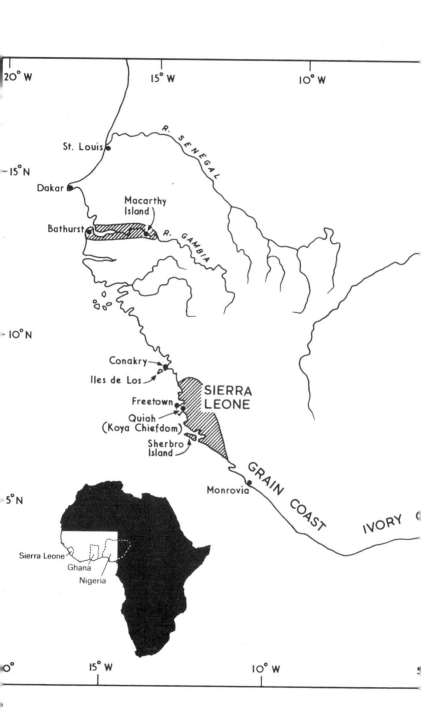